Information and Communication Technology for Competitive Intelligence

Dirk Vriens
University of Nijmegen, The Netherlands

IRM Press
Publisher of innovative scholarly and professional
information technology titles in the cyberage
Hershey • London • Melbourne • Singapore

Acquisition Editor: Mehdi Khosrow-Pour
Senior Managing Editor: Jan Travers
Managing Editor: Amanda Appicello
Development Editor: Michele Rossi
Copy Editor: Ingrid Widitz
Typesetter: Jennifer Wetzel
Cover Design: Michelle Waters
Printed at: Integrated Book Technology

Published in the United States of America by
        IRM Press (an imprint of Idea Group Inc.)
        701 E. Chocolate Avenue, Suite 200
        Hershey PA 17033-1240
        Tel: 717-533-8845
        Fax: 717-533-8661
        E-mail: cust@idea-group.com
        Web site: http://www.irm-press.com

and in the United Kingdom by
        IRM Press (an imprint of Idea Group Inc.)
        3 Henrietta Street
        Covent Garden
        London WC2E 8LU
        Tel: 44 20 7240 0856
        Fax: 44 20 7379 3313
        Web site: http://www.eurospan.co.uk

Library of Congress Cataloging-in-Publication Data

Information and communication technology for competitive intelligence /
[edited by] Dirk Vriens.
        p. cm.
Includes bibliographical references and index.
  ISBN 1-59140-214-X (s/c)
 1. Business intelligence. 2. Information storage and retrieval
systems--Management. 3. Information resources management--Data
processing. 4. Communication in management--Data processing. I.
Vriens, Dirk Jaap. 1963-
   HD38.7.I53 2004b
   658.4'7'0285--dc22

                                                    2003017690

British Cataloguing in Publication Data
A Cataloguing in Publication record for this book is available from the British Library.

All work contributed to this book is new, previously-unpublished material. The views
expressed in this book are those of the authors, but not necessarily of the publisher.

Information and Communication Technology for Competitive Intelligence

Table of Contents

Preface

Competitive Intelligence can be described as producing and processing information about the environment of an organization for strategic purposes. To formulate a strategy, an organization needs to collect and process information about its environment—about, for instance, competitors, customers, suppliers, governments, technological trends or ecological developments. Collecting and processing environmental information has always been important. However, because of the increasing complexity and dynamics of the environment, the pressure to produce relevant, timely 'actionable' intelligence increases as well. To collect and process strategically relevant environmental information in a structured fashion, a large number of organizations are currently implementing a competitive intelligence function.

To structure the process of competitive intelligence, several authors propose a cycle of four stages. This "intelligence cycle" contains the following stages:

1. **Direction.** In this stage the organization determines its "strategic information requirements." It determines about what aspects in the environment data should be collected.
2. **Collection.** In this stage, it is determined what sources can be used for data collection and the data are actually collected.
3. **Analysis.** In the analysis stage the data collected in the previous stage are analyzed to assess whether they are useful for strategic purposes. Here, the actual "production" of intelligence (data relevant for strategy) takes place.
4. **Dissemination.** The intelligence (produced in stage 3) is forwarded to the strategic decision-makers and used to formulate their strategic plans.

To support these stages, different Information and Communication Technology (ICT) applications may be employed. These ICT tools include the Internet as a tool for direction or collection activities; groupware applications for uncovering strategic information requirements; data warehouses and associated data mining tools for collecting and analyzing data; specific applications for supporting the analysis (e.g., System Dynamics software); the use of an Intranet for disseminating intelligence; or even specific CI applications covering all the four stages. The number of possible ICT tools for CI is large—and an important question for organizations is what tools they should select and implement for their own CI activities. In fact, an uncritical implementation and use of certain tools may be problematic—it can lead, for instance, to an information overload or to large collections of irrelevant data.

To select ICT tools for competitive intelligence activities, an organization needs an understanding of the role of ICT in these activities. This involves an understanding of the relation between ICT and CI activities and of the (current) possibilities of ICT for supporting CI activities.

This book intends to address this need. The chapters in this book all contribute to an improved understanding of the role and contribution of ICT regarding CI activities. The coverage provided in this book ranges from conceptual issues (addressing the relation of strategy formulation, viability and ICT) to practical issues (such as guidelines for implementing ICT tools to monitor strategy or case studies on Intranet usage for CI activities).

The following paragraphs provide an overview of the chapters of this book and their coverage of issues and applications.

Chapter I, titled *The Role of Information and Communication Technology in Competitive Intelligence*, by Dirk Vriens of the Nijmegen School of Management, University of Nijmegen, The Netherlands, provides an introduction in the relevant concepts used in this book. He presents a definition of competitive intelligence and reviews current literature on the use of ICT in intelligence activities. In this review, special attention is paid to the role of the Internet and to data warehouses and associated tools. The chapter ends with a discussion of criteria organizations can use to select ICT tools for supporting their intelligence processes.

Chapter II, titled *Sharp by Connection: Linking Competitive Intelligence and Intranets*, by Paul Hendriks of the Nijmegen School of Management, University of Nijmegen, The Netherlands, and Wendy Jacobs of PricewaterhouseCoopers, The Netherlands, assesses the usefulness of the concept of acceptability to secure an adequate conception of ICT's value to competitive intelligence. They use the Technology Acceptance Model and Task-

Technology Fit model to judge the acceptance of ICT (applications) in the context of the CI function. They use a case of an intranet application for CI to support their argument.

Chapter III, titled *Using Web Link Analysis to Detect and Analyze Hidden Web Communities*, by Edna Reid of Nanyang Business School, Nanyang Technological University, Singapore, explains that organizations have implicit Web communities, i.e., "hyperlinked" communities of Web users expressing an interest in the organization. According to the author, analyzing these communities may produce valuable knowledge about (hidden) stakeholders. The author proposes a framework for analyzing these communities and discusses how results from this analysis can be used for competitive intelligence. A case study is provided to demonstrate the use of the framework.

Chapter IV, titled *Enabling Strategy Formulation by ICT: A Viable Systems Approach*, by Dirk Vriens and Jan Achterbergh of the Nijmegen School of Management, University of Nijmegen, The Netherlands, approaches the use of ICT for CI from the perspective of strategy formulation. CI is a necessary part of strategy formulation and the authors hold the view that an understanding of the process of strategy formulation helps in understanding what intelligence is needed in this process. They use the viable systems model to derive the necessary knowledge that should be produced and processed for strategy formulation. Next, they discuss an "ICT-architecture" for supporting the knowledge processes, producing the relevant knowledge for strategy formulation.

Chapter V, titled *Using Groupware to Gather and Analyze Intelligence in a Public Setting: Development of Integral Safety Plans in an Electronic Meeting*, by Etiënne Rouwette and Jac Vennix of the Nijmegen School of Management, University of Nijmegen, The Netherlands, discusses a case in which groupware was used to support CI activities in a municipality in The Netherlands. Local Dutch municipalities encourage the participation of stakeholders in the development of safety plans. Relevant parties (representatives of, for instance, the police force, municipality, fire department or health care) participate in directing the information search, collection of data and analysis of data to arrive at a safety plan which can be forwarded to relevant members of responsible organizations. To support this group intelligence process, the authors describe the use of a specific kind of groupware application. They conclude that this application effectively supported the intelligence process.

Chapter VI, titled *Improving Competitive Intelligence Through System Dynamics*, by Özge Pala, Dirk Vriens and Jac Vennix of the Nijmegen School of Management, University of Nijmegen, The Netherlands, proposes the use of system dynamics to improve intelligence activities. The authors state that a "model of the organization in its environment" is needed in intelligence activities. In the direction stage, this model is used to determine the relevance of the environmental cues and in the analysis stage it is needed to determine the strategic impact of the values of these cues. Ideally, this model should capture the complexity and dynamics of the "real world." The authors explore the usefulness of system dynamics in arriving at such a model, because system dynamics seem suited for dealing with complexity and dynamics of systems. The authors present a method for using SD for CI. To build and analyze system dynamics-based models and to use them for CI purposes requires ICT support. At the end of the chapter, the authors deal with the issue of ICT support.

Chapter VII, titled *A Framework for Business Performance Management*, by Marco van der Kooij, Hyperion Solutions, The Netherlands, presents a method for tying ICT to the organization's intelligence needs, its management and to the collaboration of people within the organization. The method provides six steps organizations should take to arrive at ICT applications delivering the intelligence for managing their business performance. The author argues that using a framework like his can help to circumnavigate the pitfalls of business intelligence applications.

Chapter VIII, titled *The Source Map: A Means to Support Collection Activities*, by Dirk Vriens and Jan Achterbergh of the Nijmegen School of Management, University of Nijmegen, The Netherlands, presents a tool to deal with "meta data" regarding the sources organizations use in their intelligence gathering. The authors describe criteria to evaluate sources and argue that scores on these criteria can be used in (1) the selection of a relevant source vis-à-vis a certain intelligence topic and (2) evaluating the total collection of sources.

In Chapter IX, titled *Intelligence from Space: Using Geographical Information Systems for Competitive Intelligence*, by Paul Hendriks of the Nijmegen School of Management, University of Nijmegen, The Netherlands, it is argued that the spatial element in data and information relevant to organizations is underused in decision-making within the domain of Competitive Intelligence. The chapter explores how the CI function may benefit from developing a spatial perspective on its domain and how building, exploring and using this perspective may be supported by a specific class of information systems designed to handle the spatial element in data: Geographical Information Systems (GIS).

Chapter X, titled *Building a Competitive Intelligence System: An Infrastructural Approach*, by Egbert Philips of the Nijmegen School of

Management, University of Nijmegen, The Netherlands, argues that for building and implementing a competitive intelligence system, the ICT tools should be treated as a part of the intelligence infrastructure. The chapter presents an approach to ensure this. Moreover, it shows how this approach was used in a large company and illustrates the resulting ICT tool.

Chapter XI, titled *It's All in the Game: How to Use Simulation-Games for Competitive Intelligence and How to Support Them by ICT*, by Jan Achterbergh and Dirk Vriens of the Nijmegen School of Management, University of Nijmegen, The Netherlands, discusses the contribution of building and using simulation games for competitive intelligence activities. The authors argue that during building and use of these games, knowledge relevant for the four intelligence stages is produced and communicated. They also discuss possible uses of ICT to support building and using simulation games for CI.

Chapter XII, titled *Using Groupware to Build a Scenario-Based Early Warning System*, by Theo van Mullekom and Jac Vennix of the Nijmegen School of Management, University of Nijmegen, The Netherlands, shows how groupware supports scenario-building in order to contribute to the direction stage of the intelligence cycle. The authors present a procedure consisting of seven steps by means of which scenarios can be built. Moreover, they show how scenarios can be used to derive early warning variables that should be monitored to produce intelligence. Next, they discuss how groupware can support scenario-building.

ACKNOWLEDGMENTS

Putting together this book would not have been possible without the assistance and cooperation of those involved in the project. First of all, I would like to thank the authors for submitting their contributions and their assistance during the process. Most of the authors also served as referees for the chapters. I want to express my gratitude to those who provided critical, constructive and comprehensive reviews. In particular, I want to thank my colleagues at the Nijmegen School of Management for reading the manuscript and providing intelligent suggestions. Special thanks also go to the team at Idea Group Publishing, in particular to Mehdi Khosrow-Pour, who invited me to take on this project and to Jan Travers, Michele Rossi and Jennifer Sundstrom for their support. Finally, I want to thank my wife and children for their love and support throughout (and beyond) the project.

Chapter I

The Role of Information and Communication Technology in Competitive Intelligence

Dirk Vriens
University of Nijmegen, The Netherlands

ABSTRACT

This chapter discusses the role of ICT for competitive intelligence activities. To this end, it starts with an introduction to competitive intelligence. Next, it discusses possible uses of ICT for intelligence activities. In this discussion attention is paid to the use of the Internet, to general purpose ICT tools, to ICT tools tailored to one or more of the intelligence stages, and to business intelligence tools (data warehouses and tools to retrieve and present data in them). Finally, the chapter describes how organizations may select ICT applications to support their intelligence activities.

INTRODUCTION

Competitive Intelligence (CI) can be described as producing and processing information about the environment of an organization for strategic purposes (cf., Kahaner, 1997). To (re-) formulate their strategy, organizations need to collect and process information about their environment—about, for instance, competitors, customers, suppliers, governments, technological trends or ecological developments. Collecting and processing environmental information for strategic purposes is by no means something new. It has always been important. Without knowing what is going on in the environment, keeping the organization viable would be impossible. In fact, as Beer (1979) asserts, the "intelligence function" (scanning the environment in order to maintain the adaptability of a system) is a necessary function of *any* viable system. However, the issue of *explicitly* building and maintaining an intelligence function in an organization has only gained importance since the last few decades (cf., Hannon, 1997; Fleisher, 2001a). Due to the increasing complexity and dynamics of the environment the need to produce relevant "actionable" intelligence is increasing as well. Because of, for instance, increased global competition, (speed and impact of) political changes, and rapid technological developments (e.g., Kahaner, 1997; Cook & Cook, 2000; Fleisher & Blenkhorn, 2001) the need for information about the environment is more pressing than ever. As McDermott (in Hannon, 1997, p. 411) puts it, "Perhaps [CI] was inevitable, given the heightened competition that prevails now [...]." Or, putting it more directly: "If you are in business, you need competitor intelligence" (Fuld, 1995, p. 1). At the same time, organizations are facing a huge amount of available data about the environment. The Internet, although a very useful source of environmental data, is growing so large that finding relevant information is hard. As many authors point out (e.g., Cook & Cook, 2000; Chen et al., 2002), this leads to the problem of information overload.

Organizations are thus faced with an increased pressure to produce relevant information about the environment and, at the same time, with an extremely large, ever-increasing amount of data about the environment. To deal with this problem, many organizations are explicitly structuring their intelligence activities. Many have, for instance, implemented so-called "competitive intelligence units" (see Prescott & Fleisher, 1991; Kahaner, 1997; Fuld, 2002; or Gilad, 1996, for examples). To structure the process of competitive intelligence, several authors (cf., Kahaner, 1997; Gilad & Gilad, 1988; Herring, 1991; Bernhardt, 1994; Fuld et al., 2002) propose an "intelligence cycle," consisting of four stages:

1. **Direction.** In this stage the organization determines its "strategic information requirements." It determines about what aspects in the environment data should be collected.
2. **Collection.** Here, it is determined what sources can be used for data collection and the data are actually collected.
3. **Analysis.** In the analysis stage collected data are analyzed to assess whether they are useful for strategic purposes. In this stage, the actual "production" of intelligence (data relevant for strategy) takes place.
4. **Dissemination.** The intelligence (produced in stage 3) is forwarded to the strategic decision-makers and used to formulate their strategic plans.

To make sure that these activities can be carried out properly, an organization should implement a so-called "intelligence infrastructure" (Vriens & Philips, 1999). This infrastructure consists of three parts: (1) a technological part, comprising the ICT applications and ICT infrastructure that can be used to support the (stages in the) intelligence cycle, (2) a structural part, referring to the definition and allocation of CI tasks and responsibilities (e.g., should CI activities be centralized or decentralized? Should CI-activities be carried out by CI professionals or can others be involved?), and (3) a human resources part, which has to do with selecting, training and motivating personnel that should perform the intelligence activities. The challenge for organizations is to find a balanced "mix" of technological, structural and human resource measures to build and maintain the infrastructure (cf., Fuld, 1995; Kahaner, 1997; Gilad & Gilad, 1988; Hannon, 1997).

In this book we focus on the technological part of the infrastructure. In particular, we focus on the Information and Communication Technology (ICT) applications supporting the intelligence activities (see for instance Cook & Cook, 2000 for an overview). Examples of such ICT tools are the systematic use of the Internet for direction or collection activities (cf., McGonagle & Vella, 1999; McClurg, 2001), groupware applications for uncovering information requirements, specific applications for supporting the analysis of information (e.g., System Dynamics software), the use of an intranet for disseminating intelligence (cf., Cunningham, 2001; Teo & Choo, 2002), and data warehouses or data mining tools (cf., Zanasi, 1998; Cook & Cook, 2000; or Ringdahl, 2001).

Although many ICT tools to support intelligence activities are available, organizations face difficulties in using them. One particular difficulty is that there tends to be an overemphasis on the role of technology in obtaining intelligence.

As a result, some organizations rely too much on the use of their ICT applications for intelligence. For instance, ICT for competitive intelligence often means 'implementing' a data warehouse with tools for (quantitative) analysis. The software industry even seems to equate the term "business intelligence" (a "former" synonym of competitive intelligence) with data warehouses and associated tools. In other cases, organizations implemented a "CI unit," consisting of one person monitoring the results of an online database. In these cases, the technology is viewed as the only or most important means to produce intelligence. This can be problematic for several reasons. First, the data from data warehouses (or from ERP applications) mostly have an internal focus (cf., Fuld, 2002; Li, 1999) while competitive intelligence is about environmental data. Second, the use of ICT as the main source for intelligence may lead to an "unjustified sense of control" or even overconfidence in ICT for obtaining CI. This sense of control may emerge because of the vast amount of (electronic) sources one hopes to have at one's disposal—e.g., by means of an online database, by means of clever search engines or by means of a large data warehouse. However, the sense of control is unjustified, because one important source of intelligence—human intelligence (cf., Kahaner, 1997; Fleisher, 2001a; Fuld et al., 2002)—is not directly accessible via ICT [although the Internet may be used as a tool for tracking down and contacting primary sources (see Kassler, 1998)]. The sense of control is also unjustified because the number of electronic sources (e.g., websites) attached to the Internet is so large that no search engine covers all of them (see Chen et al., 2002). Moreover, their content is also (continuously) changing. Overconfidence in ICT for producing intelligence may also emerge because of the belief that intelligence activities can be automated. This is not true (yet) (see Fuld et al., 2002; Cook & Cook, 2000). As Cook and Cook (2000) remark: What you get from ICT-applications is data that still have to be put in a proper context to obtain intelligence. Direction and analysis remain the work of humans.

Another difficulty with using ICT in intelligence activities is that it can increase the information overload. If the collection stage is not properly directed, the Internet becomes "the intelligence-highway to hell": without a clear focus one can go on searching and mining forever.

A last problem with employing ICT in intelligence activities we want to mention here is that ICT is sometimes implemented without paying attention to the human resource and structural parts of the infrastructure. For example, a persistent problem with the use of an intranet for intelligence gathering and dissemination is that some "refuse" to use it. The reasons are various: ranging from "lack of time," "no part of my job-description," to "I don't see the point in using this system." In such cases, the importance of additional human resource measures to motivate personnel to use the intranet application is not recognized (see e.g., Bukowitz & Williams, 1999, for a treatment of this motivation issue). A way to deal with such problems is to treat ICT as a part of the whole infrastructure.

Despite such problems, however, ICT is a valuable part of the intelligence infrastructure. ICT offers many opportunities to support (and sometimes carry out parts of) intelligence activities. However, to avoid problems, organizations should be careful in selecting and implementing ICT applications for CI purposes. They should know the possibilities of ICT to deliver internal and external data and its capacity for supporting (and carrying out) CI activities, and they should treat ICT as a part of the whole infrastructure. In short, to support organizations in using ICT properly for their intelligence activities, an understanding of the role of ICT in intelligence activities is needed—both in terms of the (im)possibilities of ICT for intelligence activities and of its being a part of the whole intelligence infrastructure. This chapter intends to address this need. Its main goals are (1) to give an overview of the use of ICT for the intelligence activities, and (2) to present criteria for selecting proper ICT applications. To reach this goal, the plan for the chapter is as follows. In the next section we discuss competitive intelligence more closely. Next, we present an overview of ICT applications for CI. And finally we discuss the issue of selecting ICT for CI.

WHAT IS COMPETITIVE INTELLIGENCE?

To determine the role of ICT in competitive intelligence, it is first necessary to define CI. Many authors use the term, but their definitions differ. Consider, for instance, the following two definitions:

1. "CI is the process of ethically collecting, analyzing and disseminating accurate, relevant, specific, timely, foresighted and actionable intelligence regarding the implications of the business environment, competitors and the organization itself" (Society of Competitive Intelligence).
2. "CI is the process of obtaining vital information on your markets and competitors, analyzing the data and using this knowledge to formulate strategies to gain competitive advantage" (Yuan & Huang, 2001).

At a first glance, these definitions seem to refer to the same thing. Both refer to a process of obtaining information, analyzing it and using (or disseminating) it. Some differences may also be noted. One definition speaks of intelligence, while the other refers to information, data and knowledge. The second definition explicitly states the goal of CI—while the first leaves it more implicit.

In this section, we examine competitive intelligence by means of the following four aspects:

1.   the contribution of competitive intelligence
2.   competitive intelligence as a product
3.   competitive intelligence as a process
4.   the nature of the obtained competitive intelligence

This enables us to define CI and, at the same time, understand the differences and similarities of different definitions in the literature.

The Contribution of Competitive Intelligence

Authors mostly refer to two reasons for obtaining competitive intelligence. The first reason is that it contributes to an "overall organizational goal" such as improving its competitiveness or maintaining the viability of the organization. The second reason refers to the contribution of CI to the organizational activities needed to reach the overall goal (e.g., decision-making or strategy formulation). For instance, the second of the above definitions of CI refers to both kinds of contributions. It states: "CI is (…) to formulate strategies [second kind of contribution] to gain competitive advantage [first kind of contribution]." The first definition does not state either of the contributions. To our knowledge, most authors seem to agree about the overall contribution of CI. Some disagreement exists, however, about the organizational activities in which CI is used to reach this overall goal. Some hold the view that CI is used in decision-making at any level in the organization [e.g., the more ICT-oriented CI definitions (cf., Dresner, 1989)] while others maintain that it is mainly used in strategic decision-making (most authors seem to fall in this category: e.g., Fuld, 1995; Kahaner, 1996; Cook & Cook, 2000; Hannon, 1997). In defining CI, we will follow these authors and state that CI is tied to strategic decision-making.

Competitive Intelligence as a Product

In the literature, it is customary make a distinction between (competitive) intelligence as a product and as a process (e.g., Gilad & Gilad, 1988; Fuld, 1995; Kahaner, 1996; Fleisher, 2001a). In treating intelligence as a product, authors refer to the "information" or "knowledge" obtained and used for strategic purposes. The process view stresses the process by means of which this information or knowledge is obtained and used. Both the above definitions stress the process aspect. The first definition also highlights intelligence as a product.

If competitive intelligence is seen as a product, it is usually compared with data, information and knowledge (cf., Fuld, 1995; Kahaner, 1997; Vriens & Philips, 1999). To define intelligence as a product (and to compare it with data, information and knowledge) we use a framework provided by Achterbergh and Vriens (2002) (see Figure 1).

For the survival of any individual, two processes are imperative: observation and the performance of actions. In the process of observation, three steps can be distinguished. First, individuals perceive signals from the environment. These signals are referred to as data. The second step is that individuals make sense of these perceived data by putting them into a context or "frame of reference." Once perceived and interpreted, individuals may evaluate whether the signal is informative (contains something new—i.e., something the individual did not know already) and whether action is required. Information is now defined as "perceived and interpreted data, containing something new to the observer." Given this description, knowledge can be seen as the background for observation (cf., Achterbergh & Vriens, 2002). The process of performing actions consists of four steps: (1) selecting a desired effect (what does the individual want to achieve by acting?), (2) formulating options for obtaining the

Figure 1. Individual Observation and Action—A Model to Clarify the Distinction Between Data, Information and Knowledge

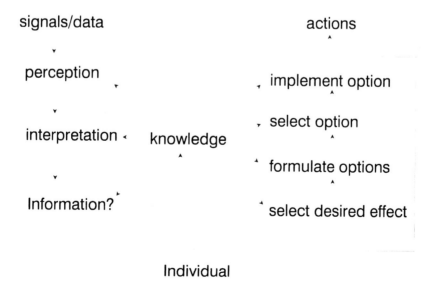

desired effect, (3) selecting an option, and (4) implementing the option. Figure 1 depicts these steps. Regarding the performance of actions, knowledge can be defined as that which serves as a background for these four steps.

In this view, knowledge has two main functions. It serves as a background for observing (or as Achterbergh & Vriens put it, the "assessment of signals") and for "performing actions." Note that knowledge is defined functionally. No attempt is made to sum up the content-elements of knowledge (see e.g., Davenport & Prusak, 1998). The reason for this is that the function of knowledge is easily pinned down, while its exact content is (still) "the subject of psychological research and philosophical debate" (Achterbergh & Vriens, 2002, p. 226).

Against the background of the definitions of data, information and knowledge, we can now define intelligence (see also Figure 2).

To do so, we transfer the above concepts from the realm of individual observing and acting to the organizational realm of strategic observing and acting. That is, we can define strategic observation as (1) "perceiving data from the environment," (2) making sense of these data—i.e., putting them in a strategic perspective, and (3) determining whether the data contain something

Figure 2. Organizational Observation and Action—A Model to Clarify the Distinction Between Data, Intelligence and Knowledge

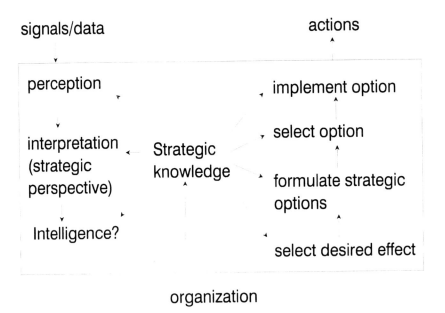

of strategic importance (something new and relevant for strategic purposes) and assessing whether strategic action is needed. In this process of "strategic observation," intelligence can be defined as the "strategic" counterpart of information. That is, if perceived and interpreted data contain something of strategic significance, and one did not already know this, the perceived and interpreted data can be defined as "intelligence." Intelligence, in turn, is evaluated in order to decide whether strategic action is needed. The four processes of (individual) action, as described above, can also be translated to strategic action. Knowledge may then refer to the background against which these strategic observations and actions occur—the "strategic knowledge" in the organization.

This view on intelligence and knowledge also makes apparent that what counts as intelligence in an organization depends on the existing strategic knowledge in the organization. This seems self-evident—but as Gilad (1996) points out, it is anything but: Incomplete or incorrect strategic knowledge often leads to the phenomenon of business blind spots.

Competitive Intelligence as a Process

Next to defining "intelligence as a product" it can also be seen as a process delivering this product. As we already stated in the introduction, authors often divide the process of competitive intelligence into four stages: (1) direction, (2) collection, (3) analysis, and (4) dissemination. The whole process (comprising these four steps) is usually called the intelligence cycle (see Figure 3).

Figure 3. The Four Stages of the Intelligence Cycle

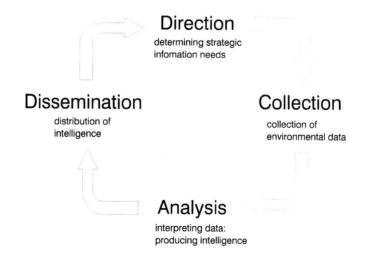

Direction
determining strategic
infomation needs

Dissemination
distribution of
intelligence

Collection
collection of
environmental data

Analysis
interpreting data:
producing intelligence

Below, we discuss these stages and illustrate them with findings from a study conducted by Lammers and Siegmund (2001). The object of this study was to give an overview of current CI practices in (large) organizations in The Netherlands. Although we are aware of the fact that these findings only represent the "Dutch" situation, we are somewhat confident in generalizing them, because many participating organizations are large multinationals (e.g., Shell, Akzo-Nobel, or Philips).

In the direction stage, the "strategic information requirements" are stated. In this stage, one determines about what aspects of the environment data should be gathered in order to produce intelligence. A distinction can be made between a "rough" data profile (indicating certain data *classes*, e.g., "We need to know something about the logistic capacity of competitor X and Y") and an exact data profile (indicating the exact data within a certain data class, e.g., "We need to know the amount of trucks and their capacity"). These topics (both in their exact or rough version) are also known as Competitive Intelligence Needs (Fleisher, 2001), Key Intelligence Topics (Kahaner, 1996) or Essential Information Elements (Sammon, 1984).

A particularly difficult aspect is determining the relevance of certain data classes before actual data about them are collected and before they can be interpreted, i.e., before intelligence can be produced. To accomplish this, some kind of model about the "organization in its environment" is needed. The challenge in the direction stage is to build and maintain such a model and to use it to define the strategically relevant data (classes) about the environment. In the literature, one often refers to the critical success factor method (or one of its variants; see for instance Sammon, 1986; Kahaner, 1997; Herring, 1999; or Cook & Cook, 2000) to build such a model and to derive environmental information needs from it.

In the second stage of the intelligence cycle, the required data are collected. To this end, two main activities are needed: (1) determining what sources are available and (2) accessing these sources and retrieving data from them. Many authors distinguish between several types of sources. For instance:

- open versus closed sources (open sources are accessible by everyone, closed sources are not);
- internal versus external sources (this distinction refers to the location where sources with data about the environment can be found: inside the organization (e.g., sales-representatives) or outside the organization);
- primary versus secondary sources [Primary sources are sources that hold the data in their original, unaltered form directly from the source from

which the original data stems. Secondary sources offer altered data (cf., Kahaner, 1997)];
- sources that differ in data carrier—i.e., paper, electronic and human sources.

To collect data that may contain strategic relevant information, many possible sources can be identified. Several authors sum up lists of possible sources. Among these are: the Internet, online databases, trade shows, consultants, customers, universities, embassies, suppliers, journals, labor unions, etc. (see for instance Cook & Cook, 2000; Vriens & Philips, 1999; or Kahaner, 1997 for a more comprehensive overview). Most organizations tend to use more than one source. In a recent study, Lammers and Siegmund (2001) asked organizations in The Netherlands what data sources they employed in their intelligence gathering. Figure 4 presents the results. As can be seen in the figure, trade journals, the Internet and online databases were found to be the three most used sources.

Figure 4. Sources Used by Large Organizations in The Netherlands for Collection Activities (Scores range from 0 (never) to 5 (always); Multiple answers are possible)

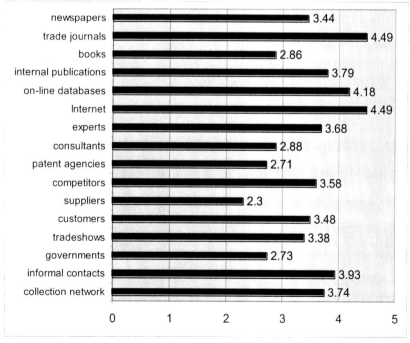

Source: Lammers & Siegmund, 2001

Gilad and Gilad (1988) stress the importance of an "intelligence collection network"—a network of people involved in collection activities. Members of this network may be dispersed throughout the organization and have all kinds of functions (e.g., service, R&D, purchase, or marketing and sales). The idea behind such a network is that individuals may collect information about the part of the environment they are closely related to. To give an impression of the nature of such networks, Table 1 summarizes the findings of Lammers and Siegmund regarding their composition in large organizations in The Netherlands. As can be seen, the study reveals a high involvement of marketing and sales, R&D and management in the collection network

To collect certain data, knowledge about the available sources should be gathered and used. This entails knowing (1) what sources may contain the requested data, (2) whether these sources can be approached and accessed adequately (measured, for instance, by means of general criteria like timeliness, costs, relevance, accuracy, whether the data is up-to-date, accessibility, etc. (cf., Gilad & Gilad, 1988), and (3) who will be involved in gathering data about the sources and in the actual collection activities. Managing the CI collection stage means ensuring that this knowledge is generated, stored and applied.

In the third stage of the intelligence cycle, the data is analyzed. In terms of the model we presented earlier (see Figure 1), the third stage focuses on interpreting the data from a "strategic point of view" to determine their strategic

Table 1.   Composition of the Intelligence Network Members of Organizations in the Lammers and Siegmund Study (The percentage refers to the percentage of organizations indicating that their collection network consisted of a specific member.)

Members of the Collection Network	Percentage
Marketing & Sales	79
Service	14
Purchase	29
R&D	50
Finance	14
Human Resources Dept.	7
Lawyers	14
Production	7
Management	57
Other	36

relevance (i.e., to determine whether the data contain intelligence). For this analysis, as with the direction stage, a model of what is relevant for the organization should be available. Many authors present both general and specific models for this purpose. Among the general models are SWOT analysis; the growth-share matrix of the Boston Consultancy Group; scenario-analysis; war-gaming; and competitor profiling (see Kahaner, 1997; Fuld, 1995; Powell & Allgaier, 1998; or Cook & Cook, 2000 for overviews of these models, and Fleisher, 2001b for a reflection on the analysis stage). More specific models are models about patent behavior (Kahaner, 1997; Poynder, 1998) or models tied to specific products. The goal of these models is to provide a context for interpreting data. For instance, an increase in R&D budget of a competitor may mean several things. A SWOT analysis may be used to put this "piece of data" in its proper context. If its R&D was analyzed to be a competitor weakness, the threat of a budget increase may be viewed as less serious than in the case where R&D was analyzed as state of the art.

In the same study we mentioned earlier, Lammers and Siegmund asked several Dutch organizations what models they used in the analysis stage. Table 2 presents the results. These results confirm the popularity of the SWOT analysis. It also turned out that organizations used models they made themselves (in the "other" category).

In the last stage of the intelligence cycle, the intelligence should be made available for strategic decision-making. That is, the intelligence should be presented clearly and distributed to relevant decision makers, using it to

Table 2. Models Used in the Analysis Stage (Lammers & Siegmund, 2001) (The percentage refers to the percentage of organizations indicating that they used a certain model for analysis.)

Models, Used in the Analysis Stage	Percentage
Simulation	35
War gaming	15
Scenario analysis	40
BCG-matrix	45
SWOT analysis	80
Financial analysis	65
Competitor profiles	90
Other	40

evaluate current strategic options and to generate, compare, select and implement new ones. Relevant in this stage is to make sure that the intelligence is actually used in strategic decision-making. All kinds of measures may be helpful in accomplishing this. For instance:

- paying attention to the format and clarity of the presentation of intelligence to strategic decision-makers (e.g., Fuld et al., 2002);
- using electronic means to store and distribute the intelligence to the right people;
- designing CI tasks and responsibilities in such a way that strategic management is involved in the intelligence activities (cf., Gilad & Gilad, 1988).

The Nature of the Obtained Competitive Intelligence

Some confusion exists about the difference between competitive intelligence and terms closely related or associated with competitive intelligence, e.g., competitor intelligence, market(ing) research or corporate espionage. One existing confusion is the difference between competitive intelligence and other kinds of intelligence. Data about many environmental aspects may be of strategic significance, e.g., data about competitors, about technological changes, about governments, about suppliers, etc. If the subject about which data is collected is not specified (if the scope is broad), one tends to speak about *competitive* intelligence. In this chapter, we will also refer to competitive intelligence in this broad sense. The common factor in data about these subjects is that they can all contain information of strategic importance. If, however, intelligence is produced and processed about a specific (environmental) subject, authors often use terms indicating this subject: e.g., *competitor* intelligence, *technological* intelligence, or *marketing* intelligence. Some authors even seem to equate competitive intelligence with competitor intelligence (e.g., Fuld, 1995). Of special interest is the term "business intelligence." This term was previously used to refer to the same issues as competitive intelligence (cf., Gilad & Gilad, 1988; Pawar & Sharda, 1997 who use the term business intelligence instead of competitive intelligence). However, lately, the software industry took over the term "business intelligence" to refer to a specific constellation of ICT tools used for organizational decision-making in general (cf., Cook & Cook, 2000; Fuld et al., 2002). We will adhere to this development and refer to BI as a specific set of ICT tools.

In defining CI, authors (cf., Gilad & Gilad, 1988; Cook & Cook, 2000) also stress the difference between CI and marketing research. This difference is partly a matter of scope. As Gilad and Gilad (1988, p. 8) put it: "Although the information produced by a market research department is intelligence, it is only a small part of the total intelligence required for decision making." Hannon, (1997, p. 411) states that marketing research is different because "it is usually undertaken within the marketing function and, obviously, is more limited in scope than the overall competitive intelligence process." Gilad and Gilad (1988) also emphasize that CI tends to be a more continuous activity than marketing research.

A last related term is corporate espionage. Although one may obtain intelligence by means of corporate espionage, the difference is that corporate espionage includes collection activities that are usually viewed as illegal and/or unethical: such as "dumpster diving," stealing information or illegal access to an intranet, to name a few. CI only employs legal activities to produce intelligence (cf., Hannon, 1997; Gilad & Gilad, 1988; Kahaner, 1997; Cook & Cook, 2000; Fleisher, 2001a).

Defining CI: A Summary

In our effort to define CI, we can now make the following statements about CI:

- As a product, CI is "environmental information relevant for strategic purposes."
- As a process, CI can be described by the intelligence cycle consisting of four stages: direction, collection, analysis and dissemination.
- The CI process aims to deliver CI as a product for strategic decision-making.
- CI differs from corporate espionage, business intelligence and other kinds of intelligence and from market(ing) research.

With this understanding of the concept of CI we can now look at the role of ICT for CI in the next section.

ICT FOR COMPETITIVE INTELLIGENCE

In this section, we discuss ICT tools for CI, i.e., ICT tools for supporting the activities in the intelligence cycle. To this end, we first try to position ICT tools for CI in the traditional classification of ICT applications. Next, we discuss four classes of ICT tools for CI.

Traditionally, ICT applications for management in organizations are classified along two well-known dimensions: the type of structure of the organizational task or decision the application is supposed to support (divided in structured, semi-structured and unstructured tasks or decisions) and the organizational (management) level at which these tasks or decisions reside (usually the operational, tactical and strategic management level) (see for instance Laudon & Laudon, 2000). Typically, transaction processing systems (TPS) are operational level systems supporting structured tasks; management information systems (MIS) support tactical (middle level) management by summarizing and reporting output of all kinds of TPS's—still supporting structured tasks. Decision support systems (DSS) typically add analytical tools to MIS for performing "what-if analysis." This analysis is said to be semi-structured. Executive support systems (EIS) refer to tools supporting high level management in their rather unstructured task of strategy making.

We acknowledge that this list of applications is incomplete and that it does not do justice to the research attempting to order ICT applications. The reason for the inclusion of this classification is to see where ICT for CI can be placed. ICT for CI aims at supporting strategic decision-making and thus supports—in the end—an unstructured organizational task. However, CI activities differ in structure: some CI tasks are highly structured (e.g., find experts on subject X); while others are not (e.g., "define the strategic information needs" or "analyze what it means that competitor X closes plant Y"). Moreover, CI tools may be employed at all levels in the organization: at the operational level (e.g., aiding sales representatives in asking questions to customers and storing the answers), at the tactical level (e.g., in supporting the management of CI professionals or supporting the analysis of environmental information) and at the strategic level (e.g., in presenting overviews of trends and their effects on the current or projected strategy). Therefore, ICT for CI (or Competitive Intelligence Systems—CIS) seem to defy an exact classification according to these dimensions. Instead, the dimensions can be used to state that CIS is best seen as a collection of electronic tools (see also Rouibah & Ould-ali, 2002):

- ultimately meant to support strategic decision-making;
- dispersed over different management levels; and
- supporting structured and unstructured intelligence activities.

In this section we will elaborate on the nature of these electronic tools. For this elaboration, we classify them according to (1) their contribution to one or more stages of the intelligence cycle and (2) the specificity of the tool. The latter "dimension" has two positions: a tool can be a general ICT tool used for intelligence activities (like groupware, used for direction activities or the Internet, used for collection or dissemination activities) or a tool specifically tailored to one or more intelligence activities. We will use this classification in our discussion of the tools below. We first discuss the Internet as a "general" ICT tool for all CI activities. Next, we pay attention to other ICT tools—both general and specific. And, finally, we discuss business intelligence applications as a specific set of ICT applications useful for CI activities.

The Internet as a Tool for CI

CI practitioners rely heavily on the use of the Internet for their intelligence activities. The Internet is sometimes seen as the most important information resource for competitive intelligence and, to our knowledge, the Internet as CI tool has received the most attention in the literature (e.g., Cronin et al., 1994; Graef, 1997; Teo & Choo, 2001; Chen et al., 2002; Cook & Cook, 2000; McCurgle, 2001). Chen et al. (2002, p. 1) state that a 1997 Futures group report identifies the Internet as one of the top five sources. Lammers and Sigmund (2001) found that, in organizations they approached, the Internet was the most preferred source for acquiring information.

The Internet can be used in numerous ways to produce intelligence. Examples are: searching certain information by using search engines (Graef, 1997; Chen et al., 2002; Cook & Cook, 2000); obtaining knowledge about costumers through interactive websites and agents (Teo & Choo, 2001); receiving feedback from customers about competitors or one's own products and services (Teo & Choo, 2001); monitoring discussion groups on competitors (Cronin et al., 1994; Graef, 1997); conducting patent search (Poynder, 1998); improving stock decisions by monitoring online stock data available from retailers (Yuan & Huang, 2001); accessing the latest news through a wire service (Cook & Cook, 2000); learning about competitors and partners by visiting their websites (Cronin et al., 1994; Graef, 1997; Chen et al., 2002; Cook & Cook, 2000), searching and contacting experts (Kassler, 1998); accessing governmental files (Kahaner, 1997; Cook & Cook, 2000); monitoring the "e-behavior" of visitors to your website (Tan & Kumar, 2002); gaining easy access to expertise through discussion groups (Teo & Choo, 2001; Cook & Cook); or "outsourcing" collection activities by using commercial online databases (Cronin et al., 1994; Graef, 1997; Gieskes, 2000; Cook & Cook, 2000; Kahaner, 1997).

To discuss the use of the Internet for one or more stages in the intelligence cycle, Teo and Choo (2001) propose to make a distinction between its internal use (Intranet), its external use (Extranet) and its use for "primary and secondary research." However, this seems to confuse two distinctions: one regarding a division of the Internet (into Intranet, Extranet and "beyond") and one regarding the stages in the intelligence cycle (of which Teo and Choo highlight the collection stage). To avoid this confusion, we would like to propose to use both distinctions. Below, we first discuss Internet tools for direction, analysis and dissemination and next devote a section to Internet tools for the collection stage.

Internet for Direction, Analysis and Dissemination

Few studies mention the use of the Internet for the direction, analysis and dissemination stages. To support the direction stage, an Intranet application may enhance communication of and collaboration regarding results of this stage [e.g., an internal discussion site may be used to define and monitor intelligence needs (see Vriens & Hendriks, 2000)]. The same sort of Internet applications may be used to support the analysis stage. Teo and Choo (2001) discuss the relevance of the Internet (Intranet and Extranet) for all CI activities: they hold the view that it (especially e-mail, Intranets, Extranets and databases) enhances internal and external collaboration in CI activities (e.g., multi-departmental analysis of intelligence and the exchange of intelligence between departments as well as the exchange of CI data with suppliers, external consultants and customers). The Internet can also be used to enhance internal and external dissemination of CI data (Teo & Choo, 2001, p. 70, 73; Graef, 1996; Cunningham, 2001). Furthermore, Teo and Choo expect an increase in external collaboration and dissemination (i.e., with relevant stakeholders for mutual benefit) through Extranets.

The Use of the Internet for Collection Activities

The Internet is mainly used for collection purposes and many different tools and uses are reported. A difference can be made between using the Internet for searching and accessing electronic data available on the Internet versus searching and accessing other sources by means of the Internet (like people, trade shows, conferences, etc.—cf., Cook & Cook, 2000; Kassler, 1997). In the first case, the Internet contains the requested data, while in the second case, the Internet is viewed as a means for referring to other sources (like a knowledge map—cf., Davenport & Prusak, 1998). To this end, Kassler (1997) explains that the Internet is invaluable as a means for locating people and contacting them. Cook and Cook (2000) give several sites where information about other sources (experts, trade shows, conferences, etc.) can be found and state their usefulness for CI.

Most attention, though, seems to be on searching and accessing directly available data. However, due to the extremely large number of sites, (and hence) the amount of information and due to the changes in this information, finding the right data is not easy. Chen et al. (2002) state that to deal with a possible information overload a number of tools are available that "analyze, categorize and visualize large collections of Web pages" and "assist in searching, monitoring and analyzing information on the Internet" (Chen et al., p. 3). Below, we discuss some of these tools.

Search Engines

Many CI authors discuss the usefulness of Web search engines for collecting data on the Internet. Typically, they refer to the difference between "common" search engines that can approach websites with some user defined information based on their own indexes (examples are Altavista.com or Yahoo.com) and "meta" search engines, using other ("common") search engines to conduct the search and integrate the results (cf., Chen et al., 2002). Among the search engines a difference is made between general and specific engines (cf., Chen et al., 2002; Cook & Cook, 2000). The specific engines cover a part of the Internet (qua content) e.g., governmental information or patents. Chen et al. (2002) also distinguish between (commercial) engines available through a browser and engines residing on user machines.

Tools for "Outsourcing" Collection Activities

A part of the collection activities can be outsourced to some (automated) service or tool offered via the Web. One way of "outsourcing" collection activities is making use of commercial online databases such as Lexis-Nexis, Dow Jones or Dialog (see Gieskes, 2000; Kahaner, 1997; Cook & Cook, 2000). As Chen et al. (2002) assert and Lammers and Siegmund (2001) found, these online databases are among the main sources for CI professionals. Another way of "outsourcing" collection activities is to employ "Web robots or agents." As Tan and Kumar (2002, p. 9) put it, "Web robots are software programs that automatically traverse the hyperlink structure of the WWW to locate and retrieve information." Cook and Cook (2000, p. 112) add, that "there are many valuable types of bots that can speed up the information gathering process including stock bots, spider bots, shopping bots, news bots [...]."

Tools for Text-Analysis

To support the collection of valuable data in (large) text files, Chen et al. (2002) mention tools for text-analysis—i.e., "automatic indexing algorithms to extract key concepts from textual data." Because of the time spent on reading textual material, these tools may greatly enhance the collection of relevant textual data.

Tools for Monitoring Changes on the Web

Another useful set of tools for collecting relevant data on the Internet are tools that help in monitoring changes in particular parts of the Internet. Among the tools monitoring the Internet are "alerting services" (see Kassler), an online service that alerts you whenever a change to a given topic in a relevant part of the Internet [like a collection of Web pages, bulletin boards, or mailing lists (cf., Kassler, 1997; Vriens & Hendriks, 2000; Chen et al., 2002)] occurs. The previously mentioned Web robots can be used for these alerting functions.

Tools for Collecting Data about the "Electronic" Behavior of Internet Users

One particular use of the Internet for analysis purposes also receiving little attention in the CI literature is monitoring the (electronic) behavior of users of the Internet [e.g., by identifying their navigational patterns or clickstreams (cf., Tan & Kumar, 2002)]. Of course, software is available to keep track of several statistics of visitors to websites, but tools to further analyze this behavior for CI purposes seem to be less available. Reid (in this volume) presents an example of such a tool.

Internet Tools for Collaboration in Search Activities

As has been put forward, the network of intelligence collectors plays an important role in collection activities (Gilad & Gilad, 1988). Internet applications can be used to facilitate the (self) management of and collaboration in these networks. As an example, one may consider an Intranet application through which a "competitor profile" is available to the members of the network, so that each member can fill in his or her part of that profile. Such applications enable monitoring the collection behavior of the members of the network and discussing and "correcting" each other's contribution (see Chapter X, for such an application).

Moving Beyond the Internet: General and Specific ICT tools for CI

Above, we discussed how the Internet (or tools exploring or mining the Internet) can be used for CI activities. We thus discussed how a general set of Internet-oriented tools can be made available for CI purposes. In this section we discuss (1) other general ICT tools that can be used for supporting CI activities and (2) specific ICT applications designed for one or more CI activities (among them are "CI-software" packages as Fuld et al. (2002) call them, and CI applications developed in-house). ICT tools from both classes may or may not use specific Internet applications as discussed above.

General ICT Tools for CI

General tools for the direction stage should aid in formulating strategic information requirements and in storing and disseminating (sub) results of this process. Among these are tools:

- supporting specific methods for identifying, storing and disseminating strategic information needs; for instance, tools that visualize the variables and their causal relations relevant for specifying the information needs. Examples are software supporting system dynamics (e.g., Vensim or Powersim—see Vennix, 1996), or software supporting, identifying or visualizing CSF's or Key Intelligence Topics (e.g., Mindmap).
- supporting the process of identifying strategic information needs—such as different types of groupware (cf., Coleman, 1997) or software supporting group model building (e.g., Vennix, 1996). An example of a suitable groupware application is GroupSystems (Nunamaker et al., 1991). This application enables different users to anonymously discuss, brainstorm about, categorize, and vote on relevant intelligence topics. Rouwette and Vennix (this volume) discuss groupware for direction purposes.

General tools for the analysis stage are comparable to those in the direction stage. They should:

- support specific methods used in analysis—e.g., SD software that enables CI professionals to run "simulations" with certain data and thus helps to establish their relevance. Other examples are applications supporting war-gaming or scenario analysis.
- support (management of and collaboration in) the process of analysis. Again, specific groupware applications may serve this purpose. In this

category one may also include applications supporting the storage and dissemination of the analysis results (for use during analysis). Many general databases with Intranet access can be used. Specific Intranet applications for dissemination and collaboration were discussed in the previous section.

For disseminating intelligence, one may identify all kinds of applications that support (1) the presentation of the intelligence in a suitable format and/or (2) transmitting reports throughout the organization. Many applications are available, including standard drawing packages or Microsoft Office, for sending and receiving documents.

Specific ICT Applications for CI

Fuld et al. (2002) produced several "intelligence software reports." In these reports they analyzed a number of software packages said to be designed specifically for (supporting) one or more CI activities. For each stage in the intelligence cycle (Fuld et al. identify five stages: they split up collection into collection of primary and of secondary sources) they derived criteria to score the applications. For the most part, these criteria link up with what has been said in this chapter. For instance, for the direction stage, Fuld et al. (2002, pp. 12-13) state that the fulfillment of the following functions acts as criteria in judging CI applications:

- Providing a framework to input Key Intelligence Topics and Key Intelligence Questions
- Receiving CI requests
- Managing a CI work process and project flow that allows collaboration among members of the CI team as well as with the rest of the company

Criteria for other stages refer to the:
- Ability to search effectively and efficiently internal or external sources
- Ability to deal with qualitative information
- Ability to support ordering, visualizing and mining information
- Ability to support several methods for analyzing data
- Ability to report and deliver reports
(For the exact criteria, the reader is referred to Fuld et al., 2002.)

Based on their analysis, Fuld et al. (2002) arrive at several conclusions. Among these are:

1.   The "CI-software cannot drive the CI-process" (p. 2), but it can help in collecting data, in reporting and communicating intelligence and in supporting the workflow and collaboration.
2.   No application can deal with all the intelligence stages adequately.
3.   No application can "truly conduct qualitative analysis" (p. 10)—but some tools seem promising in assisting CI analysts to see novel linkages (p. 2). This conclusion seems to fit comments of other authors about the possibility of ICT applications in replacing human intelligence activities. As Cook and Cook (2000) point out: "innovative applications for analyzing competitive factors and forecasting the outcomes of strategic decisions may seem like the unrealistic dreams of CEOs and CIOs alike" (p. 165). However, they expect changes in the future. It is our conjecture that CI activities remain the work of humans. ICT can facilitate them—but it can never replace them.

Fuld et.al. (2002) analyzed commercially available CI applications and concluded that there exists no "one-size-fits-all" solution. They add that the technology needs of organizations differ depending on their specific CI requirements. This may be the reason for organizations to build and maintain CI applications themselves.

Business Intelligence Applications

For some time, the terms competitive intelligence and business intelligence have been used as synonyms (e.g., Gilad & Gilad, 1988; Vriens & Philips, 1999; Pawar & Sharda, to name a few authors). However, the software industry has taken over the term business intelligence (BI) to indicate a specific set of ICT tools. These BI tools refer to ICT tools enabling (top) management to produce overviews of and analyze relevant organizational data needed for their (strategic) decision-making. As a BI vendor defines it: "Business intelligence (BI) takes the volume of data your organization collects and stores, and turns it into meaningful information that people can easily use. With this information in accessible reports, people can make better and timelier business decisions in their everyday activities" (www.cognos.com). As early as 1989 the Gartner group specified the nature of BI tools: "Today's [BI] technology categories include EISs, DSSs, query and reporting tools and online analytical processing (OLAP)." These categories currently include data warehouses (cf., Mahony, 1998) and new tools for analysis (e.g., data mining, cf., Zanasi, 1998) and reporting.

Data warehouses seem to have gained a central position in BI. Moreover, most vendors seem to equate BI with the use of data warehouse and tools for access and analysis of the data in it. Inmon (1993) defines a data warehouse as "a subject oriented, integrated, nonvolatile, and time variant collection of data in support of management's decisions." In an organization, possible relevant data for strategic decision-making is scattered in many databases (e.g., transactional databases, financial databases, personnel databases, etc.). Long and Long (2002, p. 425) point out that such data, which are not integrated and may contain redundancies, are hard to access. To cope with these problems, these data are collected and copied to a data warehouse and 'reorganized into a format that gives decision-makers ready access to valuable, time-sensitive information' (ibid). To keep the data in the data warehouse up to date, data from the source databases should be copied to it on a regular (weekly or sometimes daily) basis.

To gain access to a data warehouse and analyze its data, three types of tools are usually identified: queries, OLAP and data mining. For queries, query languages (like SQL) can be used. However, most of these are cumbersome for easy end-user access and not really suited for analysis. Online analytical processing (OLAP) is a tool for online analysis and manipulation of data. A user does not specify a query, but specifies so-called "dimensions" (like customer, product, region, time) and is able to relate these dimensions to each other in a very user-friendly way. The results can be shown directly in several formats (graphs, tables, numbers) and manipulated.

Data mining refers to a set of (statistical or artificial intelligence) tools to detect (new) relations in data (cf., Zanasi, 1998). Through data mining, for instance, elusive patterns in customer behavior may be detected. For example, a large retailer in The Netherlands discovered that buying a certain brand of diapers was positively correlated to buying a certain brand of beer. Such discoveries may be used for all kinds of purposes—ranging from identifying cross-selling opportunities or specifying marketing campaigns to improving shop layouts (cf., Long & Long, 2000). The basic architecture of a data warehouse (and tools for its use) is given in Figure 5.

The figure makes apparent that the source databases can be internal (transactional databases, financial databases, CRM data, or data from ERP systems, etc.) and external (e.g., databases from business partners, (commercially available) databases containing economic statistics, patent information, etc., or even online databases). However, most data warehouses only cover internal data—i.e., data generated in the transactions of the organization. As Fuld et al. (2002) put it: "BI software [...] typically deals with data warehouses

Figure 5. Basic Architecture of a Data Warehouse

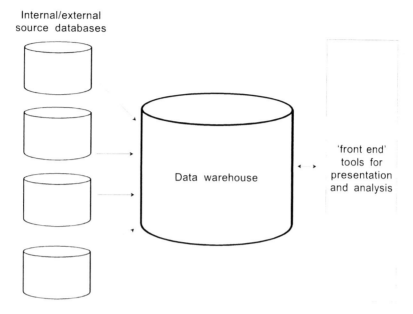

Internal/external
source databases

Data warehouse

'front end'
tools for
presentation
and analysis

and quantitative analysis, almost exclusively of a company's internal data" (p. 7). This, of course, is a major drawback when treating BI tools as CI tools. However, we feel that once data warehouses are used for storing (and updating) relevant *external* data, they may become valuable CI tools as well.

Next to their internal focus, other drawbacks with BI software can be mentioned. In the previous quotation of Fuld, a second problem arises: BI software primarily deals with quantitative analysis, while CI relies heavily on qualitative data. Other problems have to do with costs and implementation: data warehouses require large budgets and much implementation time and effort. Cook and Cook (2000, Chapter IX) also refer to the "high expectations" organizations have regarding BI software. In particular, one cannot expect BI software to produce intelligence. In their view, the results from analyzing data in a warehouse produce data that should "be analyzed and directly applied to a specific problem" to become intelligence. Therefore, "human intervention" is still needed.

HOW TO SELECT ICT FOR CI?

Now that an overview of ICT tools for CI has been presented, the question can be raised of what ICT tools are appropriate, given specific organizational

CI needs. In this section we discuss three classes of criteria organizations can use to select ICT tools for CI. These classes are: (1) criteria regarding the contribution of ICT applications to one or more stages of the intelligence cycle, (2) criteria regarding the CI infrastructure and (3) criteria pertaining to costs. These three classes correspond roughly to the criteria used in the selection of ICT applications in general according to the information economics approach (cf., Parker, Benson & Trainor, 1988).

Criteria Regarding the Contribution to One or More Stages of the Intelligence Cycle

An (candidate) ICT application should contribute to one or more stages of the intelligence cycle. Criteria to judge the contribution of a particular ICT application to a certain stage (or to several stages) may refer to its appropriateness to deliver the desired *products* for the stage and to whether it fits the *process* leading to these products. For example, collection applications should be evaluated regarding their appropriateness to collect the desired data (e.g., patent data). Applications should also match process aspects—for example, a particular application should support the particular methods (to be) used in the intelligence activities—e.g., a SWOT analysis or a system dynamics analysis. For more examples of such criteria, we refer to the criteria used by Fuld et al. (2002) to judge CI applications.

Criteria Regarding the Relation with the CI Infrastructure

The (CI) infrastructure may be decomposed into three sub-infrastructures: the ICT-infrastructure (this consists of the 'technological infrastructure' (ICT hardware, software and telecommunications technology) and the applications running on the technological infrastructure (cf., Earl, 1989), the human resources infrastructure and the organizational infrastructure; i.e., the structure of the organization qua CI-tasks and responsibilities. For each of these sub-infrastructures, specific sets of criteria can be given.

The criteria regarding the ICT infrastructure focus on the question of whether the application fits the current ICT infrastructure. This fit depends, among other things, on the current set of ICT tools used to support the CI activities. Does the application fit into this set? Does it deliver more functionalities than this set? Is an easy link between the applications in this set (if desirable) possible? Other questions for judging the fit to the ICT infrastructure have to do with the "technological" fit (does the current hard- and software permit the implementation of the application—or does it require large changes? Is the application reliable? Maintainable?). Yet another question for judging the fit to the ICT infrastructure has to do with the contribution of an application to the improvement of the infrastructure—e.g., through a particular application obsolete applications are replaced (or may be replaced more easily), or, through a particular application other state of the art applications can be implemented and used more easily. A data warehouse, for instance, can be seen as a contribution to the current infrastructure, because it enables all kinds of tools for visualizing and analyzing (internal) data.

The second set of criteria reflects the fit of the application to the human resources infrastructure—i.e., whether it fits existing skills, knowledge and attitudes of those who are carrying out CI activities. Important questions are, for instance, whether the required knowledge and skills (if any) are acquired easily, or whether the CI staff is motivated to integrate the ICT application into their routines. Criteria regarding the human infrastructure relate to the concept of "social acceptability" of an application [cf., Hendriks & Davis (this volume); Nielsen, 1999; Hartwick & Barki, 1994; Venkatesh & Speier, 1999]. This refers to standards or to the existence or absence of pressure to use an application. Authors on the subject of knowledge management have formulated criteria to diagnose and design solutions regarding problems with motivational aspects regarding the use of ICT for supporting knowledge processes (see e.g., Bukowitz & Williams, 1999).

The third set of infrastructural criteria reflects the fit of the application to the current definition and allocation of CI tasks and responsibilities (see Gilad & Gilad, 1988 for several ways of defining and allocating them). It does not make sense to install groupware for the direction stage if direction is not seen as a group process. The same holds for using ICT tools structuring collection and analysis activities if the whole CI process has a highly informal nature. In some cases, a task structure may be designed poorly and ICT for CI may act as a leverage to change the current task structure. An ICT tool can be valued because of its contribution to the improvement of the task infrastructure. A common example of a non-CI application said to improve the task-structure is workflow management systems (cf., Laudon & Laudon, 2000). In a similar vein, a groupware application may be valued for contributing to implementing the direction stage as a group process. Philips (this volume) discusses an example of an organization using the implementation of a competitive intelligence system to analyze and change its whole CI infrastructure (including its human resources; technological and organizational structure).

Criteria Pertaining to Costs

These criteria refer to the costs of the application itself, its implementation (e.g., project costs, training, etc.) and its maintenance. These costs may be calculated by different methods (cf., Parker et al.).

Selecting ICT for CI Using the Three Types of Criteria

To judge the appropriateness of an application for CI in a particular organization, the application should be "scored" regarding all three classes of criteria. To this end, the individual criteria in a class should all be identified, valued, and integrated into an overall score for the class. We will not treat all these sub-steps in this section—rather, we show how these overall scores can be used to select ICT for CI.

The overall scores of each class express (1) the contribution of a particular application to one or more of the intelligence stages, (2) the fit of the contribution to the CI infrastructure, and (3) the costs related to an application. These scores can be plotted in a graph (see Figure 6) — the size of the circle indicates the costs of an application.

In this figure, the scores of several applications are depicted (the size of the circles reflects the costs related to the application). For instance, application 1 may be a data warehouse (with an internal focus). This application is very expensive and contributes only partly to the intelligence stages (it contributes to the collection stage, but due to its internal focus its contribution to the CI stages is low). The data warehouse may contribute to the general infrastructure,

Figure 6. Classification of ICT Applications for CI Using Three Dimensions (See text)

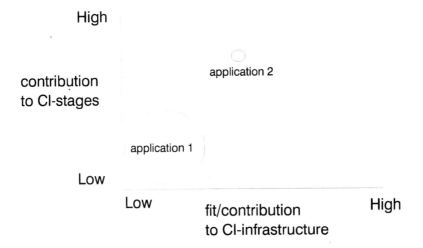

but, in our view, contributes only partly to the CI infrastructure. By contrast, a data warehouse with explicit external linkages would still be very expensive, but may score higher on both other dimensions. Application 2 may be a groupware application. These applications are moderately expensive, may contribute to the direction stage and fit the infrastructure in several ways.

An organization may treat several ICT tools for the support of its CI activities in this way and eventually select some of them.

CONCLUSION

To select and use proper ICT tools for supporting the CI process, organizations should know (1) what the CI process is, (2) what the role of ICT (tools) in this process can be, and (3) judge the role of ICT (tools) for their own CI process. In this chapter, we discussed these three aspects. We defined CI both as a product and as a process. We then discussed the role of ICT tools in the CI process. Here, we presented four types of ICT tools relevant for supporting (and sometimes even replacing) CI activities: the Internet, general applications to be used in CI activities, specific CI applications and business intelligence applications. In the last part of this chapter we discussed three classes of criteria organizations can use in evaluating and selecting ICT tools for their CI process.

Although the definition of CI and the criteria for selecting ICT tools for CI seem to have stabilized, the possibilities of using ICT for CI increase rapidly. Some of the trends that may be acknowledged are:

- A convergence of BI and CI applications (e.g., data warehouses and associated software also tied to external and qualitative data) (cf., Li, 1999)
- Using ICT for qualitative data may increase (e.g., Chen et al., 2002)
- Using the Internet for more than just collection activities (e.g., for collaboration and dissemination purposes) (cf., Teo & Choo, 2001; Cunningham, 2001)
- Improvement of Internet applications for collection (more efficient and effective collection applications will continue to emerge)
- Implementing CI applications can be seen as a process by means of which the CI process and infrastructure can be re-analyzed
- Improvement of analysis applications (cf., Fuld et al., 2002)

Despite all the possibilities of ICT for CI, we would like to end this chapter with remarking that producing intelligence still remains the work of humans who are the only "machines" able to put the data from the applications in their proper strategic perspective. ICT tools, however, are invaluable in supporting this task.

REFERENCES

Achterbergh, J.M.I.M. & Vriens, D. (2002). Managing viable knowledge. *Systems Research and Behavioral Science, 19,* 223-241.

Bernhardt, D.C. (1994). 'I want it fast, factual, actionable'—Tailoring competitive intelligence to executive needs. *Long Range Planning, 27*(1), 12-24.

Bukowitz, W.R. & Williams, R.L. (1999). *The Knowledge Management Fieldbook.* Edinburgh: Pearson.

Chen, H., Chau, M., & Zeng, D. (2002). CI-spider: A tool for competitive intelligence on the Web. *Decision Support Systems, 34,* 1-17.

Coleman, D.D. (1997). *Groupware: Collaborative Strategies for Corporate LANs and Intranets.* Upper Saddle River, NJ: Prentice Hall.

Cook, M. & Cook, C. (2000). *Competitive Intelligence.* London: Kogan Page.

Cronin, B., Overfelt, K., Fouchereaux, K., Manzvanzvike, T., Cha, M., & Sona, E. (1994). The Internet and competitive intelligence: a survey of current practice. *International Journal of Information Management, 14*(3), 204-222.

Cunningham, R. (2001). A toolbox for communicating competitive intelligence via the Internet. In C.G. Fleisher & D.L. Blenkhorn (Eds.), *Managing Frontiers in Competitive Intelligence* (pp. 90-99). Westport: Quorum.

Davenport, T.H. & Prusak, L. (1998). *Working Knowledge.* Boston, MA: Harvard Business School Press.

Dresner, H. (1993). *Business Intelligence: Competing Against Time.* Twelfth Annual Office Information Systems Conference, Gartner Group.

Earl, M.J. (1989). *Management Strategies for Information Technology.* Englewood Cliffs: Prentice Hall.

Fleisher, C.G. (2001a). An introduction to the management and practice of competitive intelligence (CI). In C.G. Fleisher & D.L. Blenkhorn (Eds.), *Managing Frontiers in Competitive Intelligence* (pp. 3-18). Westport: Quorum.

Fleisher, C.G. (2001b). Analysis in competitive intelligence: Process, progress and pitfalls. In C.G. Fleisher & D.L. Blenkhorn (Eds.), *Managing Frontiers in Competitive Intelligence* (pp. 77-89). Westport: Quorum.

Fleisher, C.G. & Blenkhorn, D.L. (2001). *Managing Frontiers in Competitive Intelligence*. Westport: Quorum.

Fuld, L.M. (1995). *The New Competitor Intelligence*. Chichester, UK: Wiley.

Fuld & Company. (2002). *Intelligence Software Report 2002*. Found at: http://www.fuld.com.

Gieskes, H. (2000). Competitive Intelligence at Lexis-Nexis. *Competitive Intelligence Review, 11*(2), 4-11.

Gilad, B. (1996) *Business Blindspots*. Calne (GB): Infonortics.

Gilad, B. & Gilad, T. (1988). *The Business Intelligence System*. New York: Amacon.

Graef, J.L. (1996). Sharing business intelligence on the world wide web. *Competitive Intelligence Review, 7*(1), 52-61.

Graef, J.L. (1997). Using the Internet for competitive intelligence: a survey report. *Competitive Intelligence Review, 8*(4), 41-47.

Hannon, J.M. (1997). Leveraging HRM to enrich competitive intelligence. *Human Resource Management, 36*(4), 409-422.

Hartwick, J. & Barki. (1994). Explaining the role of user participation in information system use. *Management Science, 40*(4), 440-465.

Herring, J.P. (1999). Key intelligence topics, a process to identify and define intelligence needs. *Competitive Intelligence Review, 10*(2), 4-14.

Inmon, W.H. (1993). *Building the Data Warehouse*. Chichester, UK: Wiley.

Kahaner, L. (1997). *Competitive Intelligence*. New York: Touchstone.

Kassler, H.S. (1997). Mining the Internet for competitive intelligence. How to track and sift for golden nuggets. *Online: The Magazine for Online Information Systems, 12*(5), 34-45.

Lammers, A. & Siegmund, J. (2001). *Business Intelligence in Nederland* [Business Intelligence in The Netherlands]. Master's thesis, University of Nijmegen (in Dutch).

Laudon, K.C. & Laudon, J.P. (2000). *Management Information Systems*. Upper Saddle River, NJ: Prentice Hall.

Li, C. (1999). ERP packages: What's next? *Information Systems Management,* (Summer), 31-35.

Long, L.E. & Long, N. (2002). *Computers: Information Technology in Perspective* (9th ed.). Upper Saddle River, NJ: Prentice Hall.

Mahony, T.M. (1998). Data warehousing and CI: An evaluation. *Competitive Intelligence Review, 9*(1), 38-43.

McClurg, R. (2001). Using the Internet for gathering competitive intelligence. In C.G. Fleisher & D.L. Blenkhorn (Eds.), *Managing Frontiers in Competitive Intelligence* (pp. 61-76). Westport: Quorum.

McGonagle, J.J. & Vella, C.M. (1999). *The Internet Age of Competitive Intelligence*. Westport: Quorum.

Nielsen, J. (1999). *Designing Web Usability*. Indianapolis: New Riders.

Nunamaker, J.F., Dennis, A.R., Valacich, J.S., Vogel, D.R., & George, J.F. (1991). Electronic meetings to support group work. *Communications of the ACM, 34*(7), 40-61.

Parker, M.M., Benson, R.J., & Trainor, H.E. (1988). *Information Economics: Linking Business Performance to Information Technology*. Englewood Cliffs: Prentice Hall.

Pawar, B.S. & Sharda, R. (1997). Obtaining business intelligence on the Internet. *Long Range Planning, 30*(1), 110-121.

Philips, E.A. & Vriens, D. (1999). *Business Intelligence*. Deventer: Kluwer.

Powell, T. & Allgaier, C. (1998). Enhancing sales and marketing effectiveness through competitive intelligence. *Competitive Intelligence Review, 9*(4), 29-41.

Poynder, R. (1998). Patent information on the Internet. *Business Information Review, 15*(1), 58-67.

Prescott, J.E. & Fleisher, C.S. (1991). SCIP: Who we are, what we do. *Competitive Intelligence Review, 2*(11), 22-26.

Ringdahl, B. (2001). The need for business intelligence tools to provide business intelligence solutions. In C.G. Fleisher & D.L. Blenkhorn (Eds.), *Managing Frontiers in Competitive Intelligence* (pp. 173-184). Westport: Quorum.

Rouibah, K. & Ould-ali, S. (2002). PUZZLE: A concept and prototype for linking business intelligence to business strategy. *The Journal of Strategic Information Systems, 11*(2), 133-152.

Sammon, W.L. (1986). Assessing the competition: Business intelligence for strategic management. In J.R. Gardner, R. Rachlin, & H.W. Sweeney (Eds.), *Handbook of Strategic Planning*. New York: Wiley.

Society of Competitive Intelligence Professionals. Found in: http://www.scip.org

Tan, P. & Kumar, V. (2002). Discovery of web robot sessions based on their navigational patterns. *Data Mining and Knowledge Discovery, 6*, 9-35.

Teo, T.S.H. & Choo, W.Y. (2001). Assessing the impact of using the Internet for competitive intelligence. *Information & Management, 39*, 67-83.

Venkatesh, V. & Speier, C. (1999). Computer technology training in the workplace: A longitudinal investigation of the effect of mood. *Organizational Behavior and Human Decision Processes, 79*(1), 1-28.

Vennix, J.A.M. (1996). *Group Model Building*. Chichester, UK: John Wiley & Sons.

Vriens, D. & Hendriks, P.H.J. (2000). Viability through Web-enabled technologies. In M. Khosrowpour (Ed.), *Managing Web-Enabled Technologies in Organizations: A Global Perspective* (pp. 122-145).
Hershey, PA: Idea Group Publishing.

Vriens, D. & Philips, E.A. (1999). Business intelligence als informatievoorziening
voor de strategievorming. In E.A. Philips & D. Vriens (Eds.), *Business
Intelligence*. Deventer: Kluwer.

Yuan, S. & Huang, M. (2001). A study on time series pattern extraction and
processing for competitive intelligence support. *Expert Systems with
Applications, 21*, 37-51.

Zanasi, A. (1998). Competitive intelligence through data mining public sources.
Competitive Intelligence Review, 9(2), 44-54.

Chapter II

Sharp by Connection: Linking Competitive Intelligence and Intranets

Paul Hendriks
University of Nijmegen, The Netherlands

Wendy Jacobs
PricewaterhouseCoopers, The Netherlands

ABSTRACT

Assessing the value of ICT to support Competitive Intelligence presumes an understanding of the relationship between the two. The chapter argues that starting from either the ICT or CI side to this relationship and linking to the other, as most studies do, cannot secure a fully adequate conception of ICT's value to CI. Instead, the challenge is to find an appropriate foundation in the relationship itself and use it as a stepping stone for developing an understanding of both ICT and CI. The chapter proposes to use and develop the concept of acceptability to provide that foundation. Acceptability offers a natural connection between the technology and CI sides. An object—e.g., a technology—cannot be acceptable in a void, but presumes a relation to a context or a subject—e.g., the CI function—to be considered acceptable or unacceptable. The Technology Acceptance Model (TAM) and Task-Technology Fit model (TTF) provide useful elements to develop this approach further. The chapter presents the case of an intranet to support CI, called IntraTel, to illustrate the argument.

INTRODUCTION

Connections play an important role in the realm of Competitive Intelligence (CI—see the definition in Chapter I). Smart connections define smart, or sharp, organizations. Connections of different kinds are at stake here. Firstly, the sharpness of an organization depends to a large degree on how well the organization manages to establish and maintain a viable connection with its environment. Secondly, CI is not just about individuals who perform CI-related tasks, roles and functions, but also about individuals connecting to others to become better at their work. The importance of these connections is indicated by such concepts as CI networks, collection networks, and analysis networks (e.g., Gilad & Gilad, 1988; Kassler, 1997). Thirdly, in this age where the Internet, intranets and associated network technology allow easy access to vast amounts of data, the sharpness of these people networks of CI professionals depends on how well they connect to these technology networks (e.g., McCrohan, 1998). How good are they in "sifting the nuggets" of ICT usage (cf., Kassler, 1997) while avoiding their pitfalls, such as information overload or loss of creativity (e.g., Gill, 1995)?

The connection between CI and ICT is the topic of this chapter. More specifically the chapter focuses on possible connections between CI and intranets as a form of ICT that aims at establishing connectivity. The chapter addresses the connection between CI and intranets from a conceptual perspective. The purpose is to develop an approach for linking CI and intranets, to identify the key concepts needed to establish such an approach, to explore the intricacies involved in defining these concepts and to elaborate how understanding the conceptual interrelationships between these concepts sets the stage for understanding the relationship between CI and intranets, or ICT in general. To avoid the risk of getting bogged down in purely abstract and theoretical discourses without a clear practical relevance to CI management, the discussion is staged in the real-life case of an organization that appeared unsuccessful in introducing an intranet to support its CI. The main argument is conceptual, using the case study for illustration purposes.

To arrive at an understanding of the relationship between CI and intranet usage the chapter is organized as follows. Firstly, we discuss alternatives for conceiving the relationship between CI and ICT leading to the choice of defining this relationship via the notion of acceptability. Secondly, we explore the concept of acceptability building on two well-researched models: the Technology Acceptance Model (TAM) and the Task-Technology Fit (TTF) model. Thirdly, we present a case study of an organization that introduced an intranet to support its CI, but found that the adoption of the intranet was unsatisfactory. The chapter builds on this case study to illustrate challenges and problems of understanding the value of an intranet for CI at a more general level. Fourthly, we discuss how applying this combined approach of TTF and TAM concepts provides a conceptually powerful perspective for linking ICT and CI. We use the case study to illustrate the elaboration and application of that perspective and give a short overview of the outcomes of applying the approach in the case study.

BACKGROUND

The chapter's purpose is to contribute to an understanding of the relationship between intranets and Competitive Intelligence (CI). Both CI practitioners and scholars have paid much attention to the linkage between ICT in general and CI. Several authors have established the importance of ICT for CI (e.g., Davenport, 2000; Guimaraes & Armstrong, 1998; Hall, 2000). The literature on the relations between CI and Information Systems support can be ordered into four classes according to the attention paid to the technology and CI behavior components of this relationship and their connection (see Figure 1). The first class, which is the most extensive of the four, concerns those studies that concentrate on the possible benefits of IS support, for instance for obtaining and analyzing vast amounts of data (some of the examples of studies falling within the first class are Sugumaran & Bose, 1999; Tan, Foo, & Hui, 2002; Tan & Kumar, 2002). Typically these studies focus on an exploration of design and use of the enabling technologies. Usually, they treat CI behavior as a black box (see Figure 1a). A second class of studies tries to remove at least part of the black box character of CI behavior (see Figure 1b). Typical examples of this class are studies that explore how using ICT may lead to new forms of CI behavior (e.g., Davenport, 2000), which implies that some model of CI behavior has to be specified. Studies that fall within this class examine the changes the use of specific ICTs has for CI behavior (e.g., Christensen & Bailey, 1998; Teo & Choo, 2001). A third class of studies—shown in Figure 1c—concerns those studies that consider the conditions and circumstances affecting the establishment of the relationship between the technology and CI behavior. For example, Hall (2000) studies some of the technological and cultural barriers that may inhibit effective IS use to support CI. The fourth class concerns those studies whose point of departure is CI behavior instead of technology (see Figure 1d). They call for a deeper understanding of CI behavior, and look at the technology through the lens of the implications of their deepened understanding of that behavior. Examples of studies in this class are Schultze (2000) and Schultze and Boland (2000). Also, the study by Bergeron (2000) may be included in this class, because of his call to develop a better understanding of information-retrieval behavior for CI before designing the tools to support it.

Figure 1. Classes of Studies Addressing the Relationship Between ICT and CI

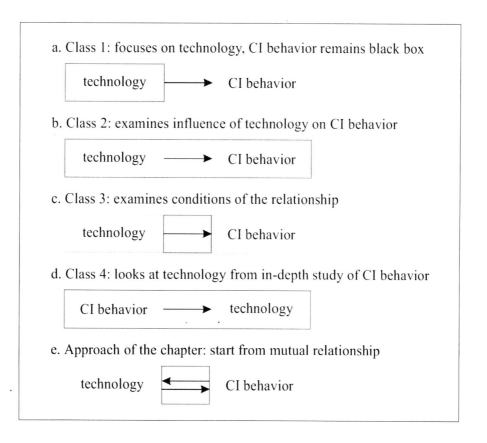

While all these classes of studies contribute useful elements for under-standing the intricacies of the relationship between ICT and CI, they share a common defect. They all treat the technology and CI behavior component as entities that may influence each other, but are conceptually independent. Their common suggestion is that we may conceive of the technology independently from our conception of CI behavior, and vice versa. The studies in all classes treat the relationship between ICT and CI as an external relationship, and not as an internal or conceptual relationship. Our argument developed here is that this understanding of the relationship is unsatisfactory, because current or potential CI behavior defines the technology and vice versa. Our argument is that one should start the process of understanding the technology and CI behavior by coming to grips with their mutual relationship, instead of treating this relationship at the bottom of the list. We propose to use the concept of acceptability to highlight the relationship between the technology and CI behavior as the focal point of attention. A definition of this concept automati-cally draws attention to the balance, and not to the ends of the balance: questions of acceptability refer to whether something—the technology—can enter into a relationship with someone—the agents of CI behavior. If we manage to define the acceptability of an intranet to the CI function of an organization, we avoid the pitfalls of one-sidedness inherent in other ap-proaches. An approach to defining the relationship between ICT and CI via acceptability has distinct integrative qualities with respect to the various approaches shown in Figures 1a through 1d. The strength of such a definition relates to how well it allows incorporating the insights of these approaches. Therefore the task we set ourselves is defining the acceptability of ICT to CI. Following Grudin (1992) and Nielsen (Nielsen, 1993, 1999) the acceptability of ISs can be split into social acceptability (standards, existence or absence of pressure to use the system, etc.; see also Hartwick & Barki, 1994; Venkatesh & Speier, 1999) and practical acceptability (costs, reliability, usefulness, etc.). In this chapter we concentrate on issues of practical acceptability.

THE ACCEPTABILITY OF AN INTRANET TO SUPPORT CI

As indicated above, the argument presented in this chapter involves that understanding the connection between CI and intranets should start by asking the question of what makes using an intranet acceptable to CI professionals. This argument should not be misunderstood. The suggestion here is not to start investigations by taking the current operation and tasks of the CI function as the template against which to measure the possible value of an intranet. What the argument suggests is that looking for clues when linking an intranet to CI, either prospective or retrospective, is basically a conceptual undertaking, and that the primary effort in this undertaking is putting the focus on the relationship between the two elements, and not on the two elements of the relationship in isolation.

The task at hand, then, is defining the acceptability of an intranet to support CI. Undoubtedly the best-researched and most widely adopted model for studying matters of practical acceptability is the Technology Acceptance Model (TAM, see Davis, 1989; Davis, Bagozzi, & Warshaw, 1989). TAM is based on a specification and adaptation of the Theory of Reasoned Action (Ajzen & Fishbein, 1980; TRA, Fishbein, & Ajzen, 1975; see also Venkatesh, 1999 for a review). TRA identifies intention to act as the main determinant of human action and attitude towards behavior as the decisive element in the intention to act. In line with this conception TAM suggests that to understand the acceptance of information technology (IT) one should look for variables explaining attitude towards IT usage and intention to use IT. TAM identifies perceived usefulness (PU) and perceived ease-of-use (PEU) as the key independent variables influencing the IT-related attitude and intention to use. PU is defined as "the prospective user's subjective probability that using a specific application system will increase his or her job performance within an organizational context" (Davis et al., 1989, p. 985). PEU refers to "the degree to which a person believes that using a particular system would be free from effort" (ibid.). Soon after its introduction in the literature TAM became a very popular model among IT researchers, resulting in hundreds of studies aimed at testing or elaborating the model (selective overviews of TAM research are, for instance, available in Lederer, Maupin, Sena, & Zhuang, 2000; Venkatesh & Davis, 2000). Part of the success of the model undoubtedly relates to its common sense nature and to its appealing simplicity. Part of the success is also explained by the robustness of the model: empirical tests invariably show significant relations between the independent and dependent variables in the model (cf., Lederer et al., 2000; Szajna, 1996; Venkatesh & Speier, 1999). However, it should also be noted that the explanatory power of the original model is not impressive, with a typical explained variance of around 40% (Dillon, 2000). Doll et al. (1998, p. 839) also note, "Despite its wide acceptance, a series of incremental cross-validation studies have produced conflicting and equivocal results that do not provide guidance for researchers or practitioners who might use the TAM for decision making." Among these conflicts and equivocalities are questions as to whether PEU affects usage directly, only through PU, or both directly and indirectly (for an overview, see Lederer et al., 2000). Also, equivocalities arise when new constructs or new variables affecting the relationships between PEU, PU, and usage are introduced (e.g., Cheung, Chang, & Lai, 2000; Gefen & Straub, 1997; Veiga, Floyd, & Dechant, 2001). Perhaps the best-known modification is a distinction between pre-implementation and post-implementation TAM (e.g., Venkatesh & Davis, 2000). The inherent discussions, while signaling the cause for caution, do not affect the importance of addressing issues of PU and PEU in system design. From the accumulated writings on TAM we draw two conclusions. Firstly, a further elaboration of the two concepts of PU and PEU at the conceptual level is called for. Secondly, using the model should not restrain the attention for additional explanatory variables. The specification of PU and PEU is discussed in the remainder of this chapter. We will not explore the class of additional variables here. The investigation in the case study adopted the pragmatic standpoint of not defining these variables beforehand but inviting respondents to name such factors after considering PU, PEU and TTF.

A model that offers useful ideas for a conceptual elaboration of PU and PEU is the task-technology fit model (TTF-model, e.g., Goodhue, 1995, 1998; Goodhue, Klein, & March, 2000; Keil, Beranek, & Konsynski, 1995; Lim & Benbasat, 2000). The basic suggestion of TTF is that whether or not the qualities of the system will induce people to use it depends on the task concerned. As Goodhue (1995, p. 1828) puts it: "A single system could get very different evaluations from users with different task needs and abilities." While TTF is newer than TAM and has not attracted as much research attention, research results for this model equally show its robustness and explanatory power (see references above). Just like TAM, TTF has a strong common sense appeal in its suggestion that IT usage can only be understood if the reason to use the IT, i.e., the task, is included in the picture. Differences between TAM and TTF concern the fact that the match between task and technology, and not attitude towards usage, is the key focus in the TTF model, as well as the fact that TTF models are mostly used to explain actual usage and not intended usage. While TTF involves a different perspective on utilization behavior than TAM, these models appear to be complementary rather than contradictory. For instance, research by Mathieson and Keil (1998) shows that neither task characteristics nor technology features in their own right can explain variations in PEU, but the interaction between the two classes can. TTF therefore influences or defines PEU. Similar suggestions can be made as to the relationship between TTF and PU (e.g., see Dishaw & Strong, 1999; see also

Venkatesh & Davis, 2000: their "interaction between job relevance and output quality" closely resembles TTF). Research by Dishaw and Strong (1999) corroborates the fruitfulness of the idea to integrate the basic concepts of TAM and TTF, as these authors show that a combined TAM/TTF model outperforms an individual TAM model as well as an individual TTF model.

In short, the research results alluded to above are interpreted as a justification to focus the elaboration of PU and PEU concepts on TTF constructs and variables.

THE CASE OF INTRATEL

To elaborate how to study the connection between CI and intranets through the concepts of PEU, PU and TTF, we present a case study. It concerns a large global consumer electronics firm, which in this chapter shall be referred to as "Consel Corporation." The organization has a center for CI research and associated operations at corporate level, called Central CMI (CMI is short for Consumer and Market Intelligence) and CMI departments for each individual business group (CMI business group TV, CMI business group Video, etc.) as well as for each individual region (CMI Europe, CMI NAFTA, etc.) located at various places all over the world. At the end of 1996 Central CMI came up with the idea of developing a database application for the data sources the department distributed. At the time, the customers of Central CMI received most data via hard copy and some data via e-mail. Both methods had several shortcomings. Delivering in hard copy implied delays because one had to wait until the full report, usually referred to as a "book," was printed. This was a time-consuming and costly process because of their size and number. Further delays were introduced by the delivery method of hard copy, particularly when destinations such as Sao Paulo or Singapore were involved. It was also very difficult, if not impossible, to make the necessary adaptations once the "books" were printed. Sending by e-mail often caused attachments to arrive in mutilated form because of the usually complex graphics included. Also, the department often ran into problems because of the size of the attachments. E-mail also involves risks of security.

Reasons such as these induced the department to develop a system to handle these problems. The underlying rationale of the system was that it should allow Central CMI to ease the delivery of data to its customers and to facilitate both distribution of data and communication among these customers without Central CMI's intercession. Early 1998 the IntraTel system that resulted from this idea was put into operation. IntraTel was built on IBM's Lotus Notes functionality and was offered to users on Consel Corporation's intranet via the Domino system. IntraTel consisted of the following five applications:

1.   Market Data: offers processed data and analyses in the form of presentations concerning markets, market shares of competitors, distribution, price movements, market predictions, and socio-economical and technological trends.

2.   Research Projects: contains the results of research projects completed by internal and external investigators.

3.   Project Informer: contains information about planned, current and completed research projects run by Central CMI.

4.   Let's Japan: provides a monitor of technological developments in Japan and follows the main competitors and their investments in consumer electronics, research and product development in that country.

5.   CMI Contacts: contains organizational charts of the organization, and a knowledge map of the connections of Central CMI inside and outside Consel Corporation.

Access to IntraTel has to be authorized by Central CMI. The home page of the system, which is accessible to all Consel Corporation employees, offers a registration form to request permission to use the system. At the time of the research some 250 people all over the world were granted this permission. The first two applications mentioned—Market Data and Research Projects—are the most popular in IntraTel. To illustrate the functionality of IntraTel some examples from Market Data will be presented. The application can be regarded as a collection of search tools on top of a large set of documents, with some additional functionality loosely linked to search actions. Search actions for documents or their authors usually start by selecting one of the categories "product," "region," "contact" or "publications," with an additional entry "new publications." Clicking for instance the option to search for documents related to specific products will offer a taxonomy of products at several hierarchical layers, which is based on the standard classification of Consel Corporation that all employees—in varying degrees of detail—are familiar with. New layers will appear when users zoom in on a specific class of products (or if they choose at any point in the hierarchy to "expand all"). Documents are typically connected to the base categories of the taxonomy. For all documents, additional meta-information is stored, including the names of the authors. Apart from the hierarchical menu system organized around products, regions, etc., some additional search functions are offered. Most of the additional functionality in IntraTel is introduced for the purpose of stimulating communication among IntraTel users. A typical example is the response button that is connected to every document. Clicking this button will open a new window allowing the user to send remarks or questions to the authors in question. When the user files his or her comments, an e-mail message is sent to the authors to notify them. To read these comments, they have to log in to IntraTel and navigate to the document to which the comments apply. These comments and reactions are accessible to all users of the system, allowing them to contribute to the discussion.

One year and a half after its introduction, the reception of IntraTel proved disappointing. The data in the login database of the system showed that only a few dozen of the 250 people authorized to use the system did so on a regular basis. The data also showed that users typically only inspected a few pages per visit and that the duration of an average stay in IntraTel was short. Although the central CMI department did not keep track of the number of e-mail and hard-copy requests for information, the undisputed impression existed that, contrary to the intentions and expectations, these numbers did not decrease during the period of IntraTel's operation. These data led Central CMI to the conclusion that the introduction of IntraTel was a failure and that the system did not live up to the expectations of its designers.

The question then is what explains the adoption-failure of IntraTel. Phrased differently, the question is which conditions favor the intranet's acceptability, and which of these conditions were not met in this case. This question concerns the evaluation of the current system, feeding into a possible diagnosis and redesign of a new version of that system. We will discuss the possible answers to these questions by exploring how acceptability can be defined and accessed. The focus in the presentation is not on the answers as such, but on the conceptual basis of the approach.

WHEN WILL AN INTRANET SUPPORT CI?

Some remarks as to reinterpreting TAM and TTF-related insights for the purpose of the subject of the current research—designing an approach to the evaluation, diagnosis, and redesign of an intranet to support CI such as IntraTel—appear fitting. The TAM and TTF models are usually studied in the literature from a different perspective than the current. The typical perspective on these models is to examine the explanatory power of the models, either theoretically or empirically. For the purpose of the current research the relevance of the models derives from their potential to provide a substantiated and integrated backbone for defining and assessing the current and potential acceptability of the intranet. These two perspectives share common ground, but they also involve shifts in their elaborations of the models and in the importance attached to individual issues. It can be noted that, when discussing implications of their research for IS design, several studies on TAM and TTF explore part of the common ground, usually in a somewhat haphazard way in a concluding discussion section (e.g., Doll et al., 1998; Kekre, Krishnan, & Srinivasan, 1995; Venkatesh & Speier, 1999). The task at hand involves identifying the constituent components of PU and PEU, rather than the "antecedents" of these concepts (cf., Agarwal & Prasad, 1998; Karahanna & Straub, 1999). What is at stake is building a convincing argument to define acceptability of a system within the context of an individual organization and to translate this definition into tangible features of the system.

When using TTF as a key component in the definition of perceived usefulness and ease-of-use, the challenge is to:

1. Identify an appropriate broad model of the tasks without fully specifying it,
2. Identify an equally broad appropriate model of the technology functionalities at a sufficiently abstract level,
3. Connect both models in order to specify them,
4. Identify, define and specify other factors in addition to PU, PEU and TTF.

The focus here is on the first three steps. As indicated above, the fourth step will not be addressed in depth. In the case study presented below we adopted the pragmatic standpoint of asking respondents to identify additional factors after considering PU, PEU and TTF.

The first step—identifying a model of the tasks—involves modeling the things the company has to do to gain and enhance its intelligence about its consumers, markets, competitors, etc. A commonly accepted model for this purpose is the Competitive Intelligence (or CI) cycle (see Chapter I). While several modifications of this cycle exist, the CI cycle typically includes four stages. Firstly, the stage of *planning and direction* sets the main course of CI activities by identifying and interpreting the mission, defining requirements, setting priorities, determining classes of indicators to be monitored and allocating resources. Secondly, the stage of *collection* refers to the activities of data collection and initial processing of these data (identifying and removing errors, matching data from different sources, removing incompatibilities in data format, etc.). Thirdly, the stage of *analysis* concerns processing the available data so they can be used for CI-related decisions, by combining information, applying statistical or mathematical analysis models, enhancing their accessibility through visualization models, etc. Finally, the CI cycle contains the stage of getting the right outcomes of the analysis stage on the right desks, referred to as *distribution, dissemination, diffusion* or *dispersal*. The first stage of the CI cycle, planning and direction, is outside the scope of the current discussion.

While the CI cycle offers an important instrument for typifying CI tasks, modeling these tasks presumes at least one further elaboration. The complexity of the "CI task" concept also derives from the fact that the definition of actions individuals perform to keep the CI cycle turning depends on how individual actions and their management are assigned to organizational units (departments, work teams, project teams, etc., see also Pirttila, 1998). In turn, the task definition of these organizational units depends on how the company as a whole conceives of the fact that it needs to give its CI flesh and blood (for instance, the various CMI departments described earlier are by no means the only spots in the company where consumer or market intelligence resides). All these elements refer to tasks in the CI cycle, and understanding each element presumes an understanding of the others. To avoid confusion we will use the following terminology: to refer to activities of individuals we will use the term "tasks." To identify the aggregate contributions of departments and groups we will use the term "roles." To indicate the overall CI task of the company we will use the term "function."

The second step in defining TTF, modeling the functionalities of the technology, refers to the need to identify the potential contributions of the intranet application. For this purpose it appears helpful to redefine an intranet as a specific type of groupware (Coleman, 1997). A useful perspective for classifying the functionalities of groupware is the 3C framework (*Groupware White Paper*, 1995), elaborated into a 4C framework (Vriens & Hendriks, 2000). The four C's are circulation, communication, coordination and collaboration. *Circulation* involves the distribution of information to a broader audience, not aimed at establishing some form of interactivity with that audience. *Communication* concentrates on the establishment of interaction between senders and receivers of information. *Coordination* deals with correspondences and conflicts between individual tasks resulting from the fact that group members work on different tasks contributing to a larger task. *Collaboration* occurs when two or more people are working together on the same task. The present or future functionalities of an intranet to support CI may refer to any of these four classes.

The distribution stage of the CI cycle offers a useful starting point for connecting the CI cycle and the 4C framework, which concerns the third step in defining TTF. Distribution concerns connecting people, which defines the basic functionality of groupware. The CI cycle introduces distribution as a sequence to analysis, which implies that it only concerns moving the outcomes of the analysis to the right desks (in other words, it concerns connecting outcome producers to interested consumers and vice versa). A closer examination shows that more distribution moments appear in the CI cycle, both within and between all other stages of the cycle. The term "collection network" that Gilad and Gilad (1988) introduce indicates that collection of data occurs by experts who have their own expertise combined with information on where they can find related expertise (see also Kassler, 1997). Similarly, they designate the connections analysts use in the course of their work as an analysis network. Ideally these two networks—or rather, sets of networks, as every individual or department may have their own networks—could or should also be mutually linked, and linked to consumers. This reinterpretation of the CI cycle provides the conceptual hooks for connecting to the intranet's functionalities. The concepts of circulation, communication, coordination and cooperation are elaborations of the network formation that is crucial for a properly operating CI cycle, as shown by Gilad and Gilad's discourse on collection and analysis networks. This leads to two conclusions. Firstly, distribution as circulation should not be studied as a final stage in the CI cycle, but should be integrated in the other stages and explicitly linked to the connection between the stages. Secondly, distribution should not just be looked at from the circulation perspective but also from the additional communication, coordination and cooperation perspectives. To understand how an intranet may affect the operation of the CI cycle, its functionalities should be studied with respect to collection, analysis and the interfaces between these two stages. This results in an elaboration of the fit between CI tasks and the functionality of the technology into the 16 classes of interest discerned in Figure 2.

The completion of the third step, defining the relationship between the intranet and CI, will consist of "filling in the cells in the matrix." Depending on the perspective taken this conceptual filling operation will take on a different form and meaning. Here TAM, with its call to distinguish between usefulness and ease-of-use, reenters the stage. To establish issues of usefulness of the intranet the perspective will be on the content of the tasks. To establish issues of ease-of-use the appropriate perspective is on the process of the tasks (that is, on the question as to how the tasks can be performed "with as little effort as necessary"). These two perspectives ensure that usefulness is not defined independent of matters of ease-of-use. Also, ease-of-use is not defined "in a void," which is the risk involved in focusing attention on isolated issues such as

Figure 2. Focal Points for Assessing the Functionalities of an Intranet to Support CI

Groupware functionalities Stages in the CI cycle	*Circulation*	*Communication*	*Coordination*	*Collaboration*
Collection	Supporting the flow of data throughout collection networks	Assisting members within and between collection networks in finding each other	Managing shared resources, identifying and handling overlap between the work of individuals, etc.	Smoothing the progress of joint data preparation
Handling collection products	Supporting the flow of data between collection and analysis networks	Supporting contact between collectors and analysts, e.g., for communicating best practices	Managing resources of mutual interest, matching the work of each party to the needs of the others, etc.	Involving analysts and collectors in each other's work
Analysis	Supporting the flow of information throughout analysis networks	Assisting members within and between analysis networks in finding each other	Handling the constraints between sequential analysis tasks	Facilitating the formation and operation of analysis teams
Handling analysis products	Supporting the flow of information from producers to consumers and vice versa	Supporting contact in information supply and command	Promoting that information requests and offers match, etc.	Mutually involving consumers and producers of information in their work

Explanation: the cells provide examples of how groupware functionalities (the columns in the matrix) may support elements of CI work (the rows in the matrix). These examples are general in nature and do not refer to the case study presented in the chapter.

clear organization of files, easy location of data, easy accessibility of data (Goodhue, 1995), training (Riemenschneider & Hardgrave, 2001), feedback, help and documentation (e.g., Nielsen, 1993, Ch. 5). Instead, both usefulness and ease-of-use are defined as specific interpretations of TTF, mutually linked through their common basis in that concept.

THE LACKING ACCEPTABILITY OF INTRATEL

In the case of IntraTel the approach sketched in the previous section was applied in practice. The matrix shown in Figure 2 served as the rationale for identifying reasons for the failed acceptance of the application, as well as for

Table 1. Description of the Sample in the Case Study

User class	Concept	Function within CMI	n
Intermediate users	Only PU	Market analysts Central CMI	3
		Market analysts Regional CMI	6
		Market analysts Business Group CMI	4
		Market analysts National Sales Organizations CMI	3
		Total	16
	PU and PEU	Market analysts Central CMI	6
		Marketing assistants Central CMI	4
		Market analysts regional CMI	8
		IT managers	3
		Total	21
End users	Only PU	Product managers	4
		Product planners	3
		Marketing managers	9
		General managers	2
		Total	18
Total	PU		55
	PEU		21

exploring possible redesign features to prepare for a successful reintroduction of the system. The data in the investigation were collected through interviews with several parties (see Table 1). The concept of PU interviews were held with both intermediate and end users of the system. The intermediate users were market analysts at the corporate, regional or business unit level. The sample was constructed so as to include a maximum variation concerning the different CMI departments, because Consel considered the differences between departments to be more important for evaluating the system than, for instance, differences between different product groups. The end users included product and marketing managers for individual classes of products and other staff members of the local consumer and market intelligence departments. Members of both the intermediate and end user groups were selected so as to include actual users, designated users who appeared to use the system hardly or not at all, and potential users who had not been included in the IntraTel-related efforts before. These three groups represented about 30%, 50% and 20%, respectively, of the intermediate and end user groups included in the sample. As for the concept of PEU, the additional questions in the interviews were more time-consuming as they involved walking through the system in sessions that lasted up to half a day. Because of the length of these interviews, they were held only with intermediate users, as this group appeared to be more easily accessible than the end users. People were selected for inclusion in this part of the sample based on the amount of experience they had with the system. The largest group (15 people, or about 70%) were experienced users who had seen most of the functionality of IntraTel at least several times. The remaining people were only just starting to use the system. They were included to assess how the system on first acquaintance will appeal to its users or deter them, which aspects of the system are the most eye-catching to novices in a positive or negative sense, and which improvements would be most needed for potential new users to be attracted to use the system.

While a discussion of the approach followed in reassessing IntraTel is the focus of attention here, the account of the case study would be incomplete without an indication of the outcomes of the research. The interviews revealed that the most important reasons why people did not use IntraTel were unfamiliarity with the existence of the system and the fact that people did not know how to use the system. They also showed that people preferred to use information on hard copy. Both elements of usefulness and ease-of-use appeared helpful in specifying reasons for disappointing usage and offering suggestions for redesign.

As for its usefulness, IntraTel was considered an appropriate system to circulate information, provided that all parties involved were willing to publish their sources. IntraTel was used for searching information. It was not used as a communication system, and respondents indicated that they would not use it as such in the future. The main reasons for this were a generally felt preference for personal contact, the resistance to broadcast personal remarks to an anonymous audience, the fact that hardly any questions that people had were related to an individual document, and the tediousness of writing down questions. IntraTel was not considered useful as a coordination or collaboration system either, because respondents indicated that they did not experience problems in these realms that the system could help resolve. As for the content of the system, a key element of usefulness, respondents stated that they missed information about competitors and distribution. They also asked for an increase in the number of analyses offered on IntraTel. Dedicated presentations linking several sources to a specific research goal are considered even more useful than sources by themselves are, either as such or as templates for performing new analyses leading into new presentations.

As for ease-of-use, the interviews showed that the user-friendliness of IntraTel left a lot to be desired. The overviews in the system were not clear and the system was not considered attractive. IntraTel even got characterized as tedious and not inviting to work with. Also, several controls were reported to malfunction: the response button was not being used and the search function had to be improved. Three facets of the system related to ease-of-use were shown to deserve special mention. Firstly, the indistinctness and intricacy of the registration procedure form appeared to deter people from requesting access to the system. Secondly, updating, while being recognized as crucial for the system to be useful, was generally considered as a cumbersome procedure, particularly because no clarity exists as to what the responsibilities of individual users and departments are regarding updating, and which documents can be updated by specific users and which cannot. Thirdly, respondents complained about deficient explanation facilities within the system, the lack of a help desk for handling individual problems and the absence of short training courses. Giving explanations, as several respondents suggested, could make clear that using IntraTel will save time and may help convince people to supply their own information.

Based on the research, the continuation of IntraTel has been recommended to Consel Corporation, a recommendation that was taken up by the company. The system may help solve several difficulties people experience in their jobs. Particularly, it may help reduce the chance of missing out on vital information. Continuation of the project is likely to fail without substantial promotion of IntraTel. Many people are unfamiliar with the system, as a result of which they obviously do not use it. Promoting IntraTel may also help promote Central CMI and may help encourage people to provide their information.

FUTURE TRENDS AND RESEARCH

ICT has the potential to support and change the CI function. However, practice shows that in the CI realm, as in other realms, the failure rate of ICT applications is high (Schultze & Boland, 2000). A more hidden ICT-related pitfall is that, even if the adoption of ICT did not fail, using ICT may impair the information-seeking behavior of CI professionals (Christensen & Bailey, 1998; Teo & Choo, 2001). Even if such negative effects of ICT usage do not surface in the short run, they may do so in the long run, reducing the organization's awareness of its environment instead of enhancing it (Gill, 1995). All these concerns indicate that our understanding of the possible value of ICT to CI is still far from satisfactory. The implication is not that we need to gain a better understanding of Competitive Intelligence Systems as such, but that we should improve our conception of the relationship between these systems and the operation of the CI function. In recent years part of the research on ICT support for CI shows a move away from purely technical issues towards a desire to comprehend the CI behavior side of the equation (Bergeron, 2000; Schultze, 2000; Schultze & Boland, 2000). We fully endorse the idea that research needs to be developed further down this path. The contribution of the chapter is to supply the signpost indicating the direction the path should take: Research should develop our understanding of ICT and CI from the perspective of their mutual relationship and not vice versa. The challenge is therefore to build a sufficiently rich conception of that mutual relationship without adopting a fully detailed model of either the technology or CI.

The chapter has explored the concept of acceptability as a possible conceptual starting point to ensure a perspective on the mutual relationship between ICT and CI. The exploration presented here by no means brings closure to the discussion on that relationship. Several open ends remain. Our argument has not been that the concept of acceptability is the only possible concept for building the appropriate perspective. The need to explore additional or alternative approaches using other concepts remains. Neither did we explore all sides of the concept of acceptability, but focused on matters of practical acceptability, sidestepping those of social acceptability. Also, we did not fully cover the ground of practical acceptability. For instance, variables outside the scope of the TAM and TTF models were addressed only in a haphazard way in the chapter. One further limitation of the present study is that we did not delve deeply into the relationship between the concept of acceptability and the overall business setting in which the value of ICT should be defined. For instance, we did not explore the connections between acceptability and business performance. The concept of PU, particularly when elaborated along TTF lines, does introduce individual performance into the picture (for an overview of studies addressing the connections between ICT acceptability and individual performance see Townsend, Demarie, & Hendrickson, 2001). However, the connection to business performance is far more complex, for instance because ICT use may well lead to individual performance going up while performance at an aggregate level goes down. Our justification for addressing the role of ICT in business via the concept of acceptability is that if a system is not acceptable to users, it cannot lead to enhanced business performance. This does not imply that the reverse relationship also holds. A more encompassing investigation of the connections between acceptability and business performance would involve including other organizational variables such as organization structure and strategy into the picture, which is beyond the scope of the present chapter. All these shortcomings show the limitations of the current research and define areas for future research.

CONCLUSION

In this chapter we have argued that an integration of the TAM and TTF models offers a powerful and workable conceptual basis for connecting CI and intranets. For the purpose of building an approach for assessing the possible or actual value of an intranet for CI rooted in this conceptual basis, we have elaborated the concept of fit between CI-related tasks and functionalities to specify elements of perceived usefulness and perceived ease-of-use of an intranet. Reactions at Consel Corporation upon the completion of the investigation into the adoption-failure of IntraTel showed that the reception of the approach and its outcomes was favorable. Particularly, appreciation was voiced as to the integrated nature of the picture that the interviews draw because of their conceptual foundation, instead of an only loosely connected collection of individual assessments and recommendations. These are indications of the value of the approach elaborated here. Perhaps more relevant to a broader public than what the outcomes of the research imply for Consel Corporation are the lessons this case study may teach about the assessment of the PU and PEU of ISs and their mutual connections through TTF. It is important to note that the concepts of PEU, PU and TTF are mutually related in a conceptual sense. For instance, what determines ease-of-use for operations within one task realm may only be partially similar to the determinants of ease-of-use in another realm. The examples described in Figure 2 that elaborate TTF in the case study provide the hooks for assessing elements of both PU and PEU, thus connecting these two concepts via TTF. While the close conceptual connections between PU, PEU and TTF call for an integrated approach in an assessment, there is also cause for a separation of usefulness and ease-of-use issues. The main reason for this is the questionable validity of pre-implementation assessments of PEU. These calls for simultaneous separation and integration appear to be causing a deadlock. Two suggestions may help reduce the paralyzing effect of this deadlock. Firstly, linking both PU and PEU to a common basis instead of only linking them mutually (cf., the rationale developed here, as pictured in Figure 2) ensures a certain separation in treatment without losing connection. Secondly, equally important is the need for a repeated consideration of all stages of the system lifecycle, an aspect that was not explicitly addressed in the description of the case study. Diagnosing and designing for acceptance on the one hand and monitoring, evaluating and explaining possible lack of acceptance on the other call for continuous and interrelated attention. Models such as TAM and TTF appear valuable because they may help safeguard the conceptual connections between the links in sequential intervention cycles.

REFERENCES

Agarwal, R. & Prasad, J. (*1998*). The antecedents and consequents of user perceptions in information technology adoption. *Decision Support Systems, 22*(1), 15-29.

Ajzen, I. & Fishbein, M. (1980). *Understanding Attitudes and Predicting Social Behavior.* Upper Saddle River, NJ: Prentice-Hall.

Bergeron, P. (2000). Regional business intelligence: The view from Canada. *Journal of Information Science, 26*(3), 153-160.

Cheung, W. M., Chang, M. K., & Lai, V. S. (2000). Prediction of Internet and World Wide Web usage at work: A test of an extended Triandis model. *Decision Support Systems, 30*(1), 83-100.

Christensen, E. W. & Bailey, J. R. (1998). Task performance using the library and Internet to acquire business intelligence. *Internet Research-Electronic Networking Applications and Policy, 8*(4), 290-302.

Coleman, D. D. (1997). *Groupware: Collaborative strategies for corporate LANs and intranets.* Upper Saddle River, NJ: Prentice Hall.

Davenport, E. (2000). Social intelligence in the age of networks. *Journal of Information Science, 26*(3), 145-152.

Davis, F. D. (1989). Perceived usefulness, perceived ease of use, and user acceptance of information technology. *MIS Quarterly, 13*(3), 319-340.

Davis, F. D., Bagozzi, R. P., & Warshaw, P. R. (1989). User acceptance of computer-technology—A comparison of 2 theoretical-models. *Management Science, 35*(8), 982-1003.

Dillon, A. (2000). Group dynamics meet cognition: Combining socio-technical concepts and usability engineering in the design of information systems. In E. Coakes, D. Willis, & R. Lloyd-Jones (Eds.), *The New SocioTech: Graffitti on the Long Wall* (pp. 119-126). London: Springer.

Dishaw, M. T. & Strong, D. M. (1999). Extending the technology acceptance model with task-technology fit constructs. *Information & Management, 36*(1), 9-21.

Doll, W. J., Hendrickson, A., & Deng, X. (1998). Using Davis's perceived usefulness and ease-of-use instruments for decision making: A confirmatory and multigroup invariance analysis. *Decision Sciences, 29*(4), 839-869.

Fishbein, M. & Ajzen, I. (1975). *Belief, Attitude, Intention and Behavior: An Introduction to Theory and Research.* Reading, MA: Addison-Wesley.

Gefen, D. & Straub, D. W. (1997). Gender differences in the perception and use of e-mail: An extension to the technology acceptance model. *MIS Quarterly, 21*(4), 389-400.

Gilad, B. & Gilad, T. (1988). *The Business Intelligence System, A New Tool for Competitive Advantage*. New York: Amacom.

Gill, T. G. (1995). High-tech hidebound: Case studies of information technologies that inhibited organizational learning. *Accounting, Management and Information Technologies, 5*(1), 41-60.

Goodhue, D. L. (1995). Understanding user evaluations of information systems. *Management Science, 41*(12), 1827-1844.

Goodhue, D. L. (1998). Development and measurement validity of a task-technology fit instrument for user evaluations of information systems. *Decision Sciences, 29*(1), 105-138.

Goodhue, D. L., Klein, B. D., & March, S. T. (2000). User evaluations of IS as surrogates for objective performance. *Information & Management, 38*(2), 87-101.

Groupware White Paper. (1995). Unpublished manuscript. Cambridge, MA.

Grudin, J. (1992). Utility and usability: Research issues and development contexts. *Interacting With Computers, 4*(2), 209-217.

Guimaraes, T. & Armstrong, C. (1998). Exploring the relations between competitive intelligence, IS support, and business change. *Competitive Intelligence Review, 9*(3), 45-54.

Hall, H. (2000). Online information sources: Tools of business intelligence. *Journal of Information Science, 26*(3), 139-143.

Hartwick, J. & Barki, H. (1994). Explaining the role of user participation in information-system use. *Management Science, 40*(4), 440-465.

Karahanna, E. & Straub, D. W. (1999). The psychological origins of perceived usefulness and ease-of- use. *Information & Management, 35*(4), 237-250.

Kassler, H. S. (1997). Mining the Internet for competitive intelligence: How to track and sift for golden nuggets. *Online: The Magazine of Online Information Systems, 21*(5), 34-45.

Keil, M., Beranek, P. M., & Konsynski, B. R. (1995). Usefulness and ease of use—Field-study evidence regarding task considerations. *Decision Support Systems, 13*(1), 75-91.

Kekre, S., Krishnan, M. S., & Srinivasan, K. (1995). Drivers of customer satisfaction for software products - Implications for design and service support. *Management Science, 41*(9), 1456-1470.

Lederer, A. L., Maupin, D. J., Sena, M. P., & Zhuang, Y. L. (2000). The technology acceptance model and the World Wide Web. *Decision Support Systems, 29*(3), 269-282.

Lim, K. H. & Benbasat, I. (2000). The effect of multimedia on perceived equivocality and perceived usefulness of information systems. *MIS Quarterly, 24*(3), 449-471.

Mathieson, K. & Keil, M. (1998). Beyond the interface: Ease of use and task/ technology fit. *Information & Management, 34*(4), 221-230.

McCrohan, K. F. (1998). Competitive intelligence: Preparing for the information war. *Long Range Planning, 31*(4), 586-593.

Nielsen, J. (1993). *Usability Engineering.* Boston, MA: Academic Press.

Nielsen, J. (1999). *Designing Web Usability.* Indianapolis, IN: New Riders.

Pirttila, A. (1998). Organising competitive intelligence activities in a corporate organisation. *Aslib Proceedings, 50*(4), 79-84.

Riemenschneider, C. K. & Hardgrave, B. C. (2001). Explaining software development tool use with the technology acceptance model. *Journal of Computer Information Systems, 41*(4), 1-8.

Schultze, U. (2000). A confessional account of an ethnography about knowledge work. *MIS Quarterly, 24*(1), 3-41.

Schultze, U. & Boland, R. J. (2000). Knowledge management technology and the reproduction of knowledge work practices. *Journal of Strategic Information Systems, 9*(2-3), 193-212.

Sugumaran, V. & Bose, R. (1999). Data analysis and mining environment: A distributed intelligent agent technology application. *Industrial Management & Data Systems, 99*(1-2), 71-80.

Szajna, B. (1996). Empirical evaluation of the revised technology acceptance model. *Management Science, 42*(1), 85-92.

Tan, B., Foo, S., & Hui, S. C. (2002). Web information monitoring for competitive intelligence. *Cybernetics and Systems, 33*(3), 225-251.

Tan, P. N. & Kumar, V. (2002). Discovery of Web robot sessions based on their navigational patterns. *Data Mining and Knowledge Discovery, 6*(1), 9-35.

Teo, T. S. H. & Choo, W. Y. (2001). Assessing the impact of using the Internet for competitive intelligence. *Information & Management, 39*(1), 67-83.

Townsend, A. M., Demarie, S. M., & Hendrickson, A. R. (2001). Desktop video conferencing in virtual workgroups: Anticipation, system evaluation and performance. *Information Systems Journal, 11*(3), 213-227.

Veiga, O. F., Floyd, S., & Dechant, K. (2001). Towards modelling the effects of national culture on IT implementation and acceptance. *Journal of Information Technology, 16*(3), 145-158.

Venkatesh, V. (1999). Creation of favorable user perceptions: Exploring the role of intrinsic motivation. *MIS Quarterly, 23*(2), 239-260.

Venkatesh, V. & Davis, F. D. (2000). A theoretical extension of the Technology Acceptance Model: Four longitudinal field studies. *Management Science, 46*(2), 186-204.

Venkatesh, V. & Speier, C. (1999). Computer technology training in the workplace: a longitudinal investigation of the effect of mood. *Organizational Behavior and Human Decision Processes, 79*(1), 1-28.

Vriens, D. J. & Hendriks, P. H. J. (2000). Viability through web-enabled technologies. In M. Khosrowpour (Ed.), *Managing Web-Enabled Technologies in Organizations: A Global Perspective* (pp. 122-145). Hershey, PA: Idea Group Publishing.

√Nɔʌɛɟʌ

Chapter III

Using Web Link Analysis to Detect and Analyze Hidden Web Communities

Edna O.F. Reid
Nanyang Technological University, Singapore

ABSTRACT

A great deal of current as well as previous studies on web links has focused mostly on improving the performance of information retrieval systems. The vast but untapped wealth of information from link-related messages generated by online communities has yet to attract the attention of the competitive intelligence researchers and practitioners. The latter groups have depended mainly on traditional intelligence sources while cognizant that much of the information which impinges upon their competitive strengths is shaped by events external to the firm. In view of the foregoing, we present in this chapter an exploratory framework for extracting and exploiting patterns of self-organizing, hyperlinked web communities for corporate intelligence purposes. More specifically, this chapter summarizes how the proposed analytical framework has been applied to MicroStrategy Inc.'s website to give us a glimpse of stakeholder communities' reactions to the enterprise's activities and identify some early warning signals. The framework can thus be considered as a prototypical approach for exploiting the Web's structure and content for Web intelligence purposes.

INTRODUCTION

The World Wide Web contains a huge amount of interconnected Web pages that are authored and made available by millions of different individuals. Consequently, it provides new opportunities for using the hyperlink structure as a creative data source for identifying and analyzing snapshots, continuously and historically, of a company's implicit stakeholder communities who share common interests in a firm. The snapshots provide bits and pieces of a jigsaw puzzle that can be assembled into patterns of relations, activities and early warning signs of developments about a firm's external environments. More importantly, capturing dispersed intelligence data about a company's implicit online communities of stakeholders should therefore be possible given the right Web mining and analytical methodologies.

The hyperlinks are reflections of social interactions between stakeholders and a company. Collectively, they represent an underlying social structure of linked communities. These hyperlinked communities are implicit and "natural" in that they are self-organizing (Flake et al., 2002).

To illustrate the notion of implicit hyperlinked communities, consider the community of Web users interested in Porsche Boxster cars (Kumar et al., 1999). There are numerous explicit online communities that are readily available and easy to identify, such as the Porsche newsgroup and Porsche owners' listserv. Porsche owners subscribe to the listserv and receive their messages via e-mail. On the other hand, there are Web users who create content and provide hypertext links to Porsche Boxster resources (www.porsche.com/english/boxster). These users may not be registered parties in the Porsche newsgroup or listserv but they share in various areas of interests in Porsche Boxster cars. This gave rise to different Web pages, e.g., www.porschefaq.com and www.autopicture.com/porsche, that are hyperlinked to a website (www.porsche-com/english/boxster). According to Kumar et al., these users can be considered as members of implicit hyperlinked communities because the communities are not obvious (hidden), lack definite membership, have spontaneously evolved, and have an implied social structure.

Since hyperlinked communities are implicit, they are often overlooked as unobtrusive data sources for intelligence analysis. Because explicit communities such as listservs and newsgroups are easier to identify, extensive analyses of contents from such communities vis-à-vis technological, sociological, managerial, and competitive intelligence perspectives have been reported in the literature (Hagel & Armstrong, 1997; Kassler, 2000; Preece, 2000).

This chapter describes a framework for detecting and analyzing relationships and activities of a company's implicit Web communities. It expands the number of competitive analysis techniques for competitor profiling. More specifically, it identifies and categorizes a company's stakeholders and maps the value-add embedded in the firm's products and services with the interested stakeholder groups.

The case study in this chapter focuses on two research questions. Using the social structure of the Web's hypertext links: (1) Can one identify the relationships and interests of implicit Web communities to a specific company? (2) How are the implicit communities, especially external stakeholders (non-customers), using the enterprise's Web resources? The focus on external stakeholders is based on Hoyt's (2002) assertion that the biggest challenges facing companies come from outside of the organization. As part of their intelligence strategies, firms need early warning systems that support the scanning of external environments to pick up on signs of change. This requires that firms gather, analyze and synthesize data about their competitors and external environmental activities.

This chapter also provides a brief review of the related literature and a conceptual framework to address the aforementioned questions. To demonstrate its feasibility, the framework was applied to MicroStrategy, Inc., a business intelligence software vendor. According to an industry survey, MicroStrategy (2000), a publicly-traded company with headquarters in the U.S., is recognized as among the top ten influential business intelligence companies. Additional information about MicroStrategy is presented in a later section. Finally, this chapter summarizes the results and competitive intelligence implications.

RELATED LITERATURE
Citation Analysis

Hyperlink analysis research has its roots in citation analysis of journal articles, legal cases and patents to identify seminal contributions and interactions (Borgman & Furner, 2002; Kleinberg, 1998). Citation analysis is based on the assumption that if a publication is cited often then it ought to be important. Citations in journal articles provide pointers (endorsements or recommendations) to other significant prior publications (Cronin et al., 1998). On the Web, pointers or referrals are provided by hypertext links.

Citation analysis is an area of bibliometrics that focuses on citation patterns that reveal who is writing what, what is popular, and which journals and authors are cited the most (Beginner's, n.d.). Bibliometrics is a quantitative methodology used for analyzing the impact of authors, publications and citation behavior. If X publishes a paper that is cited 45 times in five years and Y publishes a paper on the same subject and is cited only eight times in five years, which paper is more influential? In competitive intelligence, bibliometrics is used to identify new competitors and emerging areas that are under investigation (Zanasi, 1998). This involves using data mining to exploit patent and citation databases.

The premier citation databases are the Social Sciences Citation Index and the Science Citation Index published by the Institute of Scientific Information (ISI). On the Web, these are called Web of Science databases. Since the databases capture authors' organizational affiliations, they are often used to analyze what competitors are publishing and how the publications are being used (ISI, 1999). In comparison, AltaVista and Google search engines support link searches that mimic the citation capability similar to those provided in the ISI databases. For instance, link searches are being conducted by CI professionals at Fuld & Co. and AstraZeneca Pharmaceutical, Canada (Kassler, 1998).

Hyperlink Analysis

Borgman and Furner (2002) define hyperlink analysis as a method for analyzing data collected primarily in the form of Web links. The volume of incoming links pointing to a website (inlinks) indicates the popularity of the site, while that of the links coming out (outlinks) of a website indicates the richness or perhaps the variety of topics covered (Zaiane, 1999).

Borgman and Furner identify two types of hyperlink analysis: relational and evaluative. Relational link analysis yields indicators of levels of connectedness or strength of the relationships among subjects such as documents, people, journals, etc., and addresses the question "Who is related (linked) to whom?" Historically, information retrieval studies have explored link analysis from a relational perspective to identify authoritative documents (those closely related to the query statement) (Yang, 2002). The use of link information to improve search performance on the Web has been demonstrated by such examples as Google and IBM's Clever project (Chakrabarti et al., 1999; Kleinberg, 1998).

Kleinberg took relational link analysis a step further by using the hyperlinked induced text search (HITS) to calculate the value of each query. The link-based model supports Web searching by identifying authoritative Web pages for broad topics. Using the HITS algorithm, Kleinberg's team has produced over a dozen studies that attempt to enhance the technique and use it to identify online communities from link topology (Chakrabarti et al., 1999; Gibson, Kleinberg, & Raghavan, 1998; Hypersearching, 1999).

Although there has been a significant amount of work directed at analyzing and building online communities (Preece, 2000; Stanoevaka-Slabeva & Schmid, 2000), the online community (or hyperlinked structures) subjects in the Clever project are never assumed to have been constructed in a centralized or planned fashion. Instead, the communities are a consequence of the way in which Web content creators link to one another in the context of topics of interest (Gibson, Kleinberg, & Raghavan, 1998). This perspective of hyperlinked community is the foundation for this study.

The concept that link structure can be used to identify implicit communities was also investigated by researchers from Xerox PARC and NEC Research Institute (Flake et al., 2002). Xerox's researchers analyzed links and the information side effects to predict social relationships between students who were listed on Stanford's and MIT's websites (Adamic & Adar, 2001). Inlinks were collected using Google and AltaVista search engines. Information side effects such as the words and phrases mentioned by the users were extracted from their homepages and analyzed for a glimpse into the social structure of university communities. For this chapter, inlinks and their information side effects are explored and categorized to identify the interests and activities of stakeholder communities.

In order for the Xerox and IBM researchers to explore link relations, sophisticated techniques for Web mining of hyperlink structures, content and Web usage have been developed (Garofalakis et al., 1999; Zaiane, 1999). Web mining involves the application of data mining processes to large collections of Web data. Hackathorn (2001) illustrates an application of Web mining in his website, which displays the Web farming of a specific URL. The link analysis studies discussed thus far represent initial attempts at applying Web mining to hyperlink structure.

Evaluative link analysis, on the other hand, aims to measure the level of importance, influence, or quality of websites. It is used to rank documents, persons, organizations, or nations (Almind & Ingwersen, 1998; Borgman & Furner, 2002; Smith, 1999). The analysis is aimed at the question "Whose research or influence is better, or has greater impact, than whose?" Almind and

Table 1. Summary of Citation and Link Analysis Approaches

Type of Analysis	Application	System	Object of Analysis
Citation Analysis	Information Retrieval, Scientific Activity Assessment, Patent Analysis, Diffusion of Intellectual Property, Study State of Discipline	Science Citation Database, Social Science Citation Database, Patent database (Van der Veer Martens)	# papers, # citations, # co-citations, impact factors
Link Analysis: Relational	Information Retrieval, Social Network	Google, IBM's Clever, Social Network of Stanford (Adamic & Adar); twURLed (Hackathorn)	# inlinks, # outlinks, domains, relations, interests, level of relevance and evolution
Link Analysis: Evaluation	Information Retrieval	Google, ResearchIndex (Flake)	# inlinks, # outlinks, # co citations, impact factors

Ingwersen coined the term "webometrics" for applying bibliometrics techniques to links (Thelwall, 2001).

Table 1 provides a summary of major applications of citation and link analysis. Citation analysis techniques are commonly used for analyzing scholarly communications in many disciplines, while Web link analysis applications have been limited to mainly information retrieval.

Online Communities

As mentioned earlier, implicit communities evolve spontaneously and do not neatly fit into the traditional classification of online communities as described by Lazar and Preece (1998). Nor do they follow the defining properties of virtual communities as portrayed in Hagel and Armstrong's (1997) research in which they describe online communities as having a clear and distinctive focus, tight integration of content and communication, strong support for member-generated content, access to competing publishers and vendors, and commercial orientation. They highlight that online communities have basic needs—interest, relation, transaction, and fantasy—that should be nurtured.

Interests are business assets that drive stakeholders to react and interact in cyberspace. They can be viewed from a value creation perspective as business assets—tangible and intangible—that stimulate the development of relationships. Tangible assets are associated with financial and physical resources while the intangible organizational assets include leadership, systems, and culture (Boulton, Libert, & Samek, 2000). Generally, managers lack insight on how external communities are using their enterprise's assets to create value.

As stakeholders interact in respect of the assets, they form relations based on value-adding features of said assets. Freeman suggests that relations be examined from a stakeholder's perspective (Elias & Cavana, 2000). He describes stakeholders as any group of individuals who may be affected by the achievement (or underachievement) of the enterprise's objective. This is especially important since organizations design Web pages to project a certain image and culture. External stakeholders express their perceptions about the enterprise through their hyperlink comments (Chakrabarti et al., 1999). Stakeholders can be organized into transactional (internal stakeholder) and contextual (external stakeholder) environments (Elias & Cavana, 2000; Wallin, 2000). The stakeholder perspective concept is used to identify and categorize relations of implicit communities in this study.

The value-creating activities vis-à-vis the information assets of a company by implicit communities provide insights to the de-facto role that each community member plays. A new way of examining further the enterprise's relationships with these communities can thus be achieved. Rayport and Sviokla (1995) classify such activities as gathering, selecting, synthesizing, and distributing valuable information within the context of the customer's marketspace needs. These virtual value activities are generic strategies that companies use from a marketing perspective to enhance information (Hanson, 2000, p. 161). For this study, they are used to identify activities that linked community members engage in to create value.

Competitive Intelligence

Competitive intelligence is the process of enhancing marketplace competitiveness through a greater understanding of a firm's competitors and competitive environment (SCIP, 2002). Several authors classify the competitive intelligence process into a four-stage cycle: (1) planning and direction, (2) data collection, (3) analysis, and (4) dissemination (Kahaner, 1998; Rouach & Santi, 2001). Hypertext link analysis is pertinent to the data collection and analysis stages because it supports the requirements of identifying, locating and synthesizing qualitative information for competitive analysis. The activities and interests of implicit community members can also provide insight for competitive intelligence.

The data collection stage involves several techniques, such as environmental scanning. It encompasses collecting both primary (interview and survey) and

secondary (literature search) information on the political, economic, technological, and social arenas (Shaker & Gembicki, 1999). These collection
approaches include in-person interviews, gathering traditional print, and online
resources. Obtaining online material information is aided by metasearch
engines and intelligent agents used to mine data from the Internet (Joureston,
2000; Shaker & Gembicki, 1999, p. 122). To deal with the challenges of
seeking resources via the Internet, Burwell (1999) provides a compendium of
tools for online CI and includes a discussion of "soft information." She defines
"soft information" as non-statistical intelligence gathered from non-traditional
sources such as editorial pages and online discussions groups. Usenets and
listservs are examples of online discussion groups and are used as cyber-
listening posts to gather opinions (Burwell, 1999, p. 170; Kassler, 2000).
Although the hypertext link analysis can be considered as a technique for
gathering "soft information," it was not included in the compendium.

Fuld & Company, a CI consultancy firm, uses hypertext link analysis to
identify competitors' relationships. Search engines such as HotBot, AltaVista
and Google support what Kassler (2000) calls the "reverse link look-up" for

Table 2. Competitor Analysis Techniques

Technique	Usage	Source
Advertising Analysis	Identify demographics competitors are targeting and where the competitors may be headed.	Britton, 2002; Burwell, 1999
Alliance Networks Analysis	Assess strength of competitors' alliance networks	deMan, 2002
Competitor Profiling	Provide a picture of the strengths & weaknesses of current and potential rivals.	Fleisher & Bensoussan, 2003; Shaker & Gembicki, 1999; Whitehead, 2002
Corporate Culture Analysis	Understand competitors' leadership styles and culture of the firms	Herring et al., 2002
Futures-Based Analysis	Use as a forecasting tool to analyze changes in irrational competitor actions	Glitman, 2000; Mogel, 2002
Media Analysis	Use as a diagnostic tool to measure and compare media coverage of competitors. Also, can use for comparing actual press coverage to company's press releases.	Naylor, 2002; Stott, 1993
Opportunity Assessment	Identify opportunities and threats as part of an early warning system. Used for SWOT analysis.	Alampalli, 2002; Holder, 2001; Hoyt, 2002; Patchett, 2002

links leading into a firm's website. The links indicate either official or unofficial relationships. Although the proliferation of the Internet is resulting in lots of attention being focused on data collection, the development of appropriate analytical processes is essential for CI and for formulating corporate strategy (Fleisher & Bensoussan, 2003). CI analysis is defined as the multi-faceted means by which information is interpreted to produce intelligence for organizational action (Fleisher & Bensoussan, 2000). It provides an abundance of techniques such as competitor profiling and issues analysis that enable organizations to analyze the strengths and weaknesses of current and potential rivals in order to identify opportunities and threats. Table 2 provides a summary of analytical techniques for profiling competitors.

In addition to tracking competitors, the social, technical, economic, and political environments must be monitored for opportunities and threats (Fleisher & Bensoussan, 2003, p. 269; Mogel, 2002). Accordingly, these opportunities and threats often take the form of strategic issues. A strategic issue, according to Fleisher and Bensoussan, occurs when a difference (or gap) of beliefs, facts, or values between a company and stakeholders could significantly impact the organization's performance. Issue analysis is an analytical technique used to identify emerging issues using survey and content analysis and requires regular scanning of a company's environment.

Analysis of emerging issues requires one to filter out essential pieces of information from noise and discern the connection between disparate people, places and events. This is also a requirement for intelligence organizations because they need to mine unstructured data such as e-mails to identify linkages and potential meaningful anomalies in the marketplace and online marketspace (Ignatius, 2002; Roberts-Witt, 2002). Hoyt (2002) interprets the process of spotting anomalies, such as irregularities and surprises, as a starting point in an early warning system.

The literature shows that hypertext link analysis enables identification of implicit communities and has been applied extensively in information retrieval. However, limited studies analyze the links and information side effects to predict relationships and interests of community members. Although link analysis is useful for the data collection and analysis stages of the competitive intelligence process, the literature is bereft of empirical studies focusing on the use of link analysis for competitive intelligence.

In the following section, we provide a discussion of the conceptual framework for analyzing hidden communities of stakeholders and how such a framework was applied to the MicroStrategy case.

Conceptual Framework and Background on MicroStrategy, Inc.

Figure 1 depicts the proposed conceptual framework for analyzing implicit communities. It builds on ideas from Web link analysis, online communities and competitive intelligence literature about analyzing shared interests and activities. The framework includes the following steps: (1) identify a target company and its URL for investigation, (2) create an industry map that identifies the company's stakeholders such as customers, suppliers, etc., (3) conduct link search using the target URL, (4) code the link data, and (5) identify and analyze patterns.

The conceptual framework was applied to MicroStrategy, Inc., in an attempt to answer the following research questions using the social structure of the Web's hypertext links: (1) Can one identify the relationships and interests of implicit Web communities to a specific company?, and (2) How are the implicit communities, especially external stakeholders, using the company's Web resources?

MicroStrategy was selected because it is a leading worldwide provider of business-critical systems such as E-business intelligence applications. It is recognized for the strength of its vision and the success of its customers and products (Simpson, 2000).

Keyword searches, industry reports, MicroStrategy's press releases, case studies, white papers, and its database of over 210 partners/suppliers

Figure 1. Conceptual Framework for Analysis of Hidden Communities

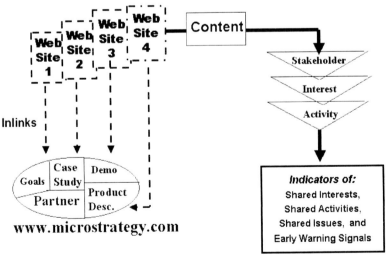

were examined to create an initial industry map of MicroStrategy's stakeholders. Table 3 provides a summary of the resources and corresponding target audience provided at MicroStrategy's website in April 2000.

METHODOLOGY

This link analysis methodology has similarities to the Xerox's study of Web communities at Stanford and MIT (Adamic & Adar, 2001). In April 2000, link searches were conducted over a four-day period using AltaVista, HotBot and Google to identify inlinks to MicroStrategy's website (Reid, 2003). For example, the Google Advanced search option was selected to conduct a link search. In response to the prompt that reads, "Find pages that link to the page," the URL www.microstrategy.com was typed into the query form. By clicking on the link from the results list, additional texts from the referral website were captured. Three search tools were used to identify the largest number of inlinks that are available in the publicly indexed section of the Web.

It should be noted that the exact number of inlinks to MicroStrategy cannot be ascertained because some organizations deny access to search engine

Table 3. Resources at MicroStrategy's Website

Resource	Target Audience
Case study	Customer, Investor, Partner, Public
CEO information	Customer, Investor, Partner, Public
Contact data -- sales	Customer, Public
Corporate overview	Customer, Investor, Partner, Public
Course data (training)	Customer, Partner, Public
Demo (product)	Customer, Investor, Partner, Public
Invitation for firms interested in partnership	Customer, Investor, Partner, Public
Mass media ads (video and print)	Customer, Investor, Partner, Public
Partners list (includes suppliers)	Customer, Investor, Partner, Public
Partners database (includes suppliers)	Customer, Investor, Partner, Public
Partners Intranet (includes suppliers)	Partners
Press releases	Customer, Investor, Partner, Public
Product description	Customer, Investor, Partner, Public
Technical support	Customer, Partner
White papers	Customer, Investor, Partner, Public

robots through the use of several techniques such as firewalls (Thelwall, 2001). The search engines are prevented from indexing the contents from those pages.

Coding

The unit of analysis in this study is a link (URL) and its associated text. Duplicate hits (same URL, same contents) were not counted as part of the sample. Data were content analyzed to develop codes based on the contexts. The data were reviewed line-by-line and coded to identify events such as E-business conferences, actions such as organizing, objects such as sponsors, and organizations such as CMP Media.

Miles and Huberman (1994) recommend using relevant theories in coding because it makes coding more manageable and ties it into a conceptual structure.

Wallin's (2000) framework provides a classification scheme that is organized from a stakeholder's perspective and indicates some relations that an enterprise has with its environmental actors. The industry map identified some of MicroStrategy's customers, competitors, and partners/ suppliers but not the external stakeholder (non-customer) groups. Boulton et al.'s (2000) model was used to segment the interest categories while the classification of activities was adapted from Rayport and Sviokla's (1995) virtual value activities scheme. The classification scheme is summarized in Table 4.

EXPERIMENTAL RESULTS

A total of 1,154 links to MicroStrategy's website were identified (see Table 5). Six hundred and thirty-three links from the host organization (MicroStrategy) were not included in the analysis because they are considered as self-citation (MicroStrategy linking to MicroStrategy). Another set of 76 duplicate links was excluded, leaving a useful sample size of 445 inlinks.

Table 6 shows that of the 445 inlinks, 264 (or 59%) companies (.com or .co) and organizations (.org) made up the largest group, followed by 76 "others," 70 educational institutions (.edu, .ac), and 17 networks (.net).

Fifty-six links from 17 non-U.S. countries, which include those from Germany, Austria, France, Switzerland, and United Kingdom, constituted 3% of the entire group. German was the most frequently cited foreign language. Three hundred eighty-nine (or 87%) links are from the U.S., while English was used in 418 (or 94%) sites.

Table 4. Classification of Link Data

Category	Major Classification	Sub-Classification	Example
1. Stakeholder Type (Wallin)	Transactional (internal environment)	Actor that the firm interacts with and influence	Customers, Employees, Investors, Partners/ Suppliers
	Contextual (external environment)	Actor that the firm has no power or influence over	Associations, Educational Institutions, SIGs, Government, Media
2. Interest (Asset) (Boulton et al.)	Tangible	Physical assets	Property, Buildings, Inventory
		Financial assets	Cash, Debt, Expense, Investment
	Intangible	Products, Services	Product Features
		Customer assets	Customer base (buying power)
		Organization assets	Culture, Strategy, Leadership, etc.
3. Activity (Rayport & Sviokla)	Gather information		Lists, Directories
	Organize information		Lists, Directories
	Select information		Reports, Events
	Synthesize information		Materials for Press Release
	Distribute information		Product Review Reports

Relations of Implicit Communities

The results are focused around the initial question: Can one identify relationships and interests of implicit Web communities of MicroStrategy? Table 7 presents the distribution of 445 stakeholders by individual sub-groups. Of these, 208 (or 46.7%) links make up the internal stakeholder communities while the remaining 237 (or 53.3%) links constitute the external stakeholder communities.

Table 5. Total and Unique Links to MicroStrategy

Search Engine	Total No. of Links	Inlinks (Less Self-Citation)	No. Unique Links (%)
AltaVista	185	185	157 (35%)
Google	872	240	218 (49%)
HotBot	97	96	70 (16%)
Total	1,154	521	445 (100%)

Table 6. Distribution of Links

Top Level Domain	Freq.	Cum. Freq.	%-Age	Cum. %-Age
1. net	17	17	3.7	3.7
2. org	18	35	4.0	7.7
3. edu, ac	70	105	15.4	23.1
4. others (.es, .it, .hn)	76	181	17.1	40.7
5. co, com	264	445	59.3	100.0
Country				
1. Japan, Korea, Singapore, S. Africa (1 each)	4	4	0.9	0.9
2. Czech Rep., Spain, Honduras, Ireland, Sweden (2 each)	10	14	2.2	3.1
3. Canada, Netherlands, Italy (3 each)	9	23	2.0	5.1
4. France	4	27	0.9	6.0
5. Switzerland	4	31	0.9	6.9
6. United Kingdom	4	35	0.9	7.8
7. Austria	7	42	1.6	9.4
8. Germany	14	56	3.1	12.6
9. USA (default)	389	445	87.4	100.0
Language Used				
1. Japanese	1	1	0.22	0.22
2. Italian	2	3	0.45	0.67
3. Spanish	2	5	0.45	1.12
4. Dutch	4	9	0.90	2.02
5. French	4	13	0.90	2.92
6. German	14	27	3.15	6.07
7. English	418	445	93.93	100.00

Partner/supplier (183), educational provider (85) and media (81) altogether accounted for 78% of all links. The largest sub-group is the partner/supplier with 183 links from 87 unique organizations such as Net Perceptions, IBM and washingtonpost.com. It should be noted that several unique links might actually emanate from a single organization. Although MicroStrategy's website provided a database of over 210 partners/suppliers, most of which were identified as U.S. partners, the inlink data we collected showed foreign partners/suppliers (not identified in MicroStrategy's database), such as a South African partner. This link turned out to be a mirror site for MicroStrategy's press releases. The mirror site is useful because of the current trend of redirecting one's competitors to a bogus site that looks like an official site.

Customer, another internal stakeholder, was made up of 15 (or 3.4%) links originating from five organizations. One such instance is the Ohio Department of Education. It has 11 links to MicroStrategy's website as it demonstrates and markets its interactive report card service for parents, educators, policymakers, and the general public.

The employee stakeholder community constituted seven (or 2.6%) links and includes employees such as Michael Saylor, MicroStrategy's CEO.

Table 7. Distribution of Links by Stakeholder Groups

Stake-Holder Group	Sub-Groups	Links (Freq)	Sub-Group			Overall		
			Cum. Freq.	%-age	Cum. %-age	Cum. Freq.	%-Age	Cum. %-Age
Internal	Partner/Supplier	183	183	87.9	87.9	183	41.1	41.1
	Customer	15	198	7.2	95.1	198	3.4	44.5
	Employee	7	205	3.3	98.5	205	1.6	46.1
	Investor	3	208	1.4	100.0	208	0.6	46.7
External	Educational Inst.	85	85	35.8	35.8	293	19.1	65.8
	Media	81	166	34.18	70.0	374	18.2	84.0
	Portal	35	201	14.8	84.8	409	7.2	91.9
	Public/Person	11	212	4.6	89.4	420	2.5	94.4
	Recruiter	11	223	4.6	94.1	431	2.4	96.8
	Unknown	8	231	2.4	97.4	439	1.8	98.6
	Reviewer	5	236	2.1	99.6	444	1.1	99.8
	Competitor	1	237	0.4	100.0	445	0.2	100.0

Another example is an employee who provided a description including pictures of his experiences in MicroStrategy's new employee training program (boot camp). The six-week boot camp and annual corporate retreat are cited as ways that MicroStrategy invests in its human capital. For the investor stakeholder sub-group, there were three (or 0.6%) links such as the link from Capital Investors which refers to Saylor's biographical data at MicroStrategy's website.

For the external stakeholders, the educational institution sub-group was represented by 85 (or 19.1%) links and included 49 unique organizations from 11 different countries such as the Royal Institute of Technology, Sweden, Telecom Paris, and University Kwangwoon Technology, Korea. Eight universities had several links to MicroStrategy from different departments such as the Database Research Group and the Career Center of the University of California, Berkeley. The media sub-group constituted 81 (or 18.2%) links and included national, international and trade press such as *Fortune*, *DBMS Magazine*, and *Nouveau*.

The portal sub-group consisted of 35 (or 7.2%) links and included firms like Yahoo and MSN. The technical portal, such as, "Open Directory— Computers" provided a gateway to database products descriptions, specialized discussion forums, white papers, and annotated analysis of current news. The public/personal sub-group has 11 links (or 2.5%) from personal home pages that focus on providing a personal view of developments in the business intelligence industry. A more interesting sub-group is the reviewer, with five (or 2.4%) links concentrating on critical assessment of MicroStrategy's products, services, and strategies. This included the OLAP Report that reviews about 30 software products. The smallest sub-group is the lone link from a competitor. It is interesting to note that MicroStrategy's traditional competitors, such as IBM and Sybase, have partnerships with the firm.

Eight links in which relationships cannot be identified were classified as "unknown." Initially, there were 50 such links whose relationships with MicroStrategy could not be identified. Each one was subjected to additional keyword searches in several databases such as Dow Jones Interactive, Yahoo, Meta-crawler, CNN, Techweb, Whois, and Lexis-Nexis. After this additional "screening," eight (or 2%) firms' relationship could not be ascertained. Four of them have been found to be dead links, while the other four provided no clues as to their relationship with MicroStrategy. The eight firms were then labeled as "unknown." Since most of these companies are in the information technology industry, they should be further analyzed through other means.

Interests of Stakeholders

Table 8 presents the sub-groups making up the hyperlinked communities and their interests in both the tangible and intangible resources of MicroStrategy. Overall, 245 links (or 55%), predominantly the partner/supplier (179) and educational provider (33) sub-groups, cite the product and services segment of MicroStrategy's website.

The assets of interest from the internal stakeholder sub-groups are fairly understandable. Partners/suppliers are firms that officially endorse MicroStrategy's products and services for the "network effect" while the employees cited and referred to the same resources to support the marketing of their expertise (Stewart, 2001). Customers cite information on their project development activities with MicroStrategy whereas the three investor-links cite the financial and biographical data resources of MicroStrategy.

Another asset drawing a lot of interest is the organizational resource, with 147 (or 33%) links. The majority of these links are from the media (54), educational provider (44), and portal (28) sub-groups. Organizational resources are intangible assets such as business intelligence (BI) systems, organizational brand, and strategy. Interests in MicroStrategy's intellectual capital, to some extent, may accrue to its charismatic and visionary CEO. In a highly competitive market dealing with expensive high-end software products, MicroStrategy's CEO is known for his plans to make interactive database access as common as the telephone (Yang, 1999).

As a reaction to the foregoing, six websites from media and public stakeholders voiced their reservations about the CEO's vision of "consumer-

Table 8.   Relations and Interests of Stakeholders

| Communities | Assets of Interest | | | | |
| | Tangible* | Intangible (Information) | | | |
	Financial	Products and Services	Customer Capital	Organi-zational	Sub-Totals
A. Internal Stakeholder Community (208 links)					
Partners and Suppliers		179		4	183
Customers			15		15
Employees		7			7
Investors	3			·	3
B. External Stakeholder Community (237 links)					
Educational Institutions		33	8	44	85
Media	18	9		54 ·	81
Portal	4		3	28	35
Public/Personal		3		8	11
Recruiter		11			11
Unknown	2	3		3	8
Reviewer				5	5
Competitor				1	1
TOTALS	27	245	26	147	445

For tangible assets, none of the links' associated texts mentioned physical assets such as buildings, equipment, etc.

ism of database"—that is, a database that can function like a crystal ball on your desk. The issues focused on privacy and implementation. For example, Lewis Perelman, President, Kanbrain Institute, provided an analysis of his in-depth interview with Michael Saylor that focused on Saylor's vision of making interactive database on the Web as common as the telephone. The critical analysis was published in *Fastcompany* magazine and as an editorial on Perelman's website.

Saylor's reputation for being a net visionary is also reflected in other websites. Moreover, nine websites mention support for Saylor's strategic announcement about establishing the "first free cyber-university." Some of these were from Germany and Austria while other U.S.-based websites were from non-IT groups such as seniorwomen.com. One website, slashdot.org, classified as a portal, had more than 100 messages discussing how the CEO could operationalize his vision of a free cyber-university. Key suggestions include using an open platform approach like Linux and the Cooper College's model of free education.

Activities of Stakeholders

Having summarized the relations and interests of the hyperlinked communities, the second research question focuses on how stakeholders are using MicroStrategy's resources. Overall, the stakeholders frequently used MicroStrategy's website to organize directories, create and disseminate news stories and press releases, and distribute information about conferences/exhibitions, as summarized in Table 9. Eighty-seven partners/suppliers used inlinks to MicroStrategy as inputs for organizing partnership and/or subject directories (webliographies). Some partner/supplier websites were referencing the same strategic alliances. For instance, Baan and the Distributor Information Systems Corporation (DISC) linked to solution partners that include MicroStrategy, IBM and Oracle.

Some organizations have several relations with MicroStrategy. *Washington Post*, for instance, acted as a partner, advertiser and affiliate of MicroStrategy's subsidiary—strategy.com. The partners/suppliers link their partnership directories, press releases, white papers, and trade shows (Web pages) to MicroStrategy's website. Through this, they promote and publicize their official affiliations with MicroStrategy.

In reference to how the 237 external stakeholders inlinks are using MicroStrategy's resources, the data show that 59 such inlinks are from universities that compile employment and business intelligence company directories. Twenty-one inlinks, from universities in U.S., Austria, Honduras and Canada, used case studies from various IT firms, including those from MicroStrategy's website, for teaching their business and engineering courses, while one university focused exclusively on MicroStrategy's cases such as Victoria Secret and Nielsen.

It was also found that the University of Saskatchewan (Canada) and the University of South Carolina used MicroStrategy's case studies in their management information systems courses. In a decision support systems course at the University of Colorado, the Web-based syllabus provided 14 links to different case studies from MicroStrategy. In addition to linking to specific cases, students provided reports on MicroStrategy's software applications. One University of Iowa student conducted a comparative analysis of OLAP architecture designs of MicroStrategy and Arbor—one of its competitors. The report included OLAP schematic images from MicroStrategy's website.

Furthermore, media outfits such as Business Week Online, Webdo (Switzerland), and cnet.com were active in synthesizing newsbytes regarding

Table 9. Usage of MicroStrategy's Website

Community	Activity	Freq.
A. Internal Stakeholder Community (208 links)		
Partners/	Organize lists of suppliers and partners, and webliographies	87
Supplier (183)	Synthesize case studies, press releases, online forum and magazine materials	43
	Distribute advertisements, product reviews, sponsorships of trade shows and conference	53
Customer (15)	Organize list of BI product vendors	5
	Synthesize press releases	2
	Distribute product demo materials	8
Employee (7)	Organize list of BI product vendors	2
	Synthesize online forum materials	4
	Distribute information on training	1
Investor (3)	Organize investor relation and press release materials	3
B. External Stakeholder Community (237 links)		
Education Provider (85)	Organize directory of technology firms and guide to BI resources	59
	Synthesize case studies, press releases, online forum and magazine materials	21
	Distribute press release and conference materials	5
Media (81)	Organize directory of technology firms	8
	Synthesize press release materials	62
	Distribute info. on job ads and trade shows	11
Portal (35)	Organize directory of BI firms	14
	Synthesize online forum materials	2
	Distribute info. on e-commerce services and news articles	19
Public (11)	Organize guide to BI resources	7
	Distribute product reviews and resumes	4
Recruiter (11)	Organize directory of BI firms and job vacancies	9
	Synthesize press release materials	2
Reviewer	Synthesize product reviews and critiques	5
Competitor	Organize directory of BI firms	1
Unknown		8

MicroStrategy's financial problems, decision support system (DSS) software, and its strategy of penetrating the consumer market by "whispering data in their ear." Business Week Online featured a company close-up on MicroStrategy's strategy of harnessing consumer data and pitted MicroStrategy against its "new competitors" such as America Online, Yahoo, and AT&T (Yang, 1999). A major strategic difference is that MicroStrategy's subsidiary, strategy.com, is selling its customized proactive wireless information services to consumer companies, such as washingtonpost.com, which in turn offer value-added services to their customers. The metaphor "whispering data in their (customers') ears," synthesized by other media such as *Fastcompany* magazine, is used to illustrate the concept of real-time intelligence.

In addition to the praises, the media and reviewer sub-groups also provided critical feedback on MicroStrategy's advertisements and software products. For example, *The Bee Newspaper* (published in Sacramento, California, USA), cynical.com and two other sites criticized MicroStrategy's Superbowl 2000 television advertisements. The Superbowl ads were used to launch a new media campaign for expanding its customer base and targeting the masses. The Superbowl is a U.S. football championship game that can be compared to the FIFA World Cup Championship. It caters to a large audience of people and provides a great opportunity for advertisers.

Some of the review sites provided video archives and their own professional critiques of MicroStrategy's 30-second ads. Other linked sites invited their users to submit feedback and vote on the best and the worst ads on those sites. Some of the review comments include: "What is MicroStrategy Selling?"; "Thoroughly Confusing!"; "Conclusion—don't buy the product."

In addition to reviews of advertisement, organizations used MicroStrategy's website to create software product review reports such as the OLAP Report. Since the OLAP Report produces more than 20 full reviews of about 30 products, it is directly linked to the software vendors for additional information needs.

DISCUSSION

This section discusses the outcomes of issue analysis, early warning signals, and their CI implications. The hyperlinked communities' comments were content analyzed to see how they share information, dramatize stories and converge on shared issues about Microstrategy. The findings showed that the issues of interest to hidden communities of stakeholders centered on MicroStrategy's advertisements, business alliances, cyber-university announcement, and strategic product development. Table 10 provides a summary of some shared issues and how they can be used for competitor profiling.

For example, the Superbowl television advertisements and stakeholders' comments can be used for analyzing MicroStrategy's marketing strategy. The tricky part in analyzing a competitor's advertisement ploy is finding current and usable data (Britton, 2002). Using Britton's approach for deconstructing a competitor's advertisement, it can provide insight into following questions.

- Who are they aiming to influence? (target)
- What do they wish to communicate? (message)
- Why will this be believed? (support)
- How are segments of the target audience reacting? (response)

Since MicroStrategy's advertisements attempted to relate to the viewer's experiences, discovering the audience's responses can provide other perspectives in respect of the strengths or weaknesses of their brand.

Another example includes shared issue about MicroStrategy's strategic vision to make proactive database access as common as the telephone. MicroStrategy's vision can be understood by analyzing changes in society, technology, economics, environment, or politics (STEEP) so that its competitors can better predict the results of its action, and what it might do next. MicroStrategy seems to be capitalizing on changes in a global society that is becoming increasingly dependent on mobile technology in a deregulated, E-business-based environment. Therefore, real-time and hassle-free mobile access to the right information may become essential to businesses and eventually for individual personal usage.

Table 10. Interests and Competitor Profiling

Interest	Example	CI Analysis	Issue
Advertisement	Superbowl 2000 Ads (four websites)	Advertisement analysis (Britton); SWOT analysis (Fleisher & Bensoussan)	Key demographics of interest to competitors; Real-time intelligence -- perceptions of needs
Alliance	Integration Partner (183 websites)	Alliance networks analysis (deMan); SWOT analysis (Fleisher & Bensoussan)	Strengths and weaknesses of competitor's alliance networks
Media Announce-ment	Announcement of "first free cyber-university" (nine websites)	Futures-based analysis (Mogel); Media Analysis (Stott); SWOT analysis (Fleisher & Bensoussan)	Unusual announcement (may indicate changes in competitor's actions); Implementation challenges
Strategy	Consumerism of databases (six websites)	Media analysis (Stott); SWOT analysis (Fleisher & Bensoussan)	Paradigm shift -- real-time intelligence for all; Privacy

In order to get increased market acceptance of its real-time business intelligence system, the stakeholders' comments indicate that MicroStrategy has to deal with the challenges of personal relevancy, affordability, ease-of-use, and privacy. The use of STEEP analysis may help competitors to see the industry the way MicroStrategy does, i.e., new opportunities, new threats, and new competitors such as Yahoo and AT&T.

Early Warning Signs

Table 11 summarizes the key early warning signs extracted from the analysis of the link-related texts, anomalies, and inferences. By identifying unusual events such as the announcements of real-time intelligence for all and

Table 11. Warning Signs

Subject	Anomaly	Inference (Illustrative Examples)
First free cyber-U (nine websites)	"Good news, especially if cyber-U uses Linux."	How do they propose to fund this? How will this project align/support their current business strategies?
Distance Education for Senior Citizens (one website: Seniorwomen.com)	"Learning notes: MicroStrategy's CEO proposes funding of a free online university with Ivy League quality."	Retirees including the "baby boom generation" with excess time and money are a rapidly growing group that has joined the cyber ranks. How can serving the demands of this niche market be of business value to MicroStrategy?
Consumerism of databases (six websites)	"MicroStrategy wants to be an angel whispering data in your ear; White House refuses auction of government databases."	Will personal intelligence system that provides proactive delivery of information become as popular and useful as the telephone? Have they invented a database killer application yet? How have they addressed the data-privacy concerns?
Superbowl Ad 2000 (four websites)	"What are they selling?"	How much marginal marketspace reach can truly be achieved by riding on the popularity of global sport events?; How does this work for firms like MicroStrategy?
Financial standing and earning report (13 websites)	"MicroStrategy overstates earnings."	Is the company in the "red"? Is this style of reporting sound? Ethical? Acceptable?
Interactive report card (11 websites)	"E-government in action. Interactive report card for parents, educators, policymakers, media, and general public."	E-government application is a market that provides additional revenue streams as well as opportunities for educating mass population on business intelligence services. How can firms like MicroStrategy tap into this market?

free cyber-university, Hoyt's (2002) technique of detecting anomalies and unusual items can be applied. He suggested moving from a great deal of data to examining small and unique events as well as using an inductive process to generate inferences.

Consider, for instance, the announcement of a free Ivy League cyber-university by MicroStrategy's CEO. From an inductive perspective, private university education is costly and since it was announced that tuition will not be charged, the pronouncement is unusual. A competitor may ask "Why will it be provided for free—what (or where) is the catch?"

By weaving information into a story, a possible scenario may emerge. For high-end business intelligence vendors, many major challenges, such as expanding the customer base, educating more mainstream people (including low-tech groups) on advantages of using the software, reducing concern about privacy, and increasing sales, etc., exist.

Over time, the free cyber-university may help allay privacy fears by creating a global community of cyber-students who 'ethically' use business intelligence software on a regular basis as part of the program requirements. The free cyber-university may provide the platform for expanding MicroStrategy's customer and human capital in the future.

CONCLUSION

This chapter discussed the feasibility of employing an analytical framework for detecting and analyzing relationships and activities of a company's implicit Web communities of stakeholders. The framework builds on ideas from Web link analysis, online communities, and competitive intelligence literature. From link analysis studies, implicit communities are defined as less visible hyperlinked communities that evolve as a consequence of the way in which Web content creators link to one another in the context of topic of interest (Gibson, Kleinberg, & Raghavan, 1998).

In order to answer the research questions, the proposed framework was applied to MicroStrategy, Inc., a business intelligence vendor. The first question focuses on whether one can identify the relationships and interests of implicit Web communities to a specific company. MicroStrategy's implicit communities were identified and categorized into internal and external stakeholder communities.

Their interests focused on tangible and intangible assets. An intangible asset drawing a lot of interest is its organizational resources, e.g., business intelligence systems, organizational brand, and strategy.

The second research question focuses on how the implicit communities are using the company's Web resources. The stakeholders frequently used MicroStrategy's website to organize directories, create and disseminate news stories and press releases, and distribute information about conferences/ exhibitions. Oftentimes when the stakeholders create directories or news stories that are hyperlinked to MicroStrategy's website, they also express their perceptions about the company. The systematic collection and analysis of such perceptions and comments—previously untapped—can be a very potent source of "soft information."

A key characteristic of the proposed framework is its use of hypertext link analysis technique to identify and mine unstructured link data. These links represent messages from less visible communities that are often not available anywhere else in cyberspace. They can be used to support competitor analysis, such as analyzing the competitor's advertisements and media coverage. The framework can be developed into a technique for listening to the external environments to pick up on opportunities and threats, and detecting early warning signals. All of these enrich the CI capability and resources of a firm.

REFERENCES

Adamic, L. A. & Adar, E. (2001). *Friends and Neighbors on the Web.* Paper presented at the KDDI.

Alampalli, S. (2002). Role of CI for opportunity assessment. *Competitive Intelligence Magazine, 5*(4), 21-24.

Almind, T. C. & Ingwersen, P. (1998). Informetric analyses on the World Wide Web: Methodological approaches to Webometrics. *Journal of Documentation, 53*(4), 404-426.

Beginner's Guide to Citation Analysis: Ten Frequently Asked Questions. [Web site]. Retrieved January, 2003, from the World Wide Web: http://alexia.lis.uiuc.edu/~standrfr/beginner.html.

Borgman, C. L. & Furner, J. (2002). Scholarly communication and bibliometrics. In B. Cronin (Ed.), *Annual Review of Information Science and Technology* (Vol. 36). Information Today, Inc.

Boulton, R. E. S., Libert, B. D., & Samek, S. M. (2000). *Cracking the Value Code: How Successful Businesses are Creating Wealth in the New Economy.* Harper Business.

Britton, C. (2002). Deconstructing advertising: What your competitor's advertising can tell you about their strategy. *Competitive Intelligence Magazine, 5*(1), 15-19.

Burwell, H. P. (1999). *Online competitive intelligence: Increase your profits using cyber-intelligence.* Tempe, AZ: Facts on Demand Press.

Chakrabarti, S., Dom, B. E., Gibson, D., Kleinberg, J., Kumar, R., Raghavan, P., Rajagopalan, S., & Tomkins, A. (1999, February). Mining the link structure of the World Wide Web.

Cronin, B., Snyder, H. W., Rosenbaum, H., Martinson, A., & Callahan, E. (1998). Invoked on the Web. *Journal of the American Society for Information Science and Technology, 49*(14), 1319-1328.

deMan, A. P. (2002). How to analyze alliance networks?·*Competitive Intelligence Magazine, 5*(4), 14-16.

Elias, A. A. & Cavana, R. Y. (2000, December). *Stakeholder Analysis for Systems Thinking and Modelling.* Paper presented at the ORSNZ 2000, New Zealand.

Flake, W. G., Lawrence, S., Giles, C. L., & Coetzee, F. M. (2002). Self-organization and identification of Web communities. *IEEE Computer, 35*(3), 66-71.

Fleisher, C. S. & Bensoussan, B. E. (2000). Far out way to manage CI analysis. *Competitive Intelligence Magazine, 3*(2), 37-40.

Fleisher, C. S. & Bensoussan, B. E. (2003). *Strategic and Competitive Analysis: Methods and Techniques for Analyzing Business Competition.* Upper Saddle River, NJ: Prentice Hall.

Garofalakis, M. N., Rastogi, R., Seshadri, S., & Shim, K. (1999). *Data Mining and the Web: Past, Present and Future.* Paper presented at the WIDM 99, Kansas City, Missouri, USA.

Gibson, D., Kleinberg, J., & Raghavan, P. (1998). *Inferring Web Communities from Link Topology.* Paper presented at the Hypertext 98: 9th ACM Conference on Hypertext and Hypermedia.

Glitman, E. (2000). Comprehending 'irrational' competitor actions through futures-based analysis. *Competitive Intelligence Magazine, 3*(4), 29-32.

Hackathorn, R. (2001). *The twURLed world of Web farming, data warehouses and Richard Hackathorn.* Retrieved 2001, from the World Wide Web: http://www.webfarming.com.

Hagel, J. & Armstrong, A. G. (1997). *Net Gain: Expanding Markets through Virtual Communities.* Harvard Business School Press.

Hanson, W. (2000). *Principles of Internet Marketing*: South-Western College Publishing.

Herring, J. P., Klein, R. D., Harris, M., & Bourey, A. T. (2002). Corporate culture as a tool for anticipating the competition. *Competitive Intelligence Magazine, 5*(4), 6-10.

Holder, B. J. (2001). Scouting: A process for discovering, creating, and acting on knowledge. *Competitive Intelligence Magazine, 4*, 17-21.

Hoyt, B. (2002). Early warning: The art of inference. *Competitive Intelligence Magazine, 5*(1), 10-14.

Hypersearching the Web. (1999). *Scientific American*. Retrieved from the World Wide Web: http://www.sciam.com.

Ignatius, D. (2002, October 11). Tools for detecting terror. Retrieved from the World Wide Web: washingtonpost.com.

ISI. (1999). *Introduction to citation indexing and citation searching*. Institute of Scientific Information (ISI). Retrieved from the World Wide Web: http://osulibrary.orst.edu/instruction/classes/engr/Mod6/impact.htm.

Joureston, J. (2000). Using intelligent search agents for CI. *Competitive Intelligence Magazine, 3*(1), 32-36.

Kahaner, L. (1998). *Competitive Intelligence: How to Gather, Analyze and Use Information to Move your Business to the Top*. Touchstone.

Kassler, H. (1998). Competitive intelligence. *Econtent*, 16-24.

Kassler, H. (2000). Competitive intelligence and the Internet: Going for the gold. *Information Outlook, 4*(2), 37-42.

Kleinberg, J. (1998). *Authoritative Sources in a Hyperlinked Environment*. Paper presented at the Proceedings of the 9th ACM-SIAM Symposium on Discrete Algorithm (SODA).

Kumar, R., Raghavan, P., Rajagopalan, S., & Tomkins, A. (1999). *Trawling the Web for Emerging Cyber-Communities*. Paper presented at the Proceedings of the 8th International World Wide Web Conference.

Lazar, J. & Preece, J. (1998). *Classification Scheme for Online Communities*. Paper presented at the Proceedings of the 1998 Association for Information Systems, American Conference.

Microstrategy Ranked as One of the 10 Most Influential Business Intelligence Companies in 2000 DM Review 100 (2000). Retrieved 2002, from the World Wide Web: http://www.microstrategy.com/News/PR_System/Press_Release.asp?ID=621.

Miles, M. B. & Huberman, A. M. (1994). *Qualitative Data Analysis: An Expanded Sourcebook* (2nd ed.). Sage.

Mogel, R. (2002). Futuristic thinking. *Competitive Intelligence Magazine, 5*(3), 12-14.

Naylor, E. (2002). X-ray your competition: Profiling, media analysis and CI [electronic newsletter]. *SCIP*. Retrieved from the World Wide Web: http://www.scip.org.

Patchett, V. (2002). May the force be with you: Michael Porter and the Five-Force Theory of Industry Analysis. *Competitive Intelligence Magazine, 5*(4), 28-30.

Preece, J. (2000). *Online Communities: Designing Usability, Supporting Sociability.* John Wiley & Sons.

Rayport, J. F. & Sviokla, J. J. (1995). Exploiting the virtual value chain. *Harvard Business Review*, 75-85.

Reid, E.O.F. (2003). *Identifying a Company's Non-Customer Online Communities.* Paper presented at the Proceedings of the 36th International Conference on Systems Sciences (HICSS), Hawaii. Retrieved from the World Wide Web: http://www.hicss.hawaii.edu/HICSS36/PGuideWeb.htm.

Roberts-Witt, S.L. (2002, November). Mining for counterterrorism. *PC Magazine.* Retrieved 2002, from the World Wide Web: http://www.pcmagcom.

Rouach, D. & Santi, P. (2001). Competitive intelligence adds value: Five intelligence attitudes. *European Management Journal, 19*(5), 552-559.

SCIP. (2002). *What is CI? Society of Competitive Intelligence Professionals.* Retrieved 2002, from the World Wide Web: http://www.scip.org/ci.

Shaker, S. M. & Gembicki, M. P. (1999). *WarRoom Guide to Competitive Intelligence.* McGraw-Hill.

Simpson, G. R. (2000, January 3). Microstrategy looks to mine untouched government data. *Wall Street Journal.*

Smith, A. (1999, January 19-21). *ANZAC Webometrics: Exploring Australasian Web Structures.* Paper presented at the Information Online & On Disc.

Stanoevaka-Slabeva, K. & Schmid, B. F. (2000). *A Typology of Online Communities and Community Supporting Platforms.* Paper presented at the Proceedings of the 34th International Conference on Systems Sciences (HICSS '01), Hawaii.

Stewart, T. A. (2001). *Wealth of Knowledge: Intellectual Capital and the Twenty-First Century Organization.* New York: Currency Book.

Stott, M. D. (1993). You can't trust what you read: Making sense of the business press. In J. E. Prescott & P. T. Gibbons (Eds.), *Global Perspectives on Competitive Intelligence* (pp. 309-321). Alexandria: Society of Competitive Intelligence Professionals (SCIP).

Thelwall, M. (2001). Extracting macroscopic information from web links. *Journal of the American Society for Information Science and Technology, 52*(13), 1157-1168.

Van der Veer Martens, B. (2001). Do citations represent theories of truth? *Information Research*, *6*(2). Retrieved 2002, from the World Wide Web: http://information.net/ir/6-2/paper92a.html.

Wallin, J. (2000). *Operationizing Competencies*. Paper presented at the 5th Annual International Conference on Competence-Based Management, Helsinki University of Technology, Finland.

Whitehead, C. (2002). Five building blocks for organizational renewal. *Competitive Intelligence Magazine*, *5*(4), 25-27.

Yang, C. (1999, 21 December). Microstrategy wants to be an angel whispering data in your ear. *Business Week Online*.

Yang, K. (2002). *How Do We Find Information on the Web?* Unpublished dissertation, University of North Carolina, Chapel Hill.

Zaiane, O. R. (1999). *Web Usage Mining*. Retrieved from the World Wide Web: http://www.cs.ualberta.ca/~zaiane.

Zanasi, A. (1998). Competitive intelligence through data mining public sources. *Competitive Intelligence Review*, *9*(1), 44-54.

Chapter IV

Enabling Strategy Formulation by ICT: A Viable Systems Approach

Dirk Vriens
University of Nijmegen, The Netherlands

Jan Achterbergh
University of Nijmegen, The Netherlands

ABSTRACT

In this chapter the role of ICT for competitive intelligence is approached from the perspective of strategy formulation. The authors hold the view that competitive intelligence can be seen as knowledge necessary for the process of strategy formulation. To determine the role of ICT, it is proposed to examine (1) the process of strategy formulation, (2) the knowledge relevant for the process of strategy formulation and (3) the knowledge processes in which the intelligence relevant for the process of strategy formulation is produced and processed. If these three elements are clear, the role of ICT for competitive intelligence can be reformulated as the support of ICT for the knowledge processes, producing and processing the necessary intelligence for strategy formulation. In the chapter, the process of strategy formulation and the knowledge it requires will be described by using the Viable Systems Model of Stafford Beer. It results in an "ICT-architecture" for supporting the knowledge processes, producing the relevant knowledge for strategy formulation.

INTRODUCTION

An adequate intelligence function is indispensable for (re)formulating strategies in a world that is getting both "larger" as new markets are opened up and "smaller" as (information and communication) technologies develop to spot these markets and profit from them. To remain viable, organizations need to identify and define their relevant environments, to scan them for opportunities and threats, to use these scans for formulating their strategies, and to act on these strategies. The contribution of business or competitive intelligence to strategy formulation (and implementation) is a key factor for organizational viability.

Because of the importance of business or competitive intelligence (BI or CI) for organizational viability, a lot has been written lately about its goals and main processes (e.g., Fuld, 1995; Kahaner, 1997; Vriens & Philips, 1999; Cook & Cook, 2000). Vriens and Philips (1999), for example, define competitive intelligence as "a process of gathering and processing information about the environment to support the process of strategy formulation." In this definition, the function of delivering relevant "external" information is central. Others, however, see BI as a process that (also) delivers "internal" information to support formulating strategies (e.g., Dresner, 1989). In this latter category, authors point, for instance, to the information provided by means of the balanced scorecard or by data warehouses.

For (re)formulating strategies, both internal and external information (and their integration) is needed. Competitive intelligence seems to be the label, in literature as well as in practice, for a function in organizations that covers the supply and processing of information for strategy formulation.

Competitive intelligence activities can be supported by information and communication technology (ICT), and most authors agree on the importance of ICT for these activities (e.g., Fuld et al., 2002; Philips & Vriens, 1999; Kahaner, 1997; Cook & Cook, 2000). Several studies show the use of ICT in competitive intelligence activities. Vriens and Hendriks (2000), for instance, show how Web-enabled technologies may enable data-collection. Teo and

Choo (2002) give an overview of how the Internet can be used for CI activities, and several authors discuss the possibilities for the electronic 'outsourcing' of search activities (e.g., Kahaner, 1997).

However, in spite of the awareness of the importance of ICT for CI, it remains unclear how the link between CI and ICT should be designed. This link is the main focus of this chapter. The chapter sets out to describe the link between ICT and the process of supplying and processing information for strategy formulation. With such a description, designers of the CI process can select proper ICT support and they can judge whether the employed ICT applications support this process appropriately.

To describe the link between ICT and CI, it is necessary to define the process of strategy formulation—otherwise, it is impossible to determine the contribution of the CI process. Next, it necessary to determine what 'intelligence' is needed in the process of strategy formulation. For us, as for other authors (see e.g., Kahaner, 1997), intelligence as a "product" is knowledge relevant for strategy (re)formulation. We will therefore approach this question from a "knowledge" point of view. If it is clear what knowledge the process of strategy formulation needs, the processes that produce and process this knowledge may be acknowledged. In knowledge management literature, these processes are normally labeled "generation," "storage," "dissemination" and "application" of knowledge (see e.g., Davenport and Prusak, 1998; Achterbergh & Vriens, 2002). Given these processes, the role of ICT in supporting them may be defined. This last step then defines ICT for CI as support tools for the processes in which knowledge relevant for strategy formulation is generated, stored, disseminated and applied.

This chapter reformulates the role of ICT for CI as the role of ICT in the knowledge processes involved in strategy formulation. It seeks to define this role of ICT in four steps. These steps are: (1) presenting a model of the process of strategy formulation, (2) deriving the knowledge relevant for the process of strategy formulation, (3) identify the knowledge processes in which the relevant knowledge for strategy formulation is processed and produced and (4) use the previous steps to arrive at an understanding of the role of ICT in the process of strategy formulation. To deal with these four issues, we organize the chapter as follows. In the following section we unfold the process of strategy formulation. To do this, we use the Viable System Model of Beer (1979, 1981). This is followed with a section discussing the derivation of the necessary knowledge domains for the process of strategy formulation. Next, we describe the knowledge processes that produce and process the relevant knowledge for strategy formulation. The chapter then uses this model to identify ICT support for strategy formulation. The last section will conclude with recommendations for using the model to derive relevant ICT for CI.

STRATEGY FORMULATION:
A VIABLE SYSTEM PERSPECTIVE

Strategy formulation aims at developing and selecting goals and plans that secure the adaptation of the organization to its environment (see for instance, Johnson & Scholes, 1999). These goals and plans may refer to specific product-market-technology combinations for which the organization hypothesizes that they ensure a stable relation with its environment. The process of strategy formulation, then, needs to generate such goals and plans, needs to reflect upon their appropriateness and needs to select certain goals and plans to guide the behavior of the organization. Moreover, it is a continuous process. Goals and plans can be seen as hypotheses about "what will work" as a means to adapt and survive. Therefore, they should be monitored constantly, and revised if necessary. In short: strategy formulation is a continuous contribution to maintaining organizational viability.

Although many authors deal with the process of strategy formulation, we choose the Viable System Model of Beer (1979, 1981) to define this process more closely. We select the VSM because Beer explicitly unfolds the functions required for the viable realization and adaptation of the organization's identity. Since strategy formulation particularly aims at organizational adaptation, we can directly use the functions described by the VSM specializing in adaptation to define strategy formulation. Based on the VSM, an explication of the process of strategy formulation in terms of the functions necessary for organizational viability is possible. A further reason for using this model is that it is an offset for deriving systematically the knowledge-domains necessary for strategy-formulation. Moreover, the model allows for an identification of these knowledge domains at many (recursive) organizational levels. Designers of the CI process can thus use it to identify the relevant knowledge domains at a corporate level, at the level of the business unit or at the level of a team. Beer's model thus provides a background for defining strategy formulation and for identifying the necessary knowledge domains for strategy formulation. In this section we introduce the VSM and use it to define strategy formulation. In Section Three, we describe the relevant knowledge domains.

Stafford Beer developed the VSM to provide a model of the functions that are needed for organizational viability. An organization is viable if it is able to maintain a separate existence in its environment (Beer, 1985, p. 113). To be viable, an organization must have the potential to adapt and realize its identity and mission. This potential crucially depends on the realization of five (related) functions. According to Beer (1985, p. 115), these five functions and their relations are necessary and sufficient conditions for organizational viability. Below, we describe these five functions and their relations. We refer to a company called "Energeco"—a company specialized in supplying eco-energy—to illustrate these functions.

Function 1: Primary Activities

Function 1 of an organization as a viable system consists of the collection of its primary activities. These primary activities constitute the system's "raison d'être" (Espejo et al., 1996, p. 110). For example, the raison d'être of "Energeco" is to service its environment with eco-energy. "Energeco" has three primary activities: supplying solar, tidal, and wind energy. These three primary activities constitute its Function 1.

The existence of a collection of primary activities as such is insufficient to maintain the viability of an organization. Somehow, these primary activities must be forged into the larger whole of the organization. To this purpose, four additional functions are required: coordination, control, intelligence, and policy.

Function 2: Coordination

In organizations, primary activities may depend on shared resources. People, machines, shared in- or output markets, or output of other primary activities, are examples of shared resources. These dependencies make the primary activities interdependent. To give an example, specialists in high voltage energy are a shared resource between "Energeco's" business units. Now suppose that there is no coordination between these business units. In this case, the allocation of high voltage specialists to a project in the business unit "Solar Energy" may require a revision of the allocation of these same specialists to a project in the business unit "Wind Energy." Without a function that supports the coordination of these interdependencies, the business units "Solar Energy" and "Wind Energy" may become entangled in a process that oscillates between allocating and revising the allocation of these specialists to projects. It is the task of Function 2 to prevent these oscillations. Function 2 facilitates the coordination of interdependencies between function one activities, hence its name: *coordination*. Examples of Function 2 activities are the introduction of quality standards, the design and implementation of shared planning systems, or the introduction of a common language to discuss coordination problems.

Function 3: Control

The primary activities and coordination are necessary, but not sufficient for the viability of an organization. Each primary activity can still pursue its own goals without contributing to the realization of the identity and mission of the viable system as a whole. For this reason, Beer (1985, 1999f) argues that there must be a third function ensuring synergy and cohesion between primary activities. He calls this function "control." Its task is to translate the identity and mission of the viable system (e.g., supplying eco-energy) into goals for the primary activities (e.g., supplying wind, solar and tidal energy) and to control the realization of these goals. In this way, control takes care of the contribution of the primary activities to the realization of the identity and mission of the viable system.

Control has three instruments to discharge for its task. First, it gives direct command to and receives direct reports from the management of the primary activities. Second, control can audit the management of the primary activities. The aim of these audits is to stay aware of problems facing the management of the primary activities and to help in finding solutions to them. Third, control ensures the synergy of the primary activities by controlling the coordination effort by Function 2.

Control not only focuses on the realization of the identity and mission of the viable system; it is also involved in the adaptation of this identity and mission. Because of control's knowledge about the modus operandi and problems of the primary activities, its second task is to review proposals for innovation produced by the intelligence function (see below) and to assess whether these proposals are realistic given the potential for change of the primary activities. For this purpose, control is involved in a continuous discussion about the feasibility of proposed innovations.

Function 4: Intelligence

Functions 1 to 3 are necessary for the realization of the identity and mission of viable organizations, yet they are not sufficient for organizational viability. Viability also means adaptation. To make adaptation possible, a fourth function is required. Beer calls this function intelligence. It is the task of intelligence to scan the environment of the organization for relevant developments and to initiate adaptation to keep the identity and mission aligned with them (doing the right thing, instead of doing things right, Espejo et al., 1996). For instance, developments in production technology may introduce the possibility of cost-effective, large-scale production of eco-energy from biomass. Intelligence should pick up these developments, assess them, and if relevant, translate them into proposals for innovation.

Function 5: Policy

The addition of the intelligence function seems to complete the list of functions required for the realization and adaptation of a viable organization's identity and mission. According to Beer (1985, p. 258ff), this is not the case. The reason for this is the particular focus of the control and intelligence function. Control focuses on the *realization* of identity and mission of the organization, while intelligence focuses on initiating *adaptation*. If it is supposed that the interaction between control and intelligence is not coordinated, three problems may occur. First, interaction is too loose. In this case, proposals for innovations are not assessed in terms of the organization's potentials for change and existing potentials for change cannot be exploited by innovations. Both the realization and adaptation of the organization's identity and strategy may slowly stop. In the second and third problem, interaction between control and intelligence is intense, but one of the functions dominates the other. If intelligence dominates control, the organization runs the risk of "innovatism." Innovative products or technologies are proposed and introduced that do not match the potential for change of the primary activities. If control dominates intelligence, the organization runs the risk of "conservatism." Proposals for innovation are rejected because of an obsession with current markets, products and production technologies.

To counter these problems, Beer introduces a final function he calls policy. Policy has the tasks of coordinating the interaction between control and intelligence and consolidating its results in a (re)definition of the identity and mission of the organization in such a way that they fit developments in its environment as well as in its own potentials for change. Policy provides closure to the adaptation and realization cycle. As such, it completes the list of functions necessary and sufficient for viable organizing.

The Process of Strategy Formulation According to the VSM

The VSM not only describes the functions needed for viability. It also describes the interactive relations that should exist between them and the characteristics these relations should have. For this purpose, it divides the functions into two groups: functions that contribute to the *realization* of the organization's strategy and functions that contribute to its *adaptation*.

The first group consists of the primary activities, coordination and control. This group deals with the *realization* of the organization's identity and strategy. The second group consists of control, intelligence, and policy. This group deals with the *adaptation* of the organization's identity and strategy: its task is "inventing the organization" (Espejo et al., 1996). Together, control, intelligence, and policy attempt to keep the organization aligned with relevant developments in its environment.

Keeping the organization aligned with relevant developments in its environment can be seen as the core objective of strategy formulation. In fact, the interplay between the VSM functions control, intelligence and policy describes the process of strategy formulation. Intelligence generates plans for adaptation and control reviews them. A discussion about the (adequacy of these) plans between intelligence and control (mediated by policy) should lead to a finalized plan for adaptation. Finally, such a plan should be consolidated by policy. Figure 1 depicts the process of strategy formulation according to the VSM (and its associated VSM functions).

Because strategy formulation is captured by the functions control, intelligence, policy, and their relations, we not only describe these relations, we also characterize them in terms of periodicity, detail, and potentials for standardization. These characteristics are relevant for designing supportive measures (among which are ICT applications) for the process of strategy formulation, as will become apparent in the last section. Table 1 summarizes and characterizes the relations between the functions in this group.

Figure 1. The Process of Strategy Formulation According to the VSM

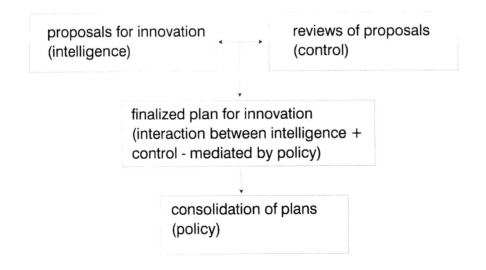

Table 1.   Relations Between Functions Focused on Adapting the Organization's Identity and Strategy

Related Functions	Relation	Normative Characteristics of Relation			
		Periodicity	*Detail*	*Standardization*	*Focus On*
Intelligence -- Control	Generating finalized proposals for innovation	Continuous	High	Low	Balancing and integrating proposals for innovation and potentials for change
Policy – Intelligence and Control	Balancing contributions by intelligence and control	Continuous	Low	Low	Supporting interaction between intelligence and control
	Consolidating proposals for innovation	Irregular intervals	Low	Low	(Re)defining the organization's identity and strategy

The VSM recommends that control and intelligence are highly interconnected and of similar complexity. The interaction between them should be continuous, intense, detailed, and balanced. Discontinuities in the interaction between intelligence and control harbor the danger of slowing down the innovation process. Feedback by control on plans for innovation or suggestions for intelligence activities by control may come too late if interaction between control and intelligence is not organized on a regular basis. Only loose and aggregate interaction between intelligence and control may lead to a culture of estrangement between 'innovators' and 'makers'. To deal with the many and complex issues related to innovation requires an intensive and detailed discussion of these issues. As has been argued, unbalanced interaction between intelligence and control can lead to either "innovatism" or "conservatism," which is detrimental to organizational viability. It is the task of the policy function to manage the interaction between intelligence and control. For this purpose, policy should focus on the process of interaction. It should minimize intervention in its content.

To summarize: Beer asserts that there are five functions necessary and sufficient for organizational viability. These have been introduced shortly. Three of them are used to define the process of strategy formulation (intelligence, control and policy). Given this description of strategy formulation, the next section deals with the knowledge required in that process.

KNOWLEDGE DOMAINS FOR
STRATEGY FORMULATION

Now that we know what functions are involved in the process of strategy formulation—or as the VSM puts it: the process of adapting and innovating organizations—we can take the next step. If ICT is to make its own contribution to this process, we need to specify the (domains of) knowledge the policy, intelligence, and control functions need to contribute to the process of strategy formulation. These domains of knowledge specify what knowledge should be generated, shared, stored and applied for strategy formulation, and are thus an offset to define the contribution of ICT to strategy formulation.

The Control Function: Knowledge Domains Required for Strategy Formulation

The control function performs two main activities. It manages the synergy of Function 1 activities and reviews proposals for innovation made by the intelligence function. Since only the second activity is relevant for the purpose of this chapter, we concentrate on this activity.

To execute this activity of reviewing proposals for innovation, control needs knowledge about these proposals. Moreover, knowledge is required that allows for the translation of these proposals into new goals for existing or new business units. These new goals have to be related to the current goals of the business units that are involved. From this confrontation, the gap between the desired and the current goals of these business units can be established. To assess this gap, knowledge is required that supports its translation into the reorganization capacity required from the business units to bridge the gap. Moreover, knowledge is required about the actual capacity for reorganization of the business units involved. From the confrontation between the required and the actual capacity for reorganization, proposals for innovation by the intelligence function can be reviewed. This review is communicated with the intelligence function. This process of communication between control and intelligence results in finalized plans for adaptation of organizational goals. Table 2 lists the knowledge domains needed by control to review proposals for innovation made by intelligence.

The Intelligence Function: Knowledge Domains Required for Strategy Formulation

It is the task of the intelligence function to initiate adaptation in such a way that the activities of the organization are aligned with relevant developments in

Table 2. Function Three and Related Domains of Knowledge

Function	Related Domains of Knowledge

F3: function three (control)	For reviewing F4 proposals:
	    Organizational goals
	    Proposals for innovation made by F4
	    Desired goals for F1 based on proposals for innovation
	    Expected performance of the primary activities (goals for F1 activities)
	    Gap between desired and current goals for F1
	    Required capacity for reorganization of F1 activities
	    Modus operandi of F1 activities
	    Actual capacity for reorganization of F1 activities
	    Gap between required and actual capacity for reorganization
	    Review of proposals for innovation
	    Finalized plans for adaptation of organizational goals (a joint F3-F4 product)
	    Regulatory measures to counter the imbalance between F3-F4 (see function five)

its environment. To be sensitive to these developments, Function 4 needs knowledge about goals and the performance of the organization. Against this background, developments can be assessed as opportunities and threats (such as economic and scientific developments, advances in production technology and innovative business concepts). Dependent on an assessment of these developments, intelligence may propose the implementation of new organizational goals or activities or the improvement of old ones (cf., Beer, 1979). To formulate the proposals for innovation that may be reviewed by the control function, intelligence also needs knowledge about goals and the actual modus operandi of the business units that are involved in these plans. Proposals for innovation also may have an internal drive (e.g., intelligence searches for ways to improve primary business activities) and proposals for innovation should somehow either fit into the activities of these business units or be a meaningful complement to them given the core business of the viable system as a whole. To finalize the proposals in a way that is acceptable to the organization, intelligence requires feedback from control. This feedback adds to the knowledge base of intelligence required for the formulation of plans. Table 3 lists the knowledge required by the intelligence function to produce proposals for innovation.

The Policy Function: Knowledge Domains Required for Strategy Formulation

It is the task of the policy function to balance the discussion between control and intelligence about the adaptation of goals and to consolidate the results of this discussion.

To assess imbalances in the discussion between control and intelligence, the policy function needs knowledge about norms for a balanced relation

Table 3. Function Four and Related Domains of Knowledge

Function	Related Domains of Knowledge
F4: function four (Intelligence)	Organizational goals Goals set by, performance and modus operandi of F1 activities Developments in the relevant environment of the organization Reviews by F3 of proposals for innovation Regulatory measures to counter the imbalance between F3-F4 (see function five) Finalized plans for adaptation of organizational goals (a joint F3-F4 product)

between control and intelligence. It also needs to know about the relative contribution of control and intelligence to the discussion about the proposals for adaptation. Against this background, actual imbalances can be established. To assess these imbalances, policy needs knowledge about their causes. To perform measures that counter imbalances, the policy function needs knowledge about actual imbalances, their causes, and about experiences with the implementation and effectiveness of actions that counter imbalances.

The consolidation of the results from the discussion between control and intelligence, i.e., finalized proposals for innovation, requires knowledge about these plans. In the VSM, it is specified that policy should minimize its interference in the substance of this discussion (Beer, 1979). Still, to consolidate proposals for innovation made by control and intelligence, policy requires an overview of the organization, its goals and relevant developments in the environment. This overview should not be an in-depth knowledge about every possible detail (control and intelligence deal with detail). It should be an informed feeling for the dynamic interplay between the organization and its environment (Beer, 1979). Table 4 lists the knowledge required by the policy function to balance the discussion about innovation between intelligence and control.

It should be noted that the knowledge domains listed in Tables 3 to 5 only refer to the knowledge that is directly necessary for viability. They do not refer to knowledge that supports producing or processing viable knowledge. An example of supportive knowledge is knowledge about methods to scan the environment. This knowledge supports the production of knowledge about relevant developments in the environment—the viable knowledge in Function 4. Other examples of supportive knowledge are knowledge about how to formulate a strategy, about how to plan, or about how to operate a particular machine. From the knowledge domains listed in the tables, supportive knowledge can be derived.

Table 4. Function Five and Its Related Domains of Knowledge

Function	Related Domains of Knowledge

F5: function five, policy	For balancing purposes:
	   Norms for balance between F3-F4
	   Proposals by F4 and their reviews by F3 (relative contribution of F3-F4 to the discussion on adaptation)
	   Actual (im)balance between F3-F4
	   Causes of imbalance between F3-F4
	   Experiences with regulatory measures to counter the imbalance between F3-F4
	   Regulatory measures to counter the imbalance between F3-F4
	For consolidation purposes:
	   Finalized plans for adaptation of organizational goals (a joint F3-F4 product)
	   Organizational goals

PRODUCING AND PROCESSING KNOWLEDGE FOR STRATEGY FORMULATION

This key question of this chapter is how to derive the role of ICT in strategy formulation. To this end, the previous sections unfolded a view on the process of strategy formulation and relevant knowledge domains for this process. Strategy formulation could be captured by the ongoing interaction between the functions of control, intelligence and policy. Relevant products in this process are proposals for innovation, reviews of these proposals, and finalized plans for innovation and their consolidation. To deliver these products, knowledge from several domains should be produced and processed. The question for this section is how the knowledge in these domains is produced and processed. Once it is clear what knowledge processes contribute in producing and processing the relevant knowledge for strategy formulation, the role of ICT in supporting these knowledge processes can be identified.

The question for this section is by means of which processes knowledge in the knowledge domains should be "produced and processed" so that the process of strategy formulation can take place. Several authors on knowledge management identify four relevant processes for producing and processing knowledge in general: generating, sharing, retaining and applying knowledge (cf., Achterbergh & Vriens, 2002; Nonaka & Takeuchi, 1995; Leonard & Barton, 1995; Davenport & Prusak, 1998; Bukowitz & Williams, 1999).

Generating organizational knowledge can be done by acquiring external knowledge (e.g., buying, renting or even stealing knowledge) (cf., Davenport & Prusak, 1998) or by means of knowledge creation in a process of learning (Davenport & Prusak, 1995; Nonaka & Takeuchi, 1995). The aim of the process "knowledge sharing" (or dissemination) is to make sure that (existing) knowledge gets to the right place in an organization. To keep knowledge available, some kind of "organizational memory" is needed. The process of "retaining knowledge" refers to the process of storing knowledge and making retrieval possible. The last process is the application or use of knowledge. The other three knowledge processes are subsidiary to applying knowledge.

These four knowledge processes can now be linked to the process of strategy formulation, as formulated according to the VSM. According to the VSM the functions of intelligence, control and policy contribute to strategy formulation. This contribution involves the application of knowledge in the knowledge domains to arrive at the four core products of strategy formulation: proposals for innovation, their reviews, the finalized plans for innovation, and their consolidation. For example, the intelligence function applies its knowledge about environmental developments to produce its proposals for innovation. The knowledge applied by each function is generated either by that function or by one of the other functions of the VSM. In the latter case, knowledge must be shared between functions. For instance, the intelligence function cannot adequately make proposals for innovation when the knowledge about organizational goals and performance is not shared with it. Likewise, the control function cannot review proposals if knowledge about them is not shared. Applying, generating and sharing knowledge requires the retention of knowledge. The policy function, for instance, benefits from storing knowledge about the measures it considered to support the discussion between intelligence and control, the reasons why some of them where chosen and the success of these measures.

Table 5 provides an overview of the relation between the five functions in the VSM, the knowledge domains and the application and generation of knowledge in these domains. Based on this table, it is possible to draw conclusions about sharing and storing knowledge. In the table we only included the relevant knowledge for strategy formulation. However, some of this knowledge is generated by Function 1, and this is the reason of its inclusion in the table. For the complete table, we refer to Achterbergh and Vriens (2002).

The first column of Table 5 summarizes the knowledge domains listed in Tables 3 to 5. In this column, we eliminated all redundant entries. Columns two to five indicate whether knowledge in a specific knowledge domain is generated (G) and/or applied (A) by a specific function. Table 5 is reminiscent of the create-use matrices used in information analysis (e.g., Jackson, 1988).

Table 5. Functions, Knowledge Domains, and Knowledge Processes for Strategy Formulation

Knowledge Domains	F1	F3	F4	F5
goals set by, performance and modus operandi of the primary activities in F1	G,A	A	A	
organizational goals	A	A	A	G,A
proposals for innovation made by F4		A	G,A	A
desired goals for F1 based on proposals for innovation		G,A		
gap between desired and current goals of F1		G,A		
required capacity for reorganization of F1 activities		G,A		
actual capacity for reorganization of F1 activities		G,A		
gap between required and actual capacity for reorganization of F1 activities		G,A		
reviews by F3 of proposals for innovation		G,A	A	A
finalized plans for adaptation of organizational goals (a joint F3-F4 product)		G,A	G,A	A
regulatory measures to counter the imbalance between F3-F4		A	A	G,A
developments in the relevant environment of the organization			G,A	
norms for balance between F3-F4				G,A
actual imbalance between F3-F4				G,A
causes of imbalance between F3-F4				G,A
experiences with regulatory measures to counter the imbalance between F3-F4				G,A

The table makes apparent that some knowledge may be generated by more than one function. For instance, the finalized plans for adaptation are a joint product of control and intelligence.

Knowledge in the domains listed in Table 5 is generated and applied for either of two reasons. The first reason is to directly contribute to the process of strategy formulation. For instance, making and reviewing proposals for innovation directly contributes to this process. The second reason for generating and applying knowledge is to regulate knowledge processes that directly contribute to the viability of the organization. For instance, knowledge about measures to counter imbalances in the discussion between control and intelligence is generated and applied to regulate the discussion that results in a direct contribution to the viability of the organization: proposals for innovation.

From Table 5, conclusions can be drawn about sharing and storing knowledge. Direct and regulatory knowledge should be shared between functions if it is applied by more than one function. In Table 5, this is indicated by more than one A in a row. For instance, control should share knowledge about its reviews of the proposals of intelligence with intelligence. Knowledge should be retained in such a way that it can be retrieved by the functions that apply it. Moreover, some knowledge is only generated and applied by one function. This knowledge should be retained in a function-related database. For instance, a database could be designed to support the balancing efforts of the policy function.

Thus far, the discussion focused on the three functions relevant for strategy formulation. We did not yet link these functions to organizational units or individuals. The discussion focused on functions because this enabled us to abstract from the specific organizational embodiment of the functions. Moreover, the model is a recursive model, and can be applied at many organizational levels: at the corporate level, at the level of a business unit and even at levels below that. However, for a practical application of the model (such as deriving ICT support for the process of strategy formulation), it is necessary that designers of ICT make a choice for the level of recursion (e.g., a specific BU) and specify the organizational units and/or individuals that are engaged in realizing the functions. In this specification more than one individual and/or more than one unit may be involved in the realization of one function, and more than one function may be realized by more than one unit and/or individual.

An example of a specific mapping is given in Table 6. This table maps the knowledge domains relevant for strategy formulation onto organizational units. In the columns, for some knowledge domains, it is indicated which units are involved in the generation (G) and application (A) of that knowledge domain. More than one G may appear in the rows, because the generation may be either a joint effort of several units, or the result of several units engaged in the generation of different knowledge in the knowledge domain. For instance, the organizational units "Research & Development," "Marketing & Sales" and the Board of Directors may all be involved in the generation of knowledge about

Table 6. Functional Knowledge Domains Tied to Organizational Units

	Organizational Units					
Knowledge Domains	*Production*	*Control*	*R&D*	*M&S*	*...*	*BoD*
goals set by, performance and modus operandi of the primary activities in F1	G,A	A	A	A		
organizational goals	A	A	A	A		G,A
proposals for innovation made by F4		A	G,A	G,A		G,A
desired goals for F1 based on proposals for innovation		G,A				
gap between desired and current goals of F1		G,A				
required capacity for reorganization of F1 activities		G,A				
actual capacity for reorganization of F1 activities		G,A				
gap between required and actual capacity for reorganization of F1 activities		G,A				
reviews by F3 of proposals for innovation		G, A	G,A	G,A		G,A
finalized plans for adaptation of organizational goals (a joint F3- F4 product)			G,A	G,A		G,A
regulatory measures to counter the imbalance between F3-F4						
developments in the relevant environment of the organization						
norms for balance between F3-F4						
actual imbalance between F3-F4						
causes of imbalance between F3-F4						
experiences with regulatory measures to counter the imbalance between F3-F4						

the environment of the organization—but all with regard to different aspects of that environment. These three units may also embody Function 3 activities—and review (parts of) the proposals.

To summarize, Table 5 captures the relation between the knowledge needed for strategy formulation and the application and generation of this knowledge in the three VSM functions. (Table 6 further specifies this in that it ties the functional activities to organizational units.) It thus indicates which relations exist between knowledge domains, and hence makes apparent what knowledge should be shared among functions for which reasons. Finally, it indicates what functional knowledge could be clustered and retained in a "functional" knowledge base. This table can be used as a start for deriving possibilities for ICT support for strategy formulation—the topic of the next section.

THE ROLE OF ICT IN STRATEGY FORMULATION

The question for this section is how ICT can support the process of strategy formulation. To answer this question we use the theory from the previous sections to formulate an "ideal" functional architecture for ICT support. Designers of ICT support for strategy formulation may use this architecture to select ICT applications. To be able to select these applications, however, one needs selection criteria. In this section we first present the "functional support architecture." Then, we discuss selection criteria, and finally we show how designers may use these criteria to select ICT applications to realize the support architecture.

An Architecture for ICT Support of the Process of Strategy Formulation

In the previous sections it became apparent that knowledge from several knowledge domains should be generated, stored, shared and applied to take the steps in the process of strategy formulation: formulating proposals for innovation; reviewing them; making finalized plans for innovation and consolidating them. We use this description to give an outline of an architecture for an information system supporting the process of strategy formulation. This outline is presented in Figure 2.

This information system consists, ideally, of several modules and knowledge and/or databases. The "modules" (at the right in Figure 2) are applications

Figure 2. Outline of an Architecture of an Information System Supporting Strategy Formulation

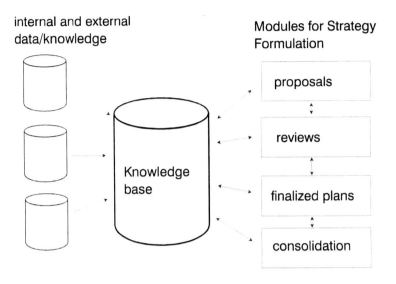

helping to generate the products of the process of strategy formulation. With the help of these modules, the knowledge from the knowledge domains is applied to produce the proposals, reviews, and (consolidated) plans. The information system further consists of a central knowledge base in which the knowledge in the knowledge domains necessary for strategy formulation (see Sections Three and Four) is stored. This central knowledge base, in turn, may receive knowledge from other internal and external knowledge and/or databases. Below, we discuss the modules and knowledge bases in more detail:

1.   *The "Proposal" Module*
      The goal of this module is to help produce a list of proposals for innovation. The main product is, therefore, a list of innovation proposals and their justification. To produce this list, one should have access to the knowledge in the relevant knowledge domains. This knowledge may be available (in the knowledge base) or it should be generated. To generate this knowledge (e.g., about technological trends or about trends in sales) the module should have access to external and internal information. For instance, it may have access to a data warehouse by means of a front-end tool or it may have access to external online databases (such as the Lexis-Nexis or Dow Jones database). Further, the module may have access to a database consisting of previously rejected or

accepted proposals. The proposals for innovation produced with this module are stored in the central knowledge base.

2.   *The "Review" Module*

The input for this module consists of the proposals for innovation. The output is a list of accepted and rejected proposals and the reasons for their acceptance or rejection. To make this list, the module should apply the knowledge in the central knowledge base. This knowledge may be available or may have to be generated. To generate the knowledge, access to several internal and external databases may be required. For instance, to get a clear view on the consequences of a certain innovation for the current production structure, it may be that internal information is required. Also, (external) data on the results of the current pmc's may be an input for rejecting or accepting innovations. The review module may benefit from a database with (a classification of) reasons for acceptance or rejection.

3.   *The "Finalized Plans" Module*

This module is mainly a means for the communication about the proposals for innovation (and their reviews) in order to arrive at a finalized plan. It overarches the proposal and review module. By means of this module, results of the review module are communicated and used as input for revising the proposals (with the aid of the proposal module). The revised proposals are, in turn, used to produce new reviews (with the aid of the review module), etc. This module should (1) facilitate the communication about the proposals and (2) ensure the finalization of an innovation plan. To these ends, this module could make available to its users:

- the rules for interaction (such as discussion format and deadlines);
- criteria for imbalance in the discussion;
- a monitoring function regarding the imbalance;
- rules/incentives for countering this imbalance;
- an overview of the history of the discussion (as well as an overview of previous discussion).

Implementation could be by means of several Intranet applications (such as a kind of internal discussion site).

4.   *The "Consolidation" Module*

This module has as its output the consolidation of (a specific selection of) the innovations on the finalized list of innovations. To make this selection, the argumentations used in the previous modules should be scanned and valued. Its main goal is to communicate the results of the strategy formulation process to relevant parties in the organization. It should communicate (1) the selected innovations, and (2) the reasons for their selection (and possibly their consequences for the current way of "doing business"). It may benefit from a database with (previously successful) communication formats.

5.   *The "Central Knowledge Base"*
This module consists of all the knowledge in the knowledge domains relevant for strategy formulation. This knowledge should be stored and made available.

Above, an outline of an architecture for an information system supporting the process of strategy formulation is given. It shows how support should be focused on the products of strategy formulation. Moreover, the focus of the support is on the four knowledge processes involved in the production of proposals, reviews, plans and consolidations. That is, application of knowledge leads to the four products (and to new knowledge). For this production, knowledge from the knowledge domains should be generated, stored and/or shared. This knowledge is (partly) stored in the knowledge base. The knowledge may be generated by using the four modules and/or by using internal/external databases. Furthermore, knowledge from the knowledge domains may be shared by using connections between the modules.

The description of the architecture states the functionalities of the different "modules" in it and how they should be connected. The question for the next two sections is how to realize this support architecture by selecting (or building) proper ICT tools.

Criteria to Select ICT Applications

To determine whether an ICT application is suitable for supporting strategy formulation, we need selection criteria. Since the ICT applications should be tied to the production and processing of knowledge relevant for strategy formulation, ICT should be tailored to the characteristics of the knowledge it should help to deliver and of the knowledge processes it should support. These two types of characteristics make up two classes of criteria. Therefore, before we select supportive ICT applications, we first need to specify these classes of criteria.

As a basis for formulating requirements to ICT applications supportive of strategy formulation, we only take into account criteria intrinsically related to the knowledge and the knowledge processes (generation, sharing, storage, and application) needed to realize the process of strategy formulation. Extrinsic criteria—for instance, criteria pertaining to costs—will not be taken into account. Moreover, the criteria to characterize knowledge and knowledge processes are chosen in such a way that—in combination—they actually can function as requirements to ICT applications. In combination, they point at some and exclude other types of ICT applications as effective tools to generate, share, store, or apply the knowledge to arrive at the products of strategy formulation.

The first class of criteria relate to the characteristics of the knowledge in question. That is, this knowledge can be:

1. Tacit or explicit (see for instance Nonaka & Takeuchi, 19xx, for this distinction). Tacit knowledge normally refers to knowledge that is not codifiable, while explicit knowledge is. Tacit knowledge, by definition, defies codification by ICT. However, ICT may be used to refer to sources of tacit knowledge—e.g., in the form of a knowledge map (cf., Davenport & Prusak, 1998).

If the knowledge is explicit, further relevant distinctions for the use of ICT are:

2. The knowledge is more of less standardizable. This criterion refers to the "uniqueness" of knowledge. Can the knowledge, for instance, be cast in a priori fixed standard formats (such as number of products under development of competitor X) or not? This clearly is important for the choice of ICT applications.

3. The knowledge is more or less aggregate. Does the knowledge refer to individual facts (client X bought Y at day Z) or to insights at a higher level of aggregation (all clients in a certain period bought so and so much of Y)? It is important to know at what level of aggregation ICT applications should help deliver knowledge. (To be sure, a great deal of ICT applications is, of course, capable of handling more than one level of aggregation.)

4. The knowledge is different in "size" (it may be that it refers to just a few rules or facts such as "Competitor X opens a production facility in region Y," or it may cover a large knowledge-area).

These characteristics are important in selecting or building any type of ICT application for supporting knowledge processes. However, to support the process of strategy formulation as put forward in this chapter, these character- istics are also important in designing or selecting ICT applications that support the interaction between functions (see Table 1), because, as has been argued, the VSM prescribes different levels of detail for different relations.

The second class of criteria refers to knowledge process characteristics. The knowledge processes:

1.   Can be more or less structured. The structuredness of a knowledge process refers to the traditional dimension of "structured versus unstructured tasks" (e.g., Simon, 1961). For instance, predicting trends in the environment may be seen as generating knowledge regarding the knowledge domain "developments in the relevant environment of the organization." This generation is not very well structured. It is not clear a priori what counts as input for such a decision and it is not clear how and when to label certain environmental events as a trend. Therefore, predicting a trend is an unstructured activity.

2.   Require more or less frequent communication. For instance, to produce a finalized plan of innovation, frequent communication is required between representatives of intelligence and control. In this communication process knowledge is shared, generated and applied. The VSM prescribes the level of communication between functions (see Table 1).

3.   Require communication between few or many parties, more or less proximate in space and/or time. Who is involved in the process of strategy formulation can be made apparent by means of matrices such as those given in Table 6. The required frequency of communication, the number of parties involved and the nature of their (lack of) proximity co-determine the selection of ICT applications.

A METHOD FOR SELECTING ICT APPLICATIONS FOR STRATEGY FORMULATION

Given the "architecture of ICT support" for strategy formulation (based on the functions and knowledge domains involved in strategy formulation) and given the criteria to characterize the knowledge and knowledge processes involved, we can now specify how a designer can formulate requirements to select (or build) proper ICT applications. This method consists of three steps: (1) determining the relevant knowledge characteristics, (2) determining the knowledge process characteristics and (3) selecting ICT support for the process of strategy formulation.

Before a designer can take these steps, however, some preliminary requirements should be met. The method presupposes that the designer has an insight into the products of the process of strategy formulation and its associated knowledge domains. The designer also needs to know which organizational units are involved in the production of the relevant knowledge for strategy formulation. A designer thus requires tables like Tables 5 and 6. In these tables the knowledge domains are given and tied to the process of strategy formulation and to organizational units.

Step 1: Establishing Knowledge Characteristics

The designer should for each activity in the process of strategy formulation specify the knowledge characteristics of the required knowledge in this domain. To this end, a designer may use Tables 2 to 6. If a knowledge domain comprises knowledge that is too heterogeneous for such a characterization, the designer should decompose the knowledge domain into sub-domains and try again.

For instance, to produce proposals for innovation one needs knowledge "about developments in the environment" (see Table 3). However, this knowledge is rather diverse. It may comprise facts about competitors or models about the impact of ecological trends. Knowledge about competitors, in turn, (in terms of facts like net sales volume, product portfolio, etc.) may have different characteristics than knowledge about "the impact of ecological trends." The latter may be less codifiable and standardizable. A designer should recognize these different types of knowledge, and identify their different characteristics (i.e., codifiability, standardization, level of aggregation).

The result of this step can be presented as a table providing an overview of characteristics of the knowledge that should be generated, shared, stored, and applied to realize the products in the process of strategy formulation in question (Table 7 gives some examples of knowledge types and their characteristics for the strategy sub-process "making proposals for innovation").

Table 7. Knowledge Characteristics: An Example

SF Activity	Knowledge Domain	Tacit	Explicit	
			Potential for Standardization	Level of Aggregation
Proposals	A …	Yes		
	B environment			
	B.1 Competitors	No	High	
	B.2 Ecological Trends	Mainly		
	C …	No	Moderate	

In the table, A, B, etc., refer to knowledge in certain knowledge domains relevant for the strategy sub-process "making proposals for innovation." B may, for instance, refer to "knowledge about the environment." B1 and B2 may refer to its re-specification into the specific knowledge-types "knowledge about competitors" and "impact of ecological trends"—which may have different knowledge characteristics. A designer should make such tables for all activities in the process of strategy formulation.

Step 2: Establishing Knowledge Process Characteristics

In this step, the designer should specify the characteristics of generating, sharing, storing and applying the knowledge specified in the previous step. To this end, the designer needs an overview of the involvement of control, intelligence, and policy in processing the knowledge needed to realize strategy formulation (Tables 2 to 5). Moreover, the designer needs to link this knowledge with the organizational units producing or processing it (Table 6). Given these prerequisites, the designer can, for all the knowledge processes regarding the knowledge in each knowledge domain, specify the process characteristics.

The main activity of the designer, then, is to determine for all classes of knowledge in the knowledge domains (1) the structuredness of generating, applying, sharing and storing the particular knowledge, (2) the required frequency of generating, applying, sharing and storing the particular knowledge, (3) the parties involved in generating, applying, sharing and storing the particular knowledge, and (4) the proximity (in time, space) of those parties.

The result of this step can be expressed in the form of Table 8. This table, again, only refers to a few knowledge domains regarding the activity "making proposals for innovation."

In the table, B1 and B2 are, as before, classes of knowledge in the knowledge domain B, "knowledge about the environment." Class B1 refers to factual knowledge about competitors and B2 to knowledge about the impact of ecological trends. To illustrate this step, only B1 is considered. Factual knowledge about competitors may refer, for example, to the sales volume of a specific customer. The generation of these facts may be highly structured and occur at a regular basis by scanning certain external information sources. The individuals involved in the generation of these facts may be dispersed among different departments in different business units. In the table, it is indicated that certain employees from business unit X1 of department Y and from business unit X2 of departments Y and Z are involved. The application of this factual

Table 8.   Knowledge Process Characteristics—An Example

SF Activity	Knowledge Domain	Knowledge Process	Structure	Frequency	Parties Involved	Distance in Space/Time
Proposals	B1: Competitors	Generating	High	Regular	BU X1; Dep. Y; Empl: ... BU X2 Dep. Y, Z Empl. ...	...
		Applying	Medium			
		Storing	High			
		Sharing	High			BU X1 and BU X2 are in different countries
	B2: Ecological trends	Generating				
		Applying				
		Storing				
		Sharing				
...	...	...				

knowledge for producing proposals for innovation may be less structured, and may be carried out centrally. For knowledge sharing it may be important to know that the parties involved are located in different countries.

In this way, for all classes of knowledge in the different knowledge domains, the characteristics of the knowledge processes may be derived. In some cases, the knowledge processes will share the same process character-istics. In other cases, the designer will have to discriminate between processes to adequately describe the process characteristics. For instance, it may be the case that *generating* knowledge requires the involvement of only a few parties that are proximate to each other in space and time, while *sharing* the generated knowledge involves many parties distant in space from each other.

Step 3: Selecting ICT Support of the Process of Strategy Formulation

The identification of proper ICT support is based on (1) the support architecture (paragraph 5.1) and (2) the requirements derived from the knowledge and knowledge characteristics (from the previous two steps). This means that the functionalities of ICT applications should match (parts of the) support architecture and the desired requirements. For instance, an application may be built that has (some of) the functionalities of the four modules from the architecture (discussed earlier). Moreover, this application should be designed to deal with the knowledge (process) characteristics.

To arrive at a list of possible ICT applications supportive of the process of strategy formulation (referring to the support architecture and to the derived knowledge and knowledge process requirements), three sub-steps can be given:

1.   Express desired ICT support;
2.   Analyze current ICT support;
3.   Select ICT applications for strategy formulation based on the gap between desired and current ICT support.

Ad. 1 Express Desired ICT Support

To express the desired ICT support, a designer should refer to the support architecture and to the requirements from the previous two steps. Ideally, one may try to find one or more ICT applications realizing the whole support architecture. This means that such applications should have the functionalities as described earlier. The knowledge and knowledge process requirements further specify how ICT applications can be used to support strategy formulation.

With regard to the knowledge requirements, the dimension of tacit versus explicit knowledge is important. For instance, if it is found that certain knowledge is mainly tacit, specific ICT applications should be used to deal with that kind of knowledge. A suitable application in this case might be a "knowledge-map" (Davenport & Prusak, 1998). Such a map does not try to capture the knowledge, but only refers to the knowledge carriers. For knowledge domains with knowledge that is highly standardizable, other applications may be used. Many authors on the subject of knowledge management give clues on how to match certain ICT applications to certain characteristics of knowledge (e.g., Davenport & Prusak, 1998).

The knowledge process requirements also further specify how ICT applications may support strategy formulation. For instance, these requirements make apparent what parties are involved and what the periodicity of the interaction of these parties is. This knowledge may be used to define access and to design the interaction between parties or applications.

Ad. 2 Analyze Current ICT Support

In this step, the desired functionalities from the support architecture and the knowledge and knowledge process requirements can be used to analyze the

adequacy of existing support applications. A designer may draw up a list of current applications and judge to what extend they contribute to the support functionalities and to what extend they meet the requirements. From this analysis, it may, for example, be concluded that:
- the knowledge in the current knowledge base is incomplete;
- there are no applications supporting the generation of a specific kind of knowledge;
- there is no support of the interaction between intelligence and control activities;
- a data warehouse is not tailored to the specific demands of strategy formulation;
- the full range of functionalities is not covered by current applications;
- sharing knowledge that should be shared among "modules" is not supported;
- knowledge is not accessible for the right people.

This list of mismatches between desired and current ICT support should be used in the next step.

Ad 3. Select ICT Applications

Based on the gap between current and desired support of the process of strategy formulation, and based on knowledge about possible ICT tools, a first list of ICT applications may be given. This list may be used for a final selection. In this selection, additional criteria (such as costs or fit in overall ICT architecture) may be used. The final list may be used to plan the development and or purchase of ICT applications (see Turban et al., 2002, for considerations regarding planning of ICT in general).

CONCLUSION

In this chapter, we approached the link between ICT and CI from an angle differing from most treatments. We "redefined" CI as the relevant knowledge used in strategy formulation and proposed to identify the role of ICT for CI as support tools for the knowledge processes involved in the process of strategy formulation. To identify the nature of such tools and to direct the selection of applications that could act as support tools for the knowledge processes involved in strategy formulation, we (1) presented a model of the process of strategy formulation, (2) derived the knowledge relevant for the process of strategy formulation, (3) identified the knowledge processes in which the relevant knowledge for strategy formulation is processed and produced, and (4) used this "theory" to arrive at an understanding of the role of ICT in the process of strategy formulation.

The model we used for describing the process of strategy formulation is the Viable System Model of Beer. This model is also the point of departure for deriving the relevant knowledge for strategy formulation and the knowledge processes in which this knowledge is produced and processed.

Given the overview of the knowledge needed to be produced and processed for strategy formulation, we formulated—in two steps—a method for tying ICT to the strategy formulation. In the first step we gave an outline of a general architecture of a system supporting the knowledge processes for strategy formulation. This architecture stated the general functionalities of (parts of) a support system. In the second step we discussed how, using the theory from the rest of the chapter, a selection of actual ICT applications for strategy formulation may be supported.

The approach in this chapter presents a different perspective on strategy formulation and the use of ICT for it. It also puts CI software in a different perspective; the approach enables the integration of both external and internal oriented ICT tools for producing intelligence through their support of the knowledge processes in formulating strategies.

REFERENCES

Achterbergh, J.M.I.M. & Vriens, D. (2002). Managing viable knowledge. *Systems Research and Behavioral Science*, *19*, 223-241.

Beer, S. (1979). *The Heart of Enterprise*. Chichester, UK: John Wiley & Sons.

Beer, S. (1981). *Brain of the Firm*. Chichester, UK: John Wiley & Sons.

Beer, S. (1985). *Diagnosing the System*. Chichester, UK: John Wiley & Sons.

Bukowitz, W.R. & Williams, R.L. (1999). *The Knowledge Management Fieldbook*. Edinburgh: Pearson.

Cook, M. & Cook, C. (2000). *Competitive Intelligence*. London: Kogan Page.

Davenport, T.H. & Prusak, L. (1998). *Working Knowledge*. Boston, MA: Harvard Business School Press.

Espejo, R., Schumann, W., Schwaninger, M., & Bilello, U. (1996). *Organizational Transformation and Learning*. Chichester, UK: John Wiley & Sons.

Fuld, L.M. (1995). *The New Competitor Intelligence*. Chichester, UK: John Wiley & Sons.

Jackson M. (1988). *Jackson System Development*. New York: Prentice Hall.

Johnson, G. & Scholes, K. (1999). *Exploring Corporate Strategy* (5th edition). Hertfordshire: Prentice Hall.

Kahaner, L. (1997). *Competitive Intelligence*. New York: Touchstone.

Leonard-Barton, D. (1995). *Wellsprings of Knowledge*. Cambridge, MA: Harvard Business School Press.

Nonaka, I. & Takeuchi, H. (1995). *The Knowledge Creating Company*. New York: Oxford University Press.

Teo, T.S.H. & Choo, W.Y. (2001). Assessing the impact of using the Internet for competitive intelligence. *Information & Management, 39*, 67-83.

Turban, E., McLean, E., & Wetherbe, J.C. (2002). *Information Technology for Management* (3rd edition). New York: Wiley.

Vriens, D. & Hendriks, P.H.J. (2000). Viability through Web-enabled technologies. In M. Khosrowpour (Ed.), *Managing Web-Enabled Technologies in Organizations: A Global Perspective* (pp. 122-145). Hershey, PA: Idea-Group Publishing.

Vriens, D. & Philips, E.A. (1999). Business intelligence als informatievoorziening voor de strategievorming. In E.A. Philips & D. Vriens (Eds.), *Business Intelligence*. Deventer: Kluwer.

Chapter V

Using Groupware to Gather and Analyze Intelligence in a Public Setting: Development of Integral Safety Plans in an Electronic Meeting

Etiënne Rouwette
University of Nijmegen, The Netherlands

Jac A. M. Vennix
University of Nijmegen, The Netherlands

ABSTRACT

This chapter focuses on the use of groupware to support local governments in activities in the intelligence cycle. Local governments in The Netherlands have a central role in developing integral safety plans for their district. However, in the implementation of safety plans the contribution of partner organizations such as the fire department and police force is indispensable. Each of the partners may have its own priorities with regard to safety. Using electronic meetings, representatives of all partner organizations identify safety problems within their district and decide on the priority of issues. In two meetings of four hours each, safety problems are analyzed and conclusions formulated to which partners feel committed. This article describes the design of the meetings and reports on results for nine municipalities. Results indicate that participants find that the electronic meetings contribute to intelligence activities. Participants feel the quality of communication in the sessions is high, and their insight into the problem is increased. The sessions support dissemination of intelligence, as shown by an increase in consensus on the problem and commitment to conclusions. Electronic meetings therefore seem an effective and practical way to support key activities in the intelligence cycle, and to develop policies that will be implemented.

INTRODUCTION

The purpose of this chapter is twofold. First, we aim to describe the approach of a local government to intelligence gathering and analysis. Second, the use of groupware to support activities in the intelligence cycle is shown. Local municipalities in The Netherlands try to encourage the participation of stakeholders in the development of policy plans on integral safety. Relevant parties jointly determine the direction of information search, collect data and analyze information. Concise reporting and direct involvement of members of responsible organizations foster dissemination of results. Representatives of the police force, municipality, fire department, health care, housing associations and inhabitants participate in an electronic meeting to identify safety problems within their district and determine priorities with regard to policy making. In two meetings of four hours each, safety problems are analyzed and conclusions formulated to which partners in integral safety feel committed. The interpretation of participants and "hard" data are combined to form the basis for performance targets for each of the parties involved. The nine city districts and local municipalities that have participated in electronic meetings so far are enthusiastic about the results. Participants indicate that the meetings increase quality of communication between stakeholders, foster insight and consensus on safety problems and create commitment to conclusions.

This chapter is structured as follows. In the following (second) section, the central problem with regard to development of safety plans in The Netherlands is outlined. Since information and responsibilities with regard to safety are shared among a number of stakeholders, a way to elicit and integrate relevant information is needed in order to arrive at a feasible plan. The third section describes a procedure based on an electronic meeting in which participants jointly identify safety problems and policy alternatives. The procedure is evaluated in a series of nine projects with local municipalities. Results of the evaluation are reported in section four. Finally, conclusions are formulated.

COMPETITIVE INTELLIGENCE ON SAFETY PROBLEMS

Dutch municipalities have a large role in developing and enforcing safety policies. Two recent catastrophes have highlighted the need for more cooperation of municipalities with other partners in safety policy making, such as the police force, fire department and health care organizations. A bar fire and the explosion of a fireworks factory in a residential area both took several casualties. An analysis of these disasters indicated a lack of clear priorities and responsibilities with regard to safety regulations. A recent recommendation to the Organization of Dutch Municipalities (VNG) argues for an integration of fire department and health care organizations into so-called safety regions, with a governing role for local municipalities. Within the municipality, the civil servant for integral safety is responsible for management of safety issues. He or she develops a policy plan on integral safety which specifies safety priorities for the area in question. To this end, the civil servant makes an analysis of the problems experienced by inhabitants, police force, fire department, health care, welfare organizations, housing associations and local schools. Most of these institutes are also partners in implementing safety policies.

The organizations responsible for enforcing safety regulations also have a large role in the identification of safety problems. Since reports are filed with these organizations, they are also the primary source for data on developments with regard to safety issues. The way in which inhabitants experience safety is, however, not covered by these data. Experience does not necessarily follow "objective" developments, which can clearly be seen in the case of violent crimes: although the number of reported violent crimes in The Netherlands has been decreasing over the past few years, the fear of becoming a victim of a violent crime has increased steadily. A policy plan solely based on "objective" or reported data therefore does not do justice to the "subjective" experience of safety by citizens. A related problem is that the combination of subjective and objective data involves a confrontation of views of "experts" and "laymen."

How should the opinions of professionals and nonprofessionals be weighed and integrated?

A second shortcoming of relying on objective facts only is the impossibility of establishing priorities. In order to weigh the importance of a long arrival time for ambulances versus a high crime rate, data need to be interpreted and the values of a policy maker come to the fore. There is a danger that other safety partners do not weigh alternatives in the same manner.

The description of Dutch public policy with regard to safety so far clearly shows local municipalities' need for strategic information about their environment. Other stakeholders in safety are needed both to provide strategic information as well as to enact selected policies. More specifically, the municipality is confronted with the following questions in each of the stages of the intelligence cycle (Philips & Vriens, 1999):

1. *Direction:* What do stakeholders see as central problems with regard to safety?
2. *Search:* How do the stakeholders interpret these problems and which reported data exist on these problems?
3. *Analysis:* Which criteria do the stakeholders employ to determine the priority of safety problems and how do the problems score on these criteria?
4. *Dissemination:* How can stakeholders learn about other viewpoints and how can commitment to a policy be achieved?

Addressing these questions in an effective and time efficient manner is not straightforward. A traditional face-to-face meeting enables participants to explain their ideas to one another, but a discussion will be complicated by differences in backgrounds and viewpoints. The municipality faces challenges such as creating realistic expectations, motivating stakeholders to participate in policy making and generating a product that is both analytically sound and acceptable to all involved. In the following section, a procedure will be outlined that aims to answer most of the questions above. Following this procedure, stakeholders participate in two four-hour sessions in an electronic meeting room and jointly identify problem elements and priorities. In the last section of this chapter, the procedure will be evaluated with regard to a number of key objectives, e.g., its ability to foster creation and sharing of knowledge and creation of commitment.

PARTICIPATION OF STAKEHOLDERS IN AN ELECTRONIC MEETING

The use of electronic meeting support to gather and analyze intelligence is well documented. Pinsonneault and Kraemer (1990) describe a number of electronic tools developed to meet the following functions:
- idea generation, collection and compilation;
- information storage and retrieval;
- representation of information.

Which tools are used depends on the meeting to be supported, as the outcomes of a meeting depend on interactions between situation (group, task, and context) and form of support used (Nunamaker et al., 1991; Jessup & Valacich, 1993). These tools are mainly used to gather and manipulate information and focus on the first three stages of the intelligence cycle. Recent publications also indicate how groupware may be used for the final stage of the intelligence cycle, dissemination of information. Increasingly electronic meeting support is used for fostering organizational change in complex and political problems (Vreede & Dickson, 2000; Appelman et al., 2002). A number of tools and insights reported in the literature were combined to form a general procedure for the development of integral safety plans. The department Management Support of the police force Gelderland-Zuid and the Methodology Section of the Nijmegen School of Management have developed a procedure in which up to twenty stakeholders can map safety issues in their area of concern in two four-hour meetings. The procedure can be adapted to fit the needs of a specific situation or area. Participants are chosen in consultation with the civil servant responsible for integral management, and are invited for an introductory meeting in which the goal and program of the two sessions are described.

The electronic meeting is different from traditional meetings with regard to facilitation, the structure and tools that are used and the report. The first difference is that the chairperson in the meetings is neutral with regard to content. He or she is a facilitator who focuses on the process without taking a position with regard to the ideas that are exchanged. In this way participants are encouraged to voice their opinions and listen to each others' contributions (Schwarz, 1994; Vennix, 1996). The facilitator develops the meeting agenda, introduces the steps in the program, asks clarifying questions, ensures that everybody has an equal opportunity to contribute to the discussion and summarizes results. During the sessions, the facilitator uses the so-called supported style in which he or she uses the projection equipment, but each participant is provided with an electronic communication channel and memory through a PC.

Another important difference with regard to a traditional meeting is the structure and tools used in the electronic meeting. The meetings take place in an electronic decision room, the VisaSkillsLab of Nijmegen University.

For participants, the decision room presents the most striking difference compared to a traditional meeting. During the sessions participants (single or in pairs) are seated behind a PC. Questions, topics and ideas are projected on a central screen, indicated in the bottom left hand side in Figure 1. Apart from using the electronic communication channel by typing in information, face-to-face discussions are used in the categorization and prioritization of ideas. In this way a number of shortcomings of traditional meetings can be overcome. First, the agenda, in which generation, categorization and prioritization of information are alternated, provides a clear focus during the meeting. This decreases the chance of the discussion being sidetracked into topics not directly relevant to safety. By referring to the agenda, the facilitator can indicate the steps in the meeting process and keep an eye on the time planning. A typical agenda for the two sessions may look as follows.

Figure 1.   The VisaSkillsLab (Nijmegen University)

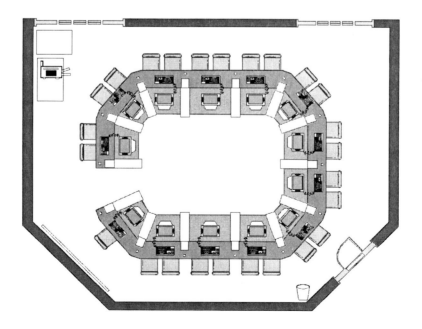

Figure 2. Agenda for the Two Sessions on Integral Safety

Agenda first session	Agenda second session
18:00 Welcome Word of welcome, goals of the session and introduction of participants **18:10 Introduction method** Introduction of decision room and tools **18:20 Example** Practice with tools **18:30 Gather ideas on integral safety** Identification and description of safety factors	**18:00 Welcome** Word of welcome and goals of the session **18:10 Analysis results workbook** Look at questions in each category **19:00 Example identification of criteria** Practice with the identification of criteria and casting a vote **19:10 Identification of criteria integral safety** Review and adjust criteria in workbook
19:30 Break	**19:30 Break**
19:45 Categorization of ideas on integral safety Identification and description of clusters of safety factors **21:15 Priotarization of ideas on integral safety** Select most important ideas in each category **21:30 Evaluation of first session - individual** Best aspects and points for improvement **21:45 Evaluation of first session – group discussion** **21:55 Close** Close of meeting and further steps	**19:45 Vote on criteria integral safety** **20:45 Discussion on results and further steps** **21:15 Evaluation - individual** Best aspects and points for improvement **21:20 Evaluation – group discussion** **21:30 Close** Close of meeting and further steps

The meetings start with a scan of problems with regard to integral safety. Participants type in ideas, after which these are collected, projected on the central screen and clarified one by one. This is an electronic application of Nominal Group Technique (Delbecq et al., 1975). In comparison to a brainstorm, this approach yields more information (Diehl & Stroebe, 1991) and has several other advantages. The participant who contributes the idea is anonymous, which separates ideas from persons. In a situation in which some persons are experts and others laymen, or in which participants work in the same organization at different hierarchical levels, this is an advantage over the traditional approach. In clarifying an idea, a participant may want to make him or herself known, but a person is free to remain anonymous. All contributions are automatically stored, which prevents loss of information. The first round of gathering ideas is followed by a plenary discussion on the categorization of ideas. The list of ideas is projected on the central screen and ideas are dragged and dropped in buckets (categories). Visualization of this step makes it easy to follow for participants, and shows the logic of getting from a list of ideas to a few central themes. In this way information converges into a set of more general categories. This step mainly contributes to the first step of the intelligence cycle: defining information needs.

Subsequently, participants are invited to open categories on their own PC, select an idea, and type in comments on the idea. In this way information is ordered in three levels (categories, ideas and comments) which are visually supported and therefore make it easy to keep an overview. This approach also enables participants to work in parallel. In comparison to a traditional meeting where only one person can speak at a time, this increases productivity. In fact this step is a search for information with regard to the topics chosen in the previous phase, which forms the second phase in the intelligence cycle. However, since ideas are related to one another in categories, this step can also be said to contribute to the analysis phase.

Analysis is continued in the last activity in the first session, where safety problems are prioritized. In this prioritization round, participants select the most important issues in each category. Except for a general indication of the importance of ideas, it is also important to consider, in more detail, the consequences of each safety problem and the possibilities to influence the problem. This is the objective of the multi-criteria analysis in the second session. In this activity, safety issues are evaluated on four criteria:

- *Impact:* To what extent does the problem have an impact on the experience of safety in the municipality or district of concern?
- *Incidental or structural:* Will the problem make itself felt at one point in time, or is it a recurring problem?
- *Scope:* Will the consequences of the problem be felt in the street, neighborhood, district or municipality?
- *Control:* To what extent can the district (in cooperation with other stakeholders) influence the problem?

Participants can score these aspects on their own PC. The meeting software makes it very easy to calculate medium scores and standard deviations, and to present these on the central screen. In the discussion of the scores, attention is paid to problems that are scored very differently by participants. Highly divergent scores are likely to point to two types of differences of opinions. Participants might interpret an aspect or problem differently; for example when for one participant "intimidation" refers to a group gathering at a street corner, while someone else interprets this as physical violence. In this case the use of more specific terminology can clarify the issue. Alternatively, participants may have a similar interpretation but put a different value on the problem being scored. This type of disagreement points to differences in priorities between (groups of) participants and needs to be taken into consideration in formulating policy options. Both types of differences are separated in a discussion, of which essentials are captured in the project report. The mean scores of problems on the four aspects mentioned above are used to identify the central conclusions of the sessions. Problems that are high in impact and occur frequently are likely to become priorities in safety policy. Scope and control indicate which parties need to be involved in working on the problem. The overall procedure, from gathering of ideas, to categorization and finally prioritization, provides participants with a transparent step-by-step process in which results of each step are clear and build on previous steps.

The project report is the final difference with a traditional meeting. After the first session, all ideas and categories are described in a short written report. The report, combined with open questions, forms a so-called workbook, which is sent to participants in order to prepare for the second session. The second session usually takes place one week after the first, enabling participants to reflect on the approach and intermediate results and contact their respective organizations. The report after the second session contains ideas, categories and prioritization of ideas. This document forms the basis for a final meeting in the district or municipality, in which the role of each of the partner organizations in implementing conclusions is discussed. Before the meeting takes place, the civil servant responsible for integral safety has summarized results of the sessions and the local council has agreed on a global action plan. In the last meeting, the municipality and other safety partners agree on performance targets and monitoring of results. The approach to reporting, but also the direct participation in the sessions, clearly influences the dissemination of results. Since representatives of the stakeholder organizations are present in the sessions, they have first-hand knowledge of the conclusions reached and the argumentation behind those conclusions. Representatives have ample time to go back to their organizations and decide on a way to go forward. One of the expected benefits of the electronic meeting approach is therefore commitment to the conclusions. Since at present nine districts and municipalities have followed the procedure, it is possible to test to what extent expected outcomes have been realized.

RESULTS FOR NINE SAFETY PLANS

So far the situation with regard to development of safety plans in The Netherlands has been described, and problems with regard to intelligence direction, search, analysis and dissemination of information have been discussed. A procedure based on electronic meetings has been proposed as a way to overcome these problems. In this section the evaluation of the procedure will be described. The first step in evaluating the electronic meetings is to decide on the central goals of the procedure. A central goal is the creation of intelligence with regard to safety problems. Two aspects of intelligence were distinguished: in the evaluation insight into safety problems and knowledge gained during the sessions. Furthermore, since intelligence is primarily created by exchanging viewpoints in the sessions, we are interested in the quality of communication in the sessions. Communication quality refers to the overall process of intelligence direction, search and analysis. The effect of creation of intelligence on stakeholders' actions is important with regard to the dissemination stage. Participants are expected to converge with regard to their safety policies. In this sense consensus can refer to convergence with regard to ideas on the problem (Stage 1 of the intelligence cycle) as well as convergence with regard to actions to be taken with regard to the problem (Stage 4 of the intelligence cycle). Since we assume that creation of a consensus view is essential for shared action (cf., Scheper, 1991), consensus will be subsumed under the dissemination stage. Finally, participants are expected to feel committed to conclusions reached in the sessions. In addition to the central goals of the sessions, it is also interesting to see how the procedure is evaluated in comparison to traditional meetings, and which elements of the procedure (e.g., the facilitator, the decision room) contribute most to the results.

The electronic meetings were evaluated individually and in a group discussion at the end of both sessions (see Figure 2). In addition, a written questionnaire was administered before and after the sessions. The pretest questionnaire contained a couple of questions on insight into safety problems. The posttest questionnaire again asked about insight into safety problems, and also contained questions on knowledge gained during the sessions, quality of communication, consensus and commitment to conclusions, a comparison to traditional meetings and the contribution of different meeting elements. All questions can be answered from 1 (strongly disagree) to 5 (strongly agree), with the exception of the contribution of session elements. Contribution of session elements is measured from -5 (obstructed the sessions) to +5 (greatly contributed to the sessions). Finally, three open questions were asked on the best aspects, greatest problems and points for improvement. The results generally indicate that participants value the electronic meetings.

*Table 1. Insight into Aspects of Safety [Cells contain median scores and standard deviations, ** significant at the .01 level, n is number of paired measurements (pretest and posttest completed).]*

	Pretest	Posttest	n
1. I am well aware of the situation with regard to safety in the area in question.	3.60 (.90)	3.92 (.81)**	65
2. I have insight into the relations between safety aspects in the area in question.	3.18 (.88)	3.74 (.75)**	65
3. I am aware of the background of the present safety situation in the area in question.	3.20 (.90)	3.59 (.87)**	64
4. I know the consequences of the present safety situation in the area in question, for persons involved.	3.32 (.86)	3.75 (.75)**	64
5. I have insight into the way in which safety in the area in question can be increased.	3.54 (.80)	3.70 (.80)	65

Intelligence on Safety Problems

Table 1 summarizes the answers on questions with regard to insight into safety problems. The first column contains the literal questions contained in the pretest and posttest questionnaires.

Table 1 shows that participants feel they have more insight into the safety situation, the relations between safety aspects, the background and the consequences for people involved. The score on the last question, on ways to increase safety, does not change significantly. This can be explained from the fact that the sessions concentrated on gathering information on the problem, while policy options were mainly addressed after the sessions.

Knowledge gained during the sessions is measured with four items in the posttest questionnaire (n = 74, alpha .57). The average score is 3.77 (sd = .55), which is significantly higher than neutral. In conclusion, the meetings seem to create intelligence on safety problems.

Communication

The posttest questionnaire contained two items on communication (n = 76, alpha .62). On average, participants agree that the sessions resulted in high quality communication. The score on communication is also significantly higher than neutral (3.87, sd = .54). The expectation that the electronic meetings resulted in high quality communication therefore seems to be confirmed.

Dissemination of Intelligence

With regard to the final stage of the intelligence cycle, dissemination of intelligence, two aspects were measured: consensus on the problem and commitment to conclusions of the sessions. Both were measured with four items (consensus n = 74, alpha .57; commitment n = 71, alpha .73). On average, participants agree that the electronic meetings resulted in consensus and commitment (consensus 4.02, sd = .54; commitment 3.91, sd = .47; both scores significantly higher than neutral). It seems therefore that the procedure of using electronic meetings has a positive contribution to make in the dissemination stage. Since the procedure has been in use for about one year now, no conclusions can be drawn with regard to actual implementation of conclusions.

Comparison to a Traditional Meeting and Meeting Elements

So far the outcomes of the electronic meetings have been described. A further interesting question is how the meetings are evaluated in comparison to traditional meetings. The posttest questionnaire included a number of questions on this topic, e.g., "Do the meetings in the decision room enable participants to gather more information than in a traditional meeting?" Above we described how the sessions resulted in high quality communication, intelligence, and the creation of consensus and commitment. From the answers to questions in the Table 2, it appears that the electronic meeting also scores better than a traditional meeting on these aspects: the electronic meetings result in higher outcomes and outcomes of a better quality.

The results with regard to efficiency and effectiveness of the procedure point in the same direction. Participants feel the procedure is efficient (mean score 4.03, sd = .63, n = 77) and think the meetings are successful (mean score 4.11, sd = .53, n = 76). The facilitators support this. The facilitators estimate that in a traditional meeting, gathering and prioritizing ideas would cost about 16 hours. According to the officials of municipalities and police force that were

Table 2. Comparison of the Electronic Meeting to Traditional Meetings

	Mean (sd)	n
Gathering more information	4.12 (.73)	77
More insight	4.05 (.72)	77
Faster insight	4.23 (.65)	77
Better communication	3.75 (.91)	76
Faster shared vision	4.17 (.77)	77
Better shared vision	3.87 (.77)	77
Faster commitment	3.66 (.78)	76
More commitment	3.72 (.79)	76

Table 3. Usefulness of Elements of the Method

	Mean (sd)	n
The fact that results were projected in a way that was visible to all participants	4.19 (1.10)	75
Presence of an outsider as a "group facilitator"	3.60 (1.86)	75
Opportunity for open discussion	3.09 (1.99)	74
Opportunity for extended discussion	2.15 (2.26)	74
The use of software for exchanging information	3.97 (1.50)	76
The written report (with questions) in between the sessions	3.24 (1.73)	74
The fact that meetings were held away from the office	2.76 (2.01)	75

involved in the sessions, the advantage of an electronic meeting is the creation of synergy among organizations involved in integral safety, if only because all contributions are valued equally. In conclusion, the efficiency and effectiveness of the electronic meetings are supported by both participants and facilitators.

Finally, the question remains as to which elements of the meetings are most successful. Please recall that the contribution of elements of the sessions is measured from -5 (obstructed the sessions) to +5 (greatly contributed to the sessions). As is shown in the Table 3, there are no large differences between session elements. The central projection (group memory), the use of software and the facilitator score slightly higher than other elements. The remarks participants made in the evaluations during the sessions support this. Participants felt the most important characteristics of the sessions were the opportunity to give large amounts of information, combined with the ability to structure information. For handling this information, the software and the facilitator were deemed most important.

In the posttest, participants were asked about problems and suggestions for improvements. Most answers point in the direction of issues outside of the sessions: ensure more time for preparation, clarify the purpose of the meetings earlier on in the process, ensure that all relevant groups are present, prevent delays due to participants who are only present part of the sessions and clarify the status of the conclusions for the municipality. As far as possible, these suggestions were used to improve later electronic meetings.

In summary, it seems that the creation of competitive intelligence with the use of electronic meetings lives up to its most important expectations.

CONCLUSION

The aims of this chapter were to show how intelligence is gathered and analyzed in a public setting, and to describe how groupware can be used to this end. The first topic was covered by sketching the problems with regard to the creation of business intelligence on integral safety issues. Local municipalities in The Netherlands have to gather information on safety problems from a number of different stakeholders, and encourage these to implement a shared action plan. With regard to the second goal, a procedure based on electronic meetings was described which aims to help in creating and disseminating business intelligence on safety problems. Application of the procedure in nine districts and municipalities has shown positive results. Participants indicate that quality of communication in the electronic meetings was high and their insight into safety problems has been increased. The discussions resulted in consensus and commitment with regard to conclusions. With regard to these aspects, the electronic meeting seems to outperform traditional meetings.

Electronic meetings therefore seem to be a promising approach to the creation of business intelligence in a public setting. Direct participation of stakeholders has many advantages with regard to gathering knowledge and implementation of policies. Electronic meeting support offers a practical way to overcome many of the obstacles to participation of key parties in the creation of intelligence.

REFERENCES

Appelman, J., Rouwette, E., & Qureshi, S. (2002). The dynamics of negotiation in a global inter-organizational network: Findings from the air transport and travel industry. *Group Decision and Negotiation, 11,* 145-163.

Delbecq, A.L., van de Ven, A.H., & Gustafson, D.H. (1975). *Group Techniques for Program Planning: A Guide to Nominal Group and Delphi Processes.* Glenview: Scott, Foresman and Co.

Diehl, M. & Stroebe, W. (1991). Productivity loss in idea-generating groups: Tracking down the blocking effect. *Journal of Personality and Social Psychology, 61*(3), 392-403.

Jessup, L. & Valacich, J.S. (1993). On the study of group support systems: An introduction to group support system research and development. In L. Jessup & J. S. Valacich (Eds.), *Group Support Systems. New Perspectives.* New York: MacMillan.

Nunamaker, J.F., Dennis, A.R., Valacich, J.S., Vogel, D.R., & George, J.F. (1991). Electronic meetings to support group work. *Communications of the ACM, 34*(7), 40-61.

Philips, E. & Vriens, D. (1999). *Business Intelligence*. Deventer: Kluwer.

Pinsonneault, A. & Kraemer, K.L. (1990). The effects of electronic meeting support on group processes and outcomes: An assessment of the empirical research. *European Journal of Operational Research, 46,* 143-161.

Scheper, W.J. (1991). *Group Decision Support Systems: An Inquiry into Theoretical and Philosophical Issues*. Unpublished doctoral dissertation. Utrecht, The Netherlands: University of Utrecht.

Schwarz, R.M. (1994). *The Skilled Facilitator. Practical Wisdom for Developing Effective Groups*. San Francisco, CA: Jossey-Bass Publishers.

Vennix, J.A.M. (1996). *Group Model Building: Facilitating Team Learning Using System Dynamics*. Chichester, UK: John Wiley & Sons.

Vreede, G.J. de & Dickson, G. W. (2000). Using GSS to support designing organizational processes and information systems: An action research study on collaborative business engineering. *Group Decision and Negotiation, 9*(2), 161-183.

Chapter VI

Improving Competitive Intelligence Through System Dynamics

Özge Pala
University of Nijmegen, The Netherlands

Dirk Vriens
University of Nijmegen, The Netherlands

Jac A. M. Vennix
University of Nijmegen, The Netherlands

ABSTRACT

To survive in a complex and dynamic world, organizations need relevant, timely, and accurate information about their environment. Due to the increasing complexity and dynamics of the environment, organizations run into several difficulties in their efforts to structure the intelligence activities. Two particularly persistent problems are (1) determining the relevant environmental cues and (2) making sense of the particular values of these cues. The current available methods for competitive intelligence do not eliminate these problems. In this chapter, system dynamics (SD) is

*proposed as an appropriate tool for competitive intelligence. System
dynamics is a simulation methodology that deals with the dynamics of
complex systems from a feedback perspective. How SD can help in dealing
with the problems in direction (selecting the relevant environmental cues)
and analysis (making sense of cues) stages and how ICT can support the
use of SD in intelligence activities are discussed.*

INTRODUCTION

To survive in a complex and dynamic world, organizations need relevant,
timely, and accurate information about their environment. Information about,
for instance, clients, competitors, and technological or ecological trends is vital
for constructing or revising strategies. The process of delivering this information
is sometimes called the "competitive intelligence" process (cf., Kahaner, 1997;
Cook & Cook, 2000). This process normally consists of four phases. In the
direction phase, an organization decides on what environmental aspects
information should be gathered. In the collection phase, the requested information is collected. In the analysis phase, the collected information is interpreted
in the light of the strategy of the organization. Authors on competitive intelligence would say that in this phase, "intelligence is produced"—meaning that
during analysis, it may be concluded that some piece of information is "relevant
strategic information" or "intelligence." In the last phase, the intelligence is
shared with strategic decision-makers and used to construct or adjust strategies. The collection of these phases is usually referred to as the "intelligence
cycle" (see, for instance, Sammon, 1986; Gilad & Gilad, 1988; Herring, 1992;
Bernhardt, 1994; Kahaner, 1997).

Obtaining information about the environment for (re)formulating strategies
has, of course, always been important. However, due to an increase in
complexity and dynamics of the environment (e.g., increased competition,
globalization, increase of amount of information, rapid political change, increased speed of technological developments), many organizations recognize
the need to *structure* the intelligence activities (cf., Gilad & Gilad, 1988;
Prescott & Fleisher, 1991; Cook & Cook, 2000). Organizations such as Shell,
Motorola, Kellog, Xerox, or Akzo-Nobel implemented or are currently
implementing so-called "intelligence units" in the hope that they can obtain the
requested intelligence.

However, in their efforts to structure the intelligence activities, organizations run into several difficulties (see e.g., Vriens & Philips, 1999, for an

overview of such problems). Two particularly persistent problems are (1) determining the relevant environmental cues (the main objective of the direction phase) and (2) making sense of the particular values of these cues (the main objective of the analysis phase). To give an example of the first problem, many organizations decide to collect data about their competitors. However, it is not straightforward to define what data should be collected. Should the collection focus be on financial data? Or on product data? Or, on something else? If it should be on financial data, one may ask: What financial data? ROI? R&D-budget? A possible reaction to this problem is that no selection is made. "All" data classes are possibly relevant, so "all" data classes should be monitored. If an organization does not select data classes, the number of data to be collected often turns out to be enormous. This, in turn, leads to an information overload, and, eventually, to questioning the relevance of the intelligence unit. Selection is, therefore, imperative. On the other hand, organizations may (implicitly or explicitly) define too few data classes. This may happen, for instance, if an organization only monitors data regarding the products and market share of the main competitor. This may lead to "environmental myopia" (cf., Levinthal & March, 1993) or to "business blindspots," as Gilad (1996) puts it. These blindspots occur because the selection of the environmental factors to be monitored is too narrow, and relevant information is missed. For instance, if only the main current competitors are monitored, newcomers may be overlooked. Gilad (1996) gives many other examples of problems occurring due to too narrow focus. In essence, the challenge is to determine the set of *relevant* environmental factors and use them to guide collection and analysis. To guide this process, methods such as the critical success factors (or one of its variants) (see Kahaner, 1997; Sammon, 1986; Herring, 1999) have been proposed. This method should help in identifying the few "important factors that must go well, for the organization to flourish" (Rockart, 1979; Robson, 1994). Based on these success factors, "key intelligence topics" in the environment can be derived.

A second persistent problem organizations run into during their intelligence activities is that of making sense of the collected data. What exactly does it mean that a competitor builds a new production plant? Or that their R&D budget increases? Or that a new technology is introduced? Determining the precise consequences for an organization's strategy is sometimes called the "study of reading tea-leaves" (Fuld, 1995). The challenge is to find a model that puts the data in a strategically relevant context (see also Gilad & Gilad, 1988, for a general approach to analysis). Several general models have been proposed to support the analysis, such as SWOT analysis or the BCG model (see e.g., Tyson, 1997; Kahaner, 1997; Fuld, 1995). Such models may help, for instance, to put the increase in R&D budget in perspective—as an indication of a threat if R&D is seen as a strength of the competitor or as less of a threat if their R&D is seen as underdeveloped. To analyze specific environmental cues, specific models have been put forward - such as tools to analyze patents (cf., Kahaner, 1997).

The two problems are, in our view, related. Both selecting relevant environmental cues and interpreting the specific values of these cues presuppose a (mental) model of the "organization in its environment." This model could be "flawed" in the sense as described above: it could be too broad or too narrow. It could also be implicit (such as the implicit assumptions about "the business we're in"—see Gilad, 1996) or explicit (in the form of a SWOT analysis, during which parts of our model of the "organization in its environment" are made explicit). The common answer in dealing with these problems is to build and maintain a model of "the organization in its environment" that is both rich and narrow enough to select relevant environmental cues and to help the interpretation of the values of these cues.

A somewhat less obvious part of this answer is the question of how this model should be built and maintained. Ideally, the model should (1) provide the arguments for the relevance of certain environmental cues and (2) provide an insight into the effect of different values of these cues on the organization's strategy. To provide these arguments and insights, the model should adequately "mirror" the complexity of the organization in its environment. One particular source of complexity is that organizational and environmental "elements" (variables) are dynamically related to each other. (More specifically: the whole system "organization in its environment" consists of variables that are dynamically related to each other.) If many variables are used to describe a system, and if they are related in a (large) network of (causal) interactions, and if, in this network, feedback loops occur, the behavior of the system is hard to understand, let alone predict. However, understanding these interactions is essential for understanding the relevance and the effect of individual variables on the organization's strategy (see for instance, Vennix, 1996; Powell & Bradford, 2000 for similar arguments). To make this argument more explicit: relevant parties in the environment (e.g., customers, competitors, technology developers, governmental organizations) constantly interact with each other and with the organization in focus and thereby change the values of variables (e.g., number of products sold, market share, investments). The change of these values, in turn, triggers new interactions, leading to a new change in values.

Understanding these interactions and their effect on different variables is important for understanding how the environment affects the organization and how the organization affects its environment. This understanding is also imperative in determining the relevance of environmental cues.

To build and maintain models that are able to deal with this complexity, a system dynamics (SD) approach seems appropriate (cf., Sterman, 1994, 2000). System dynamics is specifically suited for understanding the dynamic behavior of systems as caused by their internal structure (cf., Vennix, 1996). It seeks to provide insight into the behavior of a system by focusing on its feedback loops. Its specific way of modeling the internal structure of a system enables researchers and policy makers to trace the impact of variables on each other when they are dynamically related in the form of feedback loops. It thus helps making explicit the reasons for the relevance of certain variables. We propose that system dynamics helps to deal with the aforementioned problems in the intelligence activities. System dynamics can be used to model the "internal structure" that is responsible for generating the behavior of an "organization in its environment" system. Such a model can help in revealing the relevance of certain environmental cues and it can help in determining the impact of specific values of these cues (see also Powell & Bradford, 2000 for attempts to use qualitative SD in intelligence activities).

A model based on system dynamics seems more suitable than existing methods for determining the relevance and impact of environmental variables. For example, the critical success factors (CSF) (or one of its variants) is a method widely used for determining the relevant environmental cues (cf., Kahaner, 1997). It leads to a (static) list of variables that are important for the organization. However, it does not provide an argumentation for why these variables are important, nor does it take into account the dynamic structure from which these variables are taken. This lack of "systemic incorporation" is also the reason why the list of CSFs is not suited for analysis; the impact of specific values of the variables cannot be traced from this list. As we said earlier, many methods are available for analyzing the strategic effect of environmental information. However, to our knowledge none of these models deal explicitly with the dynamic interaction between the organizational and environmental elements. Moreover, little attention has been paid to using models in both direction *and* analysis (an exception is the use of scenarios in intelligence—e.g., Tessun, 1997). Such models, however, are desirable because they enable analysis *ex ante* and *ex post*. Analysis *ex ante* may give an insight into the relevance of (particular values of) certain variables in certain contexts, and directs the collection activities. Analysis *ex post* should confirm this relevance for the specific, actual values of the variables. In this sense, the model can be used to build and check scenarios.

In our research, we propose that system dynamics supports the direction and analysis phases of the intelligence cycle. However, to deliver this contribution, we have to show how SD supports these activities. Moreover, for SD to contribute to intelligence activities, ICT support of SD modeling is indispensable. More specifically, ICT helps (1) in building the SD model (quantification of the model), (2) in using the model for determining the effect of certain variables (analysis), (3) in identifying the relevance of the variables, and (4) as a means for distributing and using the models throughout the organization. Without ICT, then, an SD approach to competitive intelligence would be impossible. In this chapter, we specifically show how ICT enhances SD support of intelligence activities.

Against this background, we can now state the goals of the chapter. First, we will shortly explain the system dynamics methodology. Second, we will show how SD can help in dealing with the problem of selecting the relevant environmental cues (direction) and in making sense of them (analysis). Third, we will discuss how ICT can support the use of SD in intelligence activities. To reach this goal, the chapter is organized as follows. In the next section, we introduce system dynamics and then present a method that shows how SD can be used in supporting intelligence activities. This is followed with a discussion on the role of ICT in supporting this method. Next, we present our conclusions and give recommendations for using the method and for further research.

SYSTEM DYNAMICS: A SHORT INTRODUCTION

Before explaining how system dynamics can be used for competitive intelligence activities, we need to explain the methodology itself. In this section, we give an overview of the history and the core assumptions of system dynamics and the model building stages. The aim of this section is neither to give a complete, exhaustive explanation of the methodology nor to explain the details of model building. It is rather to familiarize the reader with the underlying ideas of the field. Readers who are interested in learning more about system dynamics modeling are referred to Forrester (1961, 1968), Richardson and Pugh (1981), and Sterman (2000).

History of System Dynamics

System dynamics was developed during the 1950s by Forrester at MIT (Massachusetts Institute of Technology in Boston) as a response to the problems with the methods used in problem-solving practice. Methods such as operations research/management science (Forrester, 1975):

- Ignored non-linear phenomena,
- Could only deal with simple situations and problems,
- Concentrated on isolated business functions instead of on the relationships between these functions, and
- Most importantly, focused on the "open-loop" approach of the decision-making processes in organizations, where decisions are considered as independent from the decisions themselves.

Forrester first published an article about the method in 1958 in the Harvard Business Review. In 1961, his book *Industrial Dynamics* was published, in which the theory and methodology of system dynamics (at that point, still called "Industrial Dynamics") was described almost in its entirety. In *Industrial Dynamics*, the method is applied to industrial companies. During the 1960s, Forrester also began to apply the method to other areas, and the books *Urban Dynamics* (Forrester, 1969) and *World Dynamics* (Forrester, 1971) were published. This latter study was the predecessor of a study carried out for the Club of Rome. It resulted in the renowned report *The Limits to Growth* (Meadows et al., 1972; Meadows et al., 1974). Since then, SD has been applied to a variety of issues such as project management (Cooper, 1980), dynamics of worker burnout (Homer, 1985), analysis of the causes of business cycles (Sterman, 1986), new product diffusion (Homer, 1987; Maier, 1998), and innovation implementation (Repenning, 2002). For a variety of SD applications, see Sterman (2000).

Core Assumptions of the System Dynamics Approach

System dynamics has four core assumptions. The first is that social systems are information feedback systems. Most non-SD problem-solving practices in organizations employ "open-loop" thinking. Such an approach means that the consequences of decisions taken are assumed to have no influence on future decisions. This, however, is not realistic since every action would cause changes in the environment, leading to a new understanding or even redefinition of the situation. As such, these changes would feed back to influence future decisions. As a result, the behavior of a feedback system would actually be influenced by its own past behavior (Forrester, 1968). System dynamics approach closes the open loops in thinking by using the notion of feedback and feedback loops which are "a closed sequence of causes and effect, a closed path of action and information" (Richardson & Pugh, 1981, p. 4). The interconnected feedback loops form the feedback system.

By focusing on the feedback loops in defining the relationships between the organization and its environment, system dynamics maintains an endogenous viewpoint: organizations are seen as part of the structure of a system which creates its own dynamics. Dynamic behavior is not caused by exogenous shocks; rather they are the result of the feedback structure of the system. This understanding leads to the second core assumption, which can be formulated most sharply as: "structure drives behavior." This assumption implies that the underlying feedback structure of a system (i.e., interconnected sets of feedback loops) is responsible for the system's behavior. Understanding this behavior is the main goal of the system dynamics approach (Richardson & Pugh, 1981).

There are two types of feedback loops: reinforcing (positive) and balancing (negative). Reinforcing loops are destabilizing. They amplify deviations and generate exponential growth. Balancing loops, on the other hand, have the tendency to stabilize a system. They are goal-seeking in the sense that they try to bring the system to equilibrium. (An example can be seen in Figure 1.)

The causal loop diagram (CLD) in Figure 1 represents two interacting processes to explain the generation of new mobile phone users. Causal loop diagramming is a tool used in system dynamics to represent feedback structures of systems. CLDs show the cause-effect relationships between variables and the interconnected feedback loops [for further information, see Chapter V of Sterman (2000)]. In Figure 1, it is assumed that the higher the number of mobile phone users, the higher the number of new users will be (this represents the word of mouth process which leads to the diffusion of the mobile phones). This

Figure 1. An Example of a Feedback System with One Reinforcing and One Balancing Loop

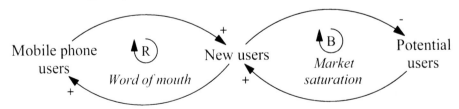

is a reinforcing loop. On the other hand, an increase in the number of new users will decrease the number of potential users (given a finite population). A smaller group of potential users will, in turn, limit the number of new users (saturation effect). This is a balancing loop. As might be clear to the reader tracing the loops, the behavior that would be generated by this structure becomes apparent. And this is exactly what the second assumption of system dynamics states.

"Structure drives behavior" means that it is the interaction of the reinforcing and balancing loops over time that generates the behavior of the system. The behavior is determined by the dominant feedback loop (in a feedback structure, "a loop that is primarily responsible for model behavior over some time interval is known as the dominant loop" (Richardson & Pugh, 1981, p. 285). As the dominance shifts from one feedback loop to another, the dynamic behavior of the system unfolds. Figure 2 shows the behavior corresponding to the feedback structure of Figure 1.

At the beginning (the first three and a half years), the number of users increases at an exponential rate; the reinforcing loop (word of mouth) is dominant. After some time (shown by the dashed line), however, the balancing loop (saturation) takes over and the growth levels off. As a result of the shift in dominance from reinforcing to balancing loop, the behavior of the system changes from exponential growth to goal seeking.

The third and fourth assumptions in system dynamics are that using mathematical models and simulation are necessary to trace the dynamics of

Figure 2. Dynamics Behavior of Mobile Phone Users

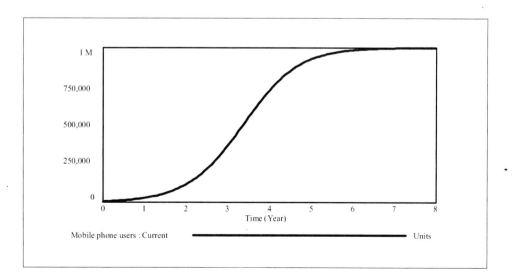

complex structures. Real problems embedded in social systems get complex so easily that understanding their behavior becomes too difficult (if not impossible) a task to perform for the human mind without an aid. Research has repeatedly demonstrated that people are not able to infer the dynamics of complex systems correctly (cf., Sterman, 1994, 2000). Hence, system dynamicists use quantified simulation models to trace the dynamics.

Model Building Process in System Dynamics

The construction of a system dynamics model is comprised, generally speaking, of the following phases:
1.   Problem statement or definition
2.   Conceptual modeling
3.   Formal modeling
4.   Testing and validating
5.   Sensitivity analysis and policy experimentation

The starting point is identifying the description of the policy problem to be modeled. This phase is crucial because the problem definition sets the boundary of the model and helps to identify the variables that will be included in the model. When using system dynamics, the problem definition is expressed in terms of the *reference modes of behavior* (Richardson & Pugh, 1981, pp. 21-25). The

Figure 3. *Example of a Reference Mode of Behavior*

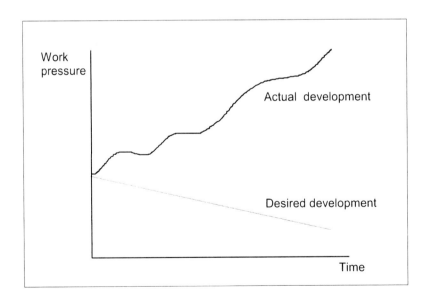

reference mode of behavior is the behavior of the problem variable over time. Figure 3 shows a hypothetical example of the increase in work pressure in a company. The discrepancy between the actual and the desired behavior shows that there exists a problem which is actually worsening over time.

For the system dynamics model building process, the reference mode of behavior serves as the starting point. And it is a very important starting point, because it shows a dynamic representation of the problem situation. Moreover, later on, this reference mode can be used for testing the validity of the simulation model. It serves to determine to what extent the developed simulation model is valid in terms of correctly simulating this reference mode of behavior.

Following the definition of the problem, the process of model construction starts with a conceptual model. The conceptual model shows the causal (feedback) structure. This can either take the form of a causal loop diagram (see Figure 1) or a stock and flow diagram (see Figure 4). Stocks and flows are a very important part of the structure of a system. Forrester (1968) differentiates four levels of structure: (1) closed boundary, (2) feedback loops (the basic elements of system structure), (3) stocks and flows, and (4) goal, actual conditions, discrepancy between goal and actual conditions, and action resulting from discrepancy. Figure 4 shows all these components. The boundary of the model is set by the clouds. These clouds represent the source and sink of the material that flow through the system. There are two balancing feedback loops: one from inventory through discrepancy and production to inventory and the other from inventory through deliveries to inventory. The variable *inventory* is a stock variable. The variables *production* (inflow) and *deliveries* (outflow) are flow variables. The goal is represented by the *desired inventory* whereas the actual condition is the current value of the *inventory*. The action is *production* and it is based on the *discrepancy* between the *inventory* and *desired inventory*.

Stocks and flows are the fundamental variables in system dynamics modeling (Forrester, 1968). Stocks represent accumulations in a system. They are also called state variables because they contain information regarding the actual state of the system on which actions and decisions are based (Sterman, 2000). Flows add to and subtract from the stocks and they represent the policies of the decision-maker. In the modeling language, stocks are represented by rectangles, and flows by valves. An important distinction between stocks and flows is that the stocks represent the amount of accumulation and the flow represents the rate of change in that accumulation. Hence, whereas a stock is 'measured' at some point in time, a flow is 'measured' over a particular time period. For example, in Figure 4, the stock (inventory) is the number of

Figure 4. Representation of a Stock-Flow Diagram

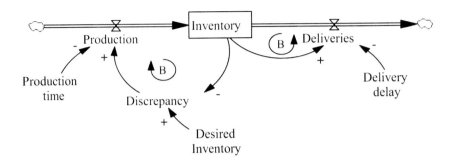

items in stock at some point in time, while the flow (deliveries) is the number of items delivered *per* time period (such as day or month).

After identifying the feedback structure of the model, the next step is to formulate the mathematical equations for the relationships between variables and estimate parameters. In this text, we will not elaborate on formulation of equations and parameter estimation since it is beyond the scope of the chapter. The interested reader may consult Forrester (1961, 1968), Richardson and Pugh (1981), Roberts et al. (1983), and Sterman (2000) for further information.

Once model formulation is completed, the validity of the model should be established. As stated before, one way of doing this is comparing the model behavior with the reference mode of behavior. However, this is only part of model testing. Since the main focus of system dynamics is the underlying feedback structure of the system, structure validity is far more important than behavior validity. Every variable should have a real-world equivalent, every equation should be checked, the model boundary should be questioned, and the model should be tested in extreme conditions. Various tests have been developed to check the validity of and increase confidence in the model (Forrester & Senge, 1980; Barlas, 1996).

The model can be used for policy experimentation after its validity is established. Sensitivity analyses and scenario runs can be conducted showing the behavior of the model under a variety of conditions. These scenario runs provide more insight into the dominant feedback processes underlying the problem. Based on such insight, new policies can be devised and tested. In addition, as we will see in the next section, it can be used in determining an organization's information need.

HOW TO USE SD FOR COMPETITIVE INTELLIGENCE

In the introduction, we explained various deficiencies in the current CI practice. The most important problems arise in identifying which information is relevant and understanding the impact of the information for the organization. By the latter, we mean identifying how the information can affect the organization's strategy/business. Both of these problems would render the CI practice ineffective. To eliminate these problems, we need to understand what causes them. In this section, we first discuss the causes of these problems and then show how SD can help in dealing with these two problems.

Identifying the relevant information would require a complete comprehension of the relationships amongst the organizational and environmental variables. Understanding the meaning of information, on the other hand, would require identifying the dynamic implications of the totality of these relationships, as they would unfold over time. At this point, two problems arise: (1) organizations are embedded in a dynamically complex system in which they continuously interact with their environment, and (2) the human mind is not able to cope with this complexity. As we have explained previously, human beings have the tendency to think in terms of linear chains of reasoning (open-loop thinking, see Figure 5a): an event taking place in the environment is seen as the cause of the organizational outcomes which then stimulates an action. What is missing in this is that whatever action the organization takes would lead to new events (hence, to changes) in the environment (see Figure 5b). These events could, for instance, be the reactions of the competitors to our action.

Any analysis performed without establishing these relationships and the feedback structure the organization is functioning in would be missing crucial links between the organization and its environment. This would lead to an erroneous understanding regarding the important information cues in the environment, the effects of these cues on the organizational outcomes, and the policies the organization should implement.

We propose system dynamics modeling as an appropriate tool for CI activities. System dynamics theory highlights the importance of feedback loops as the basis of systems structure. Moreover, through simulations, it enables us to make a link between the structure and the behavior produced by this structure. As a result, it aids in identifying the dynamics and a causal explanation for it. The advantage of a simulation model is that it gives a safe environment where various scenarios can be tried to identify the effects of different possible events.

Figure 5. (a) Linear Cause-Effect Chains (b) Interrelationships Among the Organizational Actions/Outcomes and Environmental Events

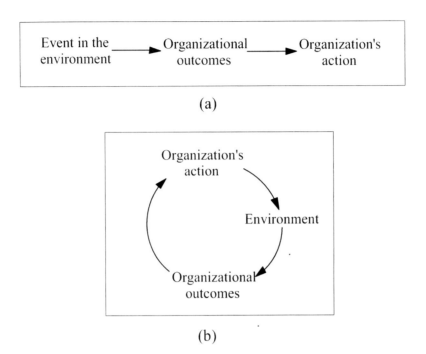

(a)

(b)

Figure 6 shows a summary of problems experienced in different stages of CI cycle and how SD can help solve these problems. Below, we explain how SD can be used to improve each stage of the intelligence cycle.

SD for the Direction and Analysis Stages

While using a system dynamics model, the direction and analysis phases can be looked at together. Any direction phase would necessitate an analysis of the effects of environmental variables to decide on their relevance. The main problem of these stages is identifying what information is relevant and the effect of relevant information on organizational policies. The system dynamics model can be used to for analyzing the effects of changes in individual variables and combinations of variables. Any scenario that is of interest to the organization can be run with the simulation model and the effects can be analyzed. For instance, the model can be run to look at the effects of increased competitor R&D expenditures on the organization's market share. The simulation run can show whether the market share would be affected by the change in competitor

Figure 6. Problems Faced During CI Activities and Possible Help from SD

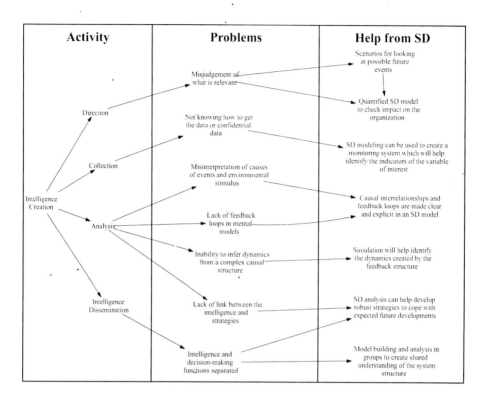

R&D expenditures and the severity of this effect. Moreover, it would help generate a causal explanation of why the effect has taken place. It would also help test policies that the organization would want to implement should the competitors increase their R&D expenditures.

SD for the Collection Stage

Once relevant variables are identified, the organization should collect information to identify the developments that are taking place in the environment. A system dynamics model cannot help with the act of collecting the information. However, the model can be used to identify indicators for the variables of interest. These indicators may prove to be very useful, especially in situations where the information of interest is difficult to obtain (for instance, due to confidentiality). In such a case, information on the indicators can be obtained to drive insight regarding the variable of interest.

SD for the Analysis Stage

After the data is collected, further analysis might be necessary. For this, the simulation model can be used. Analyzing the model with the collected data would give insights into what is happening in the environment and what the organization can do about it. One word of caution is necessary here. By definition, every model is a simplification of reality. An SD model should not be used as a forecasting tool. The behavior it will generate will come from the model structure but not the real world. Hence, the analyst should be careful about insight generated and this insight should always be supplemented with knowledge of reality that is not included in the model. Moreover, the validity of the model should be established and the model should be updated to represent the changes that take place in the system structure.

SD for the Intelligence Dissemination Stage

The last stage of the cycle is intelligence dissemination. Gilad et al. (1993) point to the current problem of the separation between intelligence created and the decisions made. He gives three reasons for this: (1) the reductionist nature of intelligence analysis techniques, (2) the difficulty of establishing clear causal relationships between a company's behavior and performance, and (3) internal social and political obstacles to information flows in a typical cooperation. System dynamics modeling could be of help here as well. First of all, the model would provide the totality of the causal relationships in a given system. It would provide a visual representation of causal relationships amongst variables, which can be used to explain the reasons behind experienced results. Second, the system dynamics approach enables a group of managers to build a model together. In situations where group model building (Vennix, 1996; Vennix et al., 1997) is used, the intelligence managers and the decision-makers can build a model together which then would represent the shared understanding. As a result, a piece of information would be judged based on the same model rather than different mental models people would possess, and thus, have the "same" meaning.

In short, using system dynamics helps to
- Make causal relationships amongst variables explicit and provide a visual representation of these relationships,
- Analyze the results of scenario-runs to show effects of environmental changes on the organization, hence, identifying the important variables or events,
- Identify a causal explanation for the causes and effects of events,

- Create a shared understanding of the system structure if the model is built with a group,
- Determine indicators for changes in the environment,
- Identify robust policies to implement in the face of environmental changes.

STEPS IN USING SD MODELING TO HELP CREATING INTELLIGENCE

In this section, we explain the stages in model building and analysis for identifying relevant environmental information. The process explained in this section aims at the identification of relevant information, but it yields several results. As explained in the previous section on the usefulness of SD in CI, different stages such as direction and analysis are performed together rather than sequentially. Hence, during the process, causal explanations are given and different scenarios are analyzed. Moreover, building the model with a group of managers would help the creation of a shared understanding.

The process is composed of the following stages:

Stage 1: Identification of the model focus

Stage 2: Causal modeling—Qualitative system dynamics

Stage 3: Quantification of the simulation model and testing

Stage 4: Identification of important variables: Sensitivity analysis and policy development

Stage 5: Identification of indicators: Future analysis and modeling

The following sub-sections explain each of these stages. Table 1 summarizes the activities that each stage is composed of.

Stage 1: Identification of the Model Focus

Before starting with model building, the focus for the model should be identified. Since the model is used for answering the information needs of the organization, it should be the model of the domain the organization is interested in. This basically means identifying what kind of information (intelligence) is required. For instance, if the organization were interested in the competitors then focusing on the suppliers would not make sense (this, however, does not mean that suppliers should be ignored altogether. If the model for competitors would require variables or structures regarding the suppliers then these should be added to the model). This might sound trivial. However, if the focus is not determined prior to the model building, the effort might be directed at wrong directions. Moreover, as explained in the introduction to system dynamics, identifying the focus of model building generates criteria for determining the boundary of the model. One or more of the following questions can be asked to determine the theme:

- Is there a problem at hand that the organization wants to tackle? For instance, a new product introduction to the market.
- Do certain parts of the environment have a priority over the others? For instance, the organization might be interested in the competitors' actions or government influence or customer preferences.
- Are there certain scenarios/developments the organization is specifically interested in? Are there any possible future developments the consequences of which should be considered?

Stage 2: Causal Modeling—Qualitative System Dynamics

In this stage, the aim is to come up with the feedback loops that explain how the organizational and environmental variables interact with each other. Identifying feedback loops is an important part of the modeling because they are the source of dynamic behavior that we would like to analyze.

The model building will constitute of the following steps: first, the organizational variables that are critical to the viability of the organization should be identified. This would result in a list of the critical organizational variables, denoted as Org. Second, the environmental variables that would affect each organizational variable should be identified. This would results in a list of environmental variables, denoted as Env. Third, the linkages amongst the organizational (Org) and environmental (Env) variables should be identified and drawn. During this last step, new organizational or environmental variables may be added.

Since the model will be used to identify the relevant environmental variables, it is important to incorporate all the necessary environmental variables that would have a possible impact on the organization and all the existing links (relationships). Therefore, throughout the model building process, the boundary of the model should be controlled. The boundary of the model depends on the modeling focus that is identified in Stage 1 of this process. Boundary control would enable the modeler to determine whether all the essential variables and links are added to the model. To control the appropriateness of the boundary, the modeler should continuously ask whether there are any other variables that would affect the organizational and environmental variables that are in the model. If there are, these should be added into the model with their corresponding links. Moreover, the modeler should also try to identify whether there are any important processes that are not represented in the model. Being aware of these questions would enable a boundary that would be appropriate for model analysis. And all throughout the process, the modeler should check whether the model covers the problematic situation/focus/the scenarios.

The output of Stage 2 will be a causal loop diagram showing the relationships of the organization with its environment. As a result, we will be able to:

- Identify the feedback/causal structure of the system. Such a model building process will make the implicit assumptions people have regarding the relationships amongst variables explicit. Yet another advantage is to have a visual representation of all the relationships together. This would decrease the probability of omitting some factors and/or relationships during the analysis stage.

- Arrive at a conceptual model representing the shared understanding of the system structure given that the model building proceeds with a group of managers. This would mean that the people who gather the intelligence and use it would have the same perceptions regarding how the system in which they are embedded functions.

- Differentiate endogenous environmental variables from the exogenous ones. Identifying endogenous variables is important because this way the organization can identify which of the variables it can affect. This knowledge can be very powerful in "fighting against" the undesired developments in the environment as well as steering the environment in the desired direction.

Stage 3: Quantification of the Simulation Model and Validation

Once the feedback structure is determined, the modeling can proceed with the quantification stage. This stage would involve specifying the equations, parameters, and initial conditions. The equations should be written following rules of modeling and each equation should be tested for consistency and conformity to real life decision-making rules. The model resulting from Stage 3 will be a stock-flow diagram with equations. This model can be used for further sensitivity and policy analysis. As explained before, since the aim of this chapter is not to explain the details of SD model building, for rules in quantification the reader is referred to Forrester (1961, 1968), Richardson and Pugh (1981), and Sterman (2000).

The quantification process can be tedious and time-consuming. However, it is very important. As explained before, human beings do not have the ability to infer dynamics correctly from a given structure. However, the CI process necessitates this. A simulation model can be a very useful tool for doing various experiments to understand a given feedback structure and the effects of environmental variables within that structure. How model analysis can be used to contribute to this understanding is explained in Stage 4.

Stage 4: Identification of Important Variables—Sensitivity Analysis and Policy Development

The identification of important variables will be done through analyzing the simulation model. The seven tasks that need to be carried out are given below. The first five describe the analysis and are iterative in nature. The result of the analysis would be the list of important variables and events and is shown as Task 6. Designing of policies, as defined in Task 7, can either be an integral part of the analysis (Tasks 2 to 4) or can be carried out on its own as a further analysis. Such analysis would generate insight into the policies the organization can devise that will endure (that is, robust policies) or cope with the possible environmental changes.

1. Identify the simulation runs to be made. The runs can involve changing individual environmental variables or implementing scenarios (possible future developments). As a rule of thumb, it might be logical to start with the highly uncertain variables.
2. Conduct the runs.
3. See the effect on the organizational variables. Look for changes in behavior patterns.
4. Explain why the change does or does not take place.
5. If necessary, think of other runs.
6. Make a list of important variables: The variables (or combination of variables) that have a high impact on the organization should be monitored.
7. Design robust policies to cope with possible environmental developments.

The analysis can be carried out at two levels. First of all, one can look at the effects of changes in individual environmental variables. For instance, what would be the consequence of a reduction in the competitor's price? An environmental variable can either be exogenous (i.e., a parameter) or endogenous. An exogenous environmental variable is one whose value is not influenced by the internal structure of the model. For example, in Figure 7, Env_3 is exogenous. We can make an analysis to answer the question "What would be the consequence(s) of changes in Env_3?" An endogenous environmental variable is one whose value is (partially) dependent on the factors that represent the internal structure of the model. Env_1 in Figure 7 is such a variable. Since the value of an endogenous environmental variable is dependent on other factors, we cannot simply change its value and re-run the model. To analyze the effects of changes in an endogenous variable, three aspects should be considered:

1. The way in which the organizational variable affects the environmental variable (e.g., what would be the consequences of changes in the effect of Org_1 on Env_1?). This would result in looking at the mathematical relation between Org_1 and Env_1.

2. The value of the other environmental factors affecting the environmental variable of interest (e.g., what would be the consequences of changes in the value of Env_2?). This step is actually the same as looking at the exogenous variables. If an exhaustive analysis of the exogenous variables has been performed there is no need for this step.

3. The way in which the other environmental factors affect the environmental variable (e.g., what would be the consequence(s) of changes in the effect of Env_2 on Env_1?). Once again, this would involve looking at the mathematical relation between Env_2 and Env_1.

Figure 7. Representation of Exogenous and Endogenous Variables

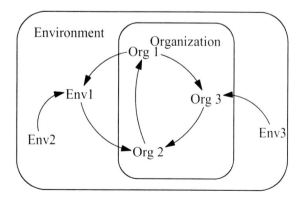

The second level of analysis refers to looking at the effects of simultaneous changes in more than one environmental variable as well as changing structural components; that is, adding or removing feedback loops. Such analysis would require developing environmental scenarios. By a scenario, we mean a combination of what can happen to different variables at the same time. This would require changing the values or equations of different environmental factors simultaneously or adding new variables and relationships into the model to simulate a certain event that might take place in the future. This type of analysis is likely to create more interesting insights with respect to the intelligence needs. This is because developments in the organizational environment hardly involve changes in one single factor. It is rather the combined effect of various changes that would affect the organization. Moreover, if the interest would lie in identifying the effects of changes in the market structure or competitor policy or involvement of an additional competitor, then this would call for more than changes in single variables. Hence, a powerful feature of scenario analysis as such is to give the analyst the possibility to alter complete structures rather than only parameter values or an equation between two variables.

The purpose of the analysis procedure is to identify the environmental factors that are important to monitor. In reality, an environmental variable becomes relevant for an organization when changes in that variable have considerable effects on the organizational outcomes. We can use the same understanding while doing the model analysis. That is, during the simulation runs, we can identify whether the organizational outcomes (as defined in the simulation model) are sensitive to the changes we make. To identify the sensitivity, we are going to look at the changes in the *behavior* of the chosen organizational variables. If a change takes place in the behavior pattern then we would say that the organization is sensitive to changes in that particular environmental variable and that variable should be monitored. The same goes for the scenarios. If an organization gets affected as a certain development in the environment unfolds then it means that the organization should be careful regarding such developments. In such a situation, the organization can do three things: (1) monitor its environment to see whether the changes will take place, (2) if possible, try to prevent the changes from happening through the influence it has on the environment, and (3) be prepared to cope with such changes by developing robust policies beforehand. The analysis process using system dynamics can assist in all these three situations. First of all, the model can point towards indicators so that the organization would know what to monitor. Second, an intrinsic property of SD modeling is focusing on an endogenous explanation for phenomenon. Thus, the modeling process will point out which environmental variables are under the (partial) control of the organization. Third, a very powerful use of modeling is designing policies and testing them under different conditions through simulation runs. The model can be seen as an environment to test as many policies as possible. As a result of such policy experimentation, the relative merits of different policies can be assessed.

All in all, the modeling process gives the organization the opportunity to think in terms of different possible futures and design different ways of coping with these futures by testing and finding robust policies.

Stage 5: Identification of Indicators—Future Analysis and Modeling

Once important environmental variables are identified, the organization might want to do further modeling to gain more insight into the determinants of these variables. It is sometimes possible that data for the environmental variable of interest are not available (e.g., due to confidentiality reasons). In these circumstances, it would be useful for the organization to have insight into how the information on the environmental variable of interest can be derived via other data that is (publicly) available. To enable this, further modeling can be done to develop causal loop diagrams that would generate insight into variables that are causally associated with the variable of interest. Such a model can be used to derive indicators for these variables.

ICT TO SUPPORT SD FOR CI

In this chapter, we discussed how SD might contribute to CI activities. However, to deliver this contribution, ICT is indispensable. Without certain ICT applications, the contribution would even be impossible. In this section, we discuss how ICT enables and enhances SD support of CI activities. We will do so by looking into each phase of the intelligence cycle separately.

Direction

As became apparent in this chapter, we proposed five steps in using SD for direction purposes. The first two steps should result in a causal model in which organizational and environmental variables are causally linked to each other (vis-à-vis a certain problem or area of interest). ICT can enhance the identification of these variables. For example, by using certain groupware (group) model building sessions can be held very effectively (cf., Rouwette et al., 2000 for the use of groupware for building SD models in groups).

Table 1. Steps of the Modeling Process

1.	*Identification of the model focus*	• Interesting sector determination: What is (are) the environment sector(s) that is interesting to analyze? • Scenario development: Are there any (environmental) developments that are expected or feared?

2.	*Causal modeling -- Qualitative system dynamics*	• Identification of organizational variables: What are the organizational variables that are viable to the survival of the organization?
		• Identification of the environmental variables: What are the environmental variables that have an effect on the organizational variables that were identified previously?
		• Identification of the links
		  • Specification of the links amongst the organizational and environmental variables
		  • Identification of other variables affecting the organizational and/or the environmental variables

3.	*Quantification of the simulation model and testing*	• Specification of the quantitative representation of the relationships • Estimation of the parameters • Validation
4.	*Identification of the important variables: Sensitivity analysis and policy development*	• Sensitivity analysis: What are the effects of changes in the environmental variables on the behavior of the organizational variables? • Scenario development: What are the possible developments that can take place in the environment? • Scenario runs • Policy development
5.	*Identification of indicators: Further analysis and modeling*	• Modeling for identifying the indicators for developments

Moreover, specific software (e.g., Vensim by Ventana Systems) is particularly suited to construct and visualize causal models. ICT can also enhance distributing and discussing the (sub) result of this step. This function is important, as building and maintaining a causal model could enhance creating a shared understanding of the 'organization in its environment' model. Once this knowledge is shared, it may direct CI professionals and strategic decision makers in their CI activities. ICT can help sharing (and updating) this knowledge through several Internet (or Intranet) applications (e.g., by e-mail or internal discussion sites, or applications tailored to distributing and updating such causal models).

The third and fourth steps include (1) the quantification of the causal model and its testing and (2) running the model to determine the impact of the values of certain variable (or variable combinations) and to determine the impact of certain policies to counter the negative effect of specific values of variables (or combinations). This would actually be impossible without specific SD software. Software packages as Powersim (by Powersim), Vensim (by Ventana Systems) or Ithink (by High Performance Systems) provide a full simulation environment where SD models can be run.

The last step in the direction stage consists of the identification of indicators of relevant environmental variables. This list of indicators should be fed into relevant ICT applications for (help) determining their actual values in the collection stage.

Collection

Although SD does not play an active part in the actual collection activities, it may be possible to establish links between the indicators appearing in the quantified model to sources containing values of these indicators (e.g., by linking them dynamically to certain online databases or other Web sources). One may even think of linking them to Web agents or robots alerting the SD software when changes in value occur.

Analysis

In this chapter, direction and analysis are treated as two highly related stages. Direction might be defined as analysis *ex ante* resulting in a list of relevant environmental indicators. In the analysis stage, the actual values of these indicators are used to simulate the performance of the system. This information, in turn, is used to (1) determine the impact of the monitored environmental variables (according to the model) and (2) test and select certain policies. To do this, the same SD-specific ICT tools as mentioned in the direction stage may be employed.

Dissemination

During the process of using SD to support CI activities, several results may be distributed: (1) the causal model (for purposes of building and maintaining it and for creating a shared understanding), (2) the list of indicators (for directing collection activities), (3) simulation results, and (4) robust policies (for purposes of decision-making). To distribute these results, ICT may help in (1) their presentation (e.g., by several SD-oriented applications, in combination with more standard presentation tools) and (2) in the distribution of these presentations (e.g., through several Web-enabled applications).

CONCLUSION

Obtaining environmental information is very important for strategic decision-making. However, the dynamic complexity of the environment and the insufficient cognitive capabilities of individuals in environmental scanning and information processing make this task very difficult. In the recent years, organizations have been trying to structure their intelligence activities. Yet, while doing so, they run into several difficulties (see e.g., Vriens & Philips, 1999, for an overview of such problems). In our view, the most important problems occur in the direction, analysis and dissemination stages. In the direction stage, it is rather difficult to determine which information is relevant and which is not. Which of the many environmental cues are important for the organization to collect data on? The problem in the analysis stage is making sense of the meaning of the collected information for the organization. In the dissemination stage, on the other hand, the separation between the intelligence and decision-making functions in an organization is problematic.

In this chapter, we have proposed system dynamics as a methodology that can be used during intelligence activities. SD is a methodology for understanding and analyzing dynamically complex problems from a feedback perspective. We believe that system dynamics has the potential to eliminate the problems faced in CI. Using system dynamics helps enable the identification of important or relevant environmental variables, analysis of the effects environmental changes have on the organization, and design of robust policies to implement to cope with undesired situations. The identification of relevant variables and the analysis of their effects can be done through the analysis of the causal structure. The simulation model can be used for scenario runs to see the effects of changes in individual variables or in combinations of variables. The environmental variables in which changes alter the behavior of the important organizational variables would be those that should be monitored. Moreover, if the model is built with a group of managers from different functions, the process would help create a shared understanding of the system structure.

We feel that employing SD for CI activities (if properly supported by ICT applications) may contribute in coping with the problems in the direction, analysis, and dissemination stages. However, future research should show the usefulness of SD in CI practice through real-life applications.

REFERENCES

Barlas, Y. (1996). Formal aspects of model validity and validation in system dynamics. *System Dynamics Review, 12*(3), 183-210.

Bernhardt, D.C. (1994). 'I want it fast, factual, actionable'—Tailoring competitive intelligence to executive needs. *Long Range Planning, 27*(1), 12-24.

Cook, M. & Cook, C. (2000). *Competitive Intelligence*. London: Kogan Page.

Cooper, K. (1980). Naval ship production: A claim settled and a framework built. *Interfaces, 10*(6), 20-36.

Forrester, J.W. (1958). Industrial dynamics: a major breakthrough for decision makers. *Harvard Business Review*, (July/August), 37-66.

Forrester, J.W. (1961). *Industrial Dynamics*. Cambridge, MA.

Forrester, J.W. (1968). *Principles of Systems*. Cambridge, MA.

Forrester, J.W. (1969). *Urban Dynamics*. Cambridge, MA/London.

Forrester, J.W. (1971). *World Dynamics*. Cambridge, MA.

Forrester, J.W. (1975). Industrial dynamics—After the first decade. In *Collected Papers of J.W. Forrester*. Cambridge, MA: Wright-Allen Press. (Original paper in *Management Science (1998), 14*(7), 398-415.

Forrester, J.W. & Senge, P.M. (1980). Tests for building confidence in system dynamics models. In A. A. Legasto, J. W. Forrester, & J. M. Lyneis (Eds.), *System Dynamics*. Amsterdam: North-Holland.

Fuld, L.M. (1995). *The New Competitor Intelligence*. Chichester, UK: John Wiley & Sons.

Gilad, B. (1996). *Business Blindspots*. Calne (GB): Infonortics.

Gilad, B. & Gilad, T. (1988). *The Business Intelligence System*. New York: Amacon.

Gilad, B., Gordon, G., & Sudit, E. (1993). Identifying gaps and blind spots in competitive intelligence. *Long Range Planning, 26*(6), 107-121.

Herring, J.P. (1992). The role of intelligence in formulating strategy. *The Journal of Business Strategy, 13*(5), 54-60.

Herring, J.P. (1999). Key intelligence topics, a process to identify and define intelligence needs. *Competitive Intelligence Review, 10*(2), 4-14.

Homer, J. (1985). Worker burnout: A dynamic model with implications for prevention and control. *System Dynamics Review, 1*(1), 42-62.

Homer, J. (1987). A diffusion model with application to evolving medical technologies. *Technological Forecasting and Social Change, 31*(3), 197-218.

Ithink. High Performance Systems Inc. Retrieved from: http://www.hps-inc.com.

Kahaner, L. (1997). *Competitive Intelligence*. New York: Touchstone.

Levinthal, D.A. & March, J.G. (1993). The myopia of learning. *Strategic Management Journal, 14*, 95-112.

Maier, F.H. (1998). New product diffusion models in innovation management—A system dynamics perspective. *System Dynamics Review, 14*(4), 285-308.

Meadows, D.H., Meadows, D.L., Randers, J., & Behrens III, W.W. (1972). *The Limits to Growth: A Report for the Club of Rome's Project on the Predicament of Mankind.* New York: Universe Books.

Meadows, D. L., Behrens III, W.W., Meadows, D.H., Naill, R.F., Randers, J., & Zahn, E.K.O. (1974). *Dynamics of Growth in a Finite World.* Cambridge, MA: Productivity Press.

Powell, J. H. & Bradford, J. P. (2000). Targeting intelligence gathering in a dynamic competitive environment. *International Journal of Information Management, 20*(3), 181-195.

Powersim. Retrieved from: http://www.powersim.com.

Prescott, J.E. & Fleisher, C.S. (1991). SCIP: Who we are, what we do. *Competitive Intelligence Review, 2*(11), 22-26.

Repenning, N. (2002). A simulation-based approach to understanding the dynamics of innovation implementation. *Organization Science, 13*(2), 109-127.

Richardson, G.P. & Pugh III, A.L. (1981). *Introduction to System Dynamics Modeling with DYNAMO.* Cambridge, MA: Productivity Press.

Roberts, N., Andersen, D.F., Deal, R., Garet, M., & Schaffer, W. (1983). *Introduction to Computer Simulation: A System Dynamics Modeling Approach.* Reading, MA.

Robson, W. (1994). *Strategic Management and Information Systems.* London: Pitman.

Rockart, J.F. (1979). Chief executives define their own data needs. *Harvard Business Review,* (March-April), 81-93.

Rouwette, E.A.J.A., Vennix, J., & Thijssen, C. (2000). Group model building. A decision room approach. *Simulation & Gaming, 31*(3), 359-479.

Sammon, W.L. (1986). Assessing the competition: Business intelligence for strategic management. In J.R. Gardner, R. Rachlin, & H.W. Sweeney (Eds.), *Handbook of Strategic Planning.* New York: John Wiley & Sons.

Sterman, J.D. (1986). The economic long wave: Theory and evidence. *System Dynamics Review, 2*(2), 87-125.

Sterman, J.D. (1994). Learning in and about complex systems. *System Dynamics Review,* 10 (2-3), 291-330.

Sterman, J.D. (2000). *Business Dynamics: Systems Thinking and Modeling for a Complex World.* Boston, MA: Irwin McGraw-Hill.

Tessun, F. (1997). Scenario analysis and early warning systems at Daimler-Benz Aerospace. *Competitive Intelligence Review, 15*(3), 139-145.

Tyson, K.W.M. (1997). *Competition in the 21st Century.* Delray Beach: St. Lucie Press.

Vennix, J.A.M. (1996). *Group Model Building: Facilitating Team Learning Using System Dynamics.* UK: John Wiley & Sons.

Vennix, J.A.M., Andersen, D.F., & Richardson, G.P. (eds.). (1997). Special issue: Group model building. *System Dynamic Review, 13*(2).

Vensim. Ventana Systems Inc. Retrieved from: http://www.vensim.com/.

Vriens, D. & Philips, E.A. (1999). Business intelligence als strategisch informatieproces. In E.A. Philips & D. Vriens (Eds.), *Business Intelligence.* Deventer: Kluwer.

Chapter VII

A Framework for Business Performance Management

Marco van der Kooij
Hyperion Solutions, The Netherlands

ABSTRACT

To manage their performance in a dynamic and complex environment, organizations need forward-looking intelligence. Forward-looking intelligence is the ability to make reliable predictions about where the business is going to and what is driving the business. To produce forward-looking intelligence, an organization should have an insight into its business drivers, an adequate management process, and skilled people able to collaborate and share knowledge. To support the production of forward-looking intelligence, the role of information technology is crucial. However, the existing decision-support infrastructures in companies often fail to support this production. In this chapter, a framework is presented that can be used to structure and organize the production of forward-looking intelligence. This framework also serves as a background for the evaluation and implementation of a supportive ICT infrastructure.

INTRODUCTION

What do airliners and companies in the food industry have in common? An abrupt crisis (9/11 and the BSE crisis) in their respective industries forced them to change their strategy dramatically. For instance, the beef sales of Dutch company Royal Wessanen suddenly decreased to zero in Germany due to the BSE crisis and the media attention about this crisis[1]. Another recent crisis—the Enron and WorldCom affair - taught us that integrity, transparency in financial figures and accountability for these figures by top management is vital. As a result of this affair, the creditability of many companies was and still is at stake. Relevant questions are whether organizations could have foreseen such crises and how they should deal with them. The ability of organizations to anticipate events and developments in their business environment and to deal with these events is the main topic of this chapter.

When business volatility increases and market conditions become more aggressive and stakeholders more demanding, organizations should optimize their resources efficiently to meet changing goals and gain or maintain competitive advantage. To do this, relevant information about the business processes and the environment is imperative. Suppose a product manager of mobile phones is introducing a new range of mobile phones that should bring his/her company back into a market-leading role within six months. In order to provide a reliable estimate about the number of phones sold and their revenue, a lot of information is required. How much of the current range of phones has been sold and during which conditions, to whom and when? What is the estimated delivery time? What is in stock and what needs to be produced? Does this have an impact on the production and introduction of the new range? What is the impact of marketing activities for the current and new product range? What is the competition doing? What is the impact of the competitor's activities? What is the impact of introducing the new product range earlier or later? To make the right decisions, forward-looking intelligence is required. Forward-looking intelligence is the ability to make reliable predictions about where the business is going to and what is driving the business. Forward-looking intelligence entails having an insight into business drivers, a management process and skilled people able to collaborate and share knowledge with the systems and organization to support this.

The existing decision-support infrastructures in companies often inhibit, rather than enable, an organization from producing forward-looking intelligence. The underlying systems are departmental in scope, focus on single business functions, fail to integrate in any meaningful business sense, lack process support and are expensive to maintain and modify. In my daily practice I have noticed that the financial consolidation process is used to collect data from the last quarter for financial and management reporting about the past, with a forecast that has a limited outlook to the future. The data from the consolidation process are of limited use in anticipating the future. These figures are meant for the statutory and financial reporting for some internal and external stakeholders. These figures explain too little about what is really going on in the business itself. Therefore, a forecast is needed, but the currently used forecasting method consists of a limited set of metrics which only grasp at the developments in sales and expenses for the remainder of the year or, if you are lucky, some quarters ahead in a rolling forecast. Just like the yearly exercise of putting a budget together, the value of this forecast is limited, as it is often completed only by the financial department and not by the people who are involved in the business on a day-to-day basis such as account, product and production managers.

Over the last couple of years many companies have invested a lot of money in enterprise resource planning (ERP), supply chain management (SCM) and customer relationship management (CRM) systems to improve operational processes. However, many systems did not meet expectations and some even failed. Next, data warehouses were built to collect data from all these operational systems in order to use the data for management information. Most data warehouses are either not able or not designed to deliver forward-looking intelligence to managers. Information technology (IT) is a core component to produce forward-looking intelligence and to support collaboration between people. The important role of IT is extensively described in this chapter.

To plan and control their organization, managers need timely, accurate and relevant intelligence. To obtain this intelligence, the following questions should be answered:

1. What are the "business drivers" and how well does the organization perform based on these drivers?
2. What are the most important uniform metrics to measure the performance of the company?
3. What does the management process look like for the entire organization?
4. How do people collaborate across all functional areas in the organization and/or outside the organization whenever necessary?

5.   Which intelligence systems are used to support the management process and collaboration?
6.   Who is responsible for and how is the support of the management process and systems arranged?

These questions enable organizations to manage their business performance. In this chapter each question is described in a separate paragraph. There is also a separate paragraph with guidelines for their practical implementation. This chapter can also be used as a checklist for business performance management and intelligence projects, as the most important aspects are described for initiating and implementing these types of projects.

BUSINESS DRIVERS

Southwest Airlines is the only airliner in the United States making a profit since 9/11. How is this possible? The reason for this is that Southwest Airlines knows exactly what the drivers in its industry are and knows what to do to remain profitable. For instance, the company knows exactly what the utilization is of each route by type of aircraft; which routes by type of aircraft are making or losing money; what the most important cost components are; what its customers' preferred service level is; what the level of customer satisfaction is, etc. The company also compares this information to the industry in general and its main competitors. Based on assumptions about developments in flight behavior and the number of passengers, Southwest Airlines was able to create reliable scenarios and predictions. These scenarios prompted immediate action to terminate routes, to decide which type of aircraft should be used to control expenses for a certain route and to determine what the effect of these actions is to the profitability of the company. Another reason why Southwest Airlines outperforms its competitors is that it was able to test assumptions, identify bottlenecks and constraints and to solve these using different "what-if" scenarios better than the competition.

An example of a business driver for a company developing and selling software is license revenue. Based on this driver, the company can evaluate its performance compared to the market. License revenue also drives revenues from services to implement the software and maintenance fees for support to assure future investments in development. License revenue is also relevant for the evaluation conducted by shareholders, business partners and (potential) customers to judge whether it's worthwhile investing in this company. Together with the metric days sales outstanding, the business driver license revenue is

may vary. For example, the budget is submitted bottom-up by a departmental manager based on top-down targets. Some of the costs such as the total IT costs are allocated to departments based on the number of computers in that department. The forecast is entered and modified over time by account, product or production managers based on their ongoing foresight in the business. Moreover, the budget data can be very specific for each product by customer, while the forecast is entered by customer group and product type. These differences set the requirements for the intelligence systems to use.

There are different methods to get the most important metrics, for example, with the help of a computerized brainstorm. With this method, different people can brainstorm anonymously using computers. Following this, the metrics are categorized into groups and duplicates are eliminated. Next, they can complete the information matrix together. The selection of the uniform metrics used in the corporation may consist of a combination of different methods used; for example, value-based management, balanced scorecard or activity-based management (Geishecker, 2002). The use of these methods for the company's strategy is described in the paragraph *Intelligence Systems*.

To satisfy managers' constant need for intelligence, the information matrix can be used. It enables the definition of a set of uniform and common metrics and supports their utilization to measure the performance of the company over time. However, for this purpose, it is vital to keep the information matrix updated. The use of and the responsibility for the information matrix should be incorporated into the organization. This will be described in the paragraph *Responsibility* of this chapter.

THE MANAGEMENT PROCESS

At any level in the organization—top-management, departments or teams—management processes are essentially the same, no matter what aspect of the organization is being addressed. Management can be seen as a cycle consisting of six sub-processes (see Figure 1) (Hyperion, 2002). This cycle is not necessarily unidirectional, since interaction and collaboration are required at every step of the process to ensure success. Common, consistent information (the "shared information" hub in the middle) is required to ensure that all decision makers are working with the same information. The six fundamental processes are:

Goal-setting: defining and confirming the criteria and measures for successful performance of the management process that bring together long-term business strategies and day-to-day business operations.

Modeling: identifying the business drivers and determining the relationship between drivers and predicted results.

Planning: establishing a set of actions or targets that are designed to meet the business goals.

Monitoring: acquiring and normalizing internal results, key performance indicators and external influencing factors (e.g., market or economic events), triggering alerts and responding to exceptions at any given point in time.

Analysis: gaining insight from results and variations in predicted outcomes and using this information to improve the process.

Reporting: providing information in an expected, predefined format.

It is critical that this approach of the business management process is fully supported by the intelligence systems, as described in that paragraph. It is important that realistic goals and objectives are set and that business models are used to test different scenarios and to validate plans. As plans are executed, it's necessary to constantly monitor the progress and not just the outcomes. If there are variances in the metrics used to measure performance, plans need to be adjusted to ensure that goals are met. End results need to be analyzed and compared to the original goals to discover deviations and variances. All information can be used to explain the reported results and to adjust models for future success. By using this approach, continuous business improvements can be applied to an organization. For example, based on the strategic target of 10% growth in license revenue, the marketing department has a goal for the number of leads to provide to the sales department. Based on the assumptions and constraints (budget, employees, etc.) modeling is conducted to determine how many campaigns by which media can be executed and what the potential results will be. After that, the best and most likely scenario is transformed into an operational plan. The outcome of the plan is monitored against the actual results. If differences are detected, they are analyzed to find out their causes and these are reported in order to make adjustments and improvements.

In the financial domain this process is known as the planning and control cycle (Mintzberg, 1994). Here it is called the management process, as this cycle applies to every manager in the entire organization. Managers secure the control aspect (monitor, analyze and report) through procedures and systems with internal checks from the financial domain and external checks from the

Figure 1. Management Process

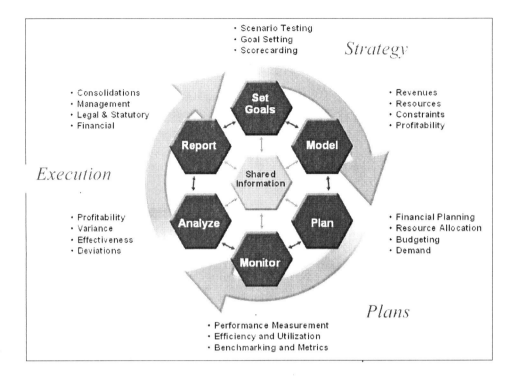

auditor. The planning function is gaining importance, as previously mentioned, with the rolling forecast. Operational managers, who are close to the business, complete the rolling forecast. In this way, a more frequent and reliable picture of what is going on in the business and the company's own position in the marketplace can be provided. A change is expected from the annual budgeting process to a monthly or even more frequent rolling forecast process. Eventually, the creation and completion of the budget will be obsolete and completely replaced by the strategic planning process and the rolling forecast.

The need for an increase in speed within the management process is an additional issue. The entire management process needs to be performed faster, especially when certain events happen and thus render the current budget and forecast irrelevant. Corrective actions must be taken quickly to avoid the company from being outperformed by the competition. This means that the planning function should be closer to the business and outside the financial domain where it often is today. The financial domain facilitates the planning process with models and systems, at most.

COLLABORATION FOR ALIGNMENT

The definition, testing and translation of strategic goals into daily operations usually start with mid-term planning for several years. In today's business environment, looking forward several years is hardly possible, with the exception of scenario analyses (Vijverberg, 1993), and has even been mentioned in press releases detailing the financial results of various companies. Moreover, increasing numbers of managers are becoming involved in the whole process at the same level and also in other levels of the organization (see Figure 2). In the planning process the output of the operational plan from one unit is the strategic plan for another unit. The same applies for control. The reporting from one unit is part of the monitoring of another. Information must be shared in the whole process and between processes to anticipate and take actions whenever events happen. This means that the process must be faster, more iterative and more interactive to ensure better collaboration between managers. The targets of the sales department mean that marketing has to supply them with enough leads. When this doesn't happen, the sales department needs to act in order to still realize its sales target. The sooner the sales department knows something is not going as planned, the faster it can act accordingly.

Shared information for collaboration is the reason why the use of uniform definitions for metrics is essential; for example, what is the definition of a lead and do sales and marketing use the same definition. Otherwise it is very difficult to share information and experiences. Subsequently, process management is also important. When hundreds or thousands of managers are involved in the rolling forecast and managers depend on the outcome of another unit, then the workflow of the process must be supported and managed. This sets requirements for the systems used.

Any business manager has five fundamental responsibilities which make up the management environment:
- Strategy setting and leadership (goals, targets, direction);
- Finances (budgets, expenses, capital requests);
- The people who make up a business (teams, business units);
- Products and services that are provided to customers;
- Customers.

The top management (leaders) of the company establishes the goals and objectives. Divisional and local management teams need to work together to make sure those goals and objectives are realistic and obtainable. Enterprise-wide collaboration is required to optimize all aspects of the business for

Figure 2. Collaboration is Essential

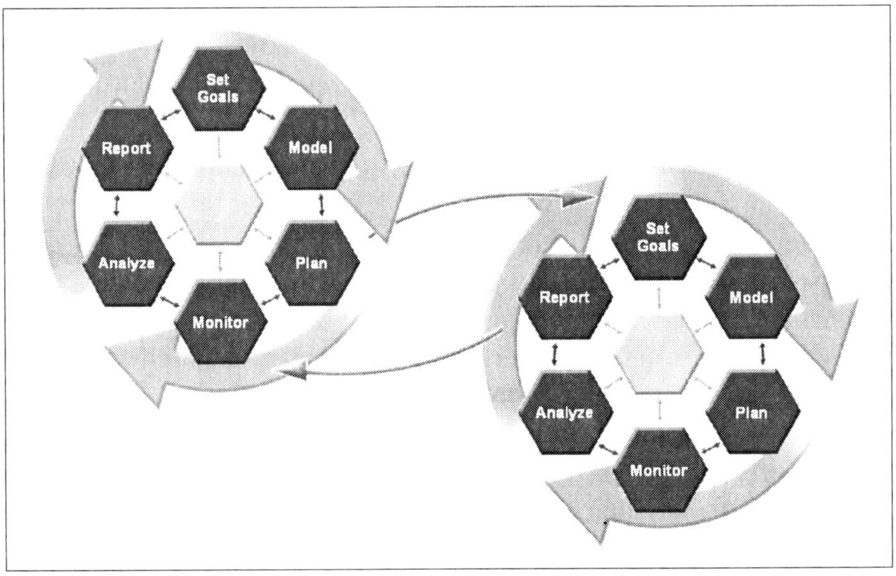

success. This means that managers must work across domains and alignment is essential, both between domains and from top to bottom and vice versa (see Figure 3). For instance, the sales forecast from the commercial domain determines the demand planning for production in the production domain. Consequently, the production determines headcount planning and/or recruitment and the budget for hiring new employees or investments in equipment when the workload becomes too high. Obtaining insight into business issues across domains sets requirements for the systems used and for the use of uniform definitions of common metrics (Oakland, 1993).

INTELLIGENCE SYSTEMS

Information technology plays a very important role in today's business and in managing the business. The first part of this section describes the developments in IT for supporting the management process. In the second part, the components of a framework for business performance management are described.

As shown in Figure 3, applications in the management environment use data coming from operational systems: These systems are used to store transactions such as sales orders, flight reservations, payments, etc. In many

Figure 3.   Collaboration Supports Management Responsibility and Alignment

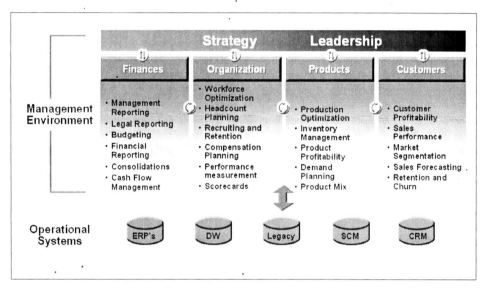

companies these transactions are also stored in a data warehouse to be used by managers to make informed decisions and set actions. Often external data about market shares, competitors, the weather, etc., are added. Managers need this information to do a better job, achieve unprecedented, better results and to surpass the competition (Porter, 1985).

Business changes every day. Managers need information to anticipate changes no matter where this information comes from, as long as it is reliable. This information must support the management process and collaboration (Vijverberg, 1993). Today, in many companies, data are stored in separate systems for each domain or even in totally different and unintegrated applications in a specific domain. Spreadsheets and PowerPoint presentations are also widely used to store strategic information used in the management process. This software is not designed to assure uniformity in metrics (formulas can easily be changed) or to be used simultaneously with other users. When data warehouses and/or OLAP tools (OnLine Analytical Processing) are used, these systems are often only used in a specific domain or in a certain unit, consisting of historic data to report and analyze what happened. Companies such as Southwest Airlines and Royal Wessanen are transforming from business intelligence to business performance management. Business performance management[2] describes the methods, metrics, processes and systems used in organizations to translate strategies into plans, monitor execution, and provide insight to improve financial

Figure 4. The Evolution to Business Performance Management

and operational performance. It represents the strategic, integrated evolution of business intelligence (BI) to support the management process. To support management decisions there must be (see Figure 4):

- A proactive approach to decision-making;
- Collaboration between peers;
- The use of information to support management decisions;
- General use for all decisions;
- An enterprise-wide approach for managing a business;
- A unified approach to the business and its information.

Business performance management is beyond historical data delivery; it is about managing the business with information. It automates and supports the workflow and decision-making involved in management. This is marrying intelligence and the management process in order to measure performance and drive profitability. The goal of business performance management is to drive business performance by supporting organizational goals to:

- Identify and exploit opportunities for investment, growth and profitability;
- Optimize deployment of organizational resources for maximum impact on the bottom line;
- Simplify the execution challenges of organizational strategy.

This means that a question such as: "How to increase profitability by 10% every year?" has huge consequences for almost every manager's business. The impact of such a question is enormous. Answers to such questions do not come from operational systems or data warehouses. To fulfill managers' ever-changing demand for information, requirements are set for the intelligence systems to be used.

As mentioned earlier, requirements are set for the intelligence systems to be used. These requirements are determined by the use of forward-looking intelligence based on uniform metrics in order to fulfill the ever-changing demand for management information, to have access to data and information no matter where it comes from, to provide all stakeholders such as customers, suppliers and partners with access to required areas of the system, to support the management process with workflow and to support and manage the collaboration between people. The net result of this is to stay ahead of the competition in a very dynamic market. To achieve this, a business performance management framework must be in place to support strategic and operational decision-making (see Figure 5).

How can systems help to dominate the business instead of being dominated by others in the marketplace and to understand what really drives the business? Also, how can they help test scenarios based on trends and business drivers in order to be prepared and to adjust the company's strategy when

Figure 5. Framework for Business Performance Management

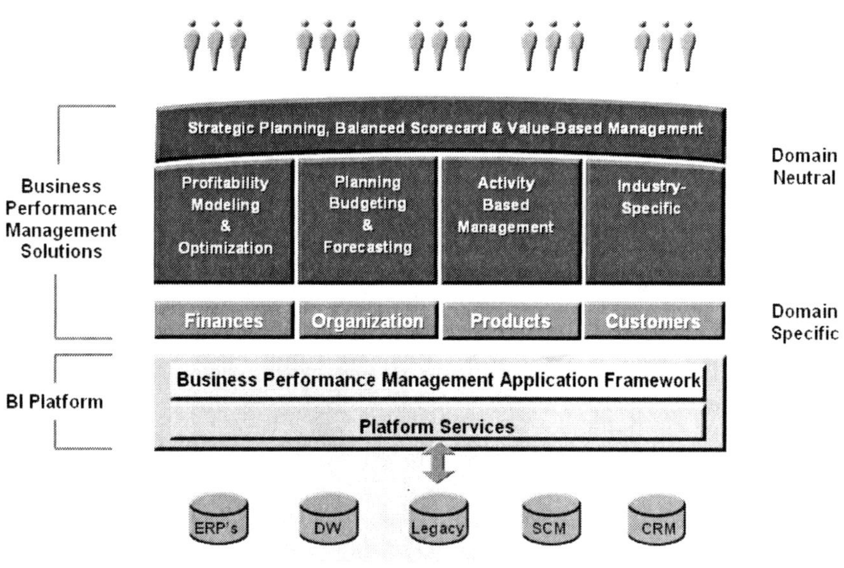

unexpected events happen? As previously stated, it all starts with the need for forward-looking intelligence. This intelligence is not available in operational systems and data warehouses. That explains the need for an additional business intelligence platform (BI platform), in which values are calculated based on assumptions, bottlenecks, constraints and the collective experience available in present and historic data.

The business performance management framework consists of different layers and these are described below.

Platform Services

These consist of a number of components for the integration of data from operational systems, the administration of users, applications (dimensions and metrics), distribution of information and enterprise-wide collaboration of the company's internal and external users. In brief, this is the technical fundament of the platform. The most important services are explained below.

Interoperability Services

Interoperability services are the most critical part of the framework in order to apply business performance management enterprise-wide. These services enable the collaboration between the different applications used for the sharing and mapping of uniform definitions (metadata). They offer version control: who changed what, when and why? Furthermore, these services enable the promotion of changes to applications from development to testing and production.

Applications do not have to be from the same supplier for collaboration to work between them. Open standards, such as XML (eXtended Markup Language), XMLA (for Analysis) and XBRL[3] (eXtensible Business Reporting Language) are used to exchange metadata and data. Therefore, it is important that the applications can support these open standards to ensure the use of uniform definitions, metrics and information enterprise-wide.

Analytic Services

This component deals with the analytic power and the applied technique to offer an enterprise-wide scalable solution. Analytic power is required for calculations and business rules to calculate the derived values used as management information, which is not available in operational systems; for instance, derived values such as market shares for individual products or services by group of customers, profitability by customer and product or complex statistical calculations for scenario testing. Therefore, it is essential to enter assumptions into the BI platform to calculate results quickly. To have write-back capabilities to the BI platform is also important for the rolling forecast. The rolling forecast is often entered on a different level of detail than the data in the operational systems or for top-down targets, or other amounts are allocated based on predefined drivers. It is even better to automatically process data from reports of industry analysts, news agencies or even competitors for a new forecast to see what the impact on the business will be, and in addition to that with proposed actions to take in different what-if scenarios with the impact of these proposed actions. In this case managers can decide very quickly about what to do and communicate with the people involved.

The applied technique is relevant for the storage of mass data. Is the data stored in the OLAP environment or can this be done in combination with relational database technology (Hybrid OLAP)? This is of great importance for analyzing millions of customers. The storage of data also has an impact on the platform to be used. Next to Windows, are Unix, Linux or a mainframe computer also viable options to store and calculate data and metadata? Is the use of multi-processors supported in order to achieve acceptable performance of complex calculations? Any failure resulting from the use of software and systems is often caused by the lack of using them. If users have to wait too long for answers to questions then they look for other ways to get answers.

Query and Reporting Services

End-users do not care where their information is coming from. They want acceptable performance and the software must be easy to use. Therefore, the use of Internet technology is crucial, as information must be disseminated worldwide in a reliable, secure way, internally in the company and also externally to stakeholders such as shareholders, customers, suppliers or business partners. In addition to all types of graphical features for presentation purposes, three things are critical to the end-user:

1.   The information must be provided proactively based on triggers such as an alert on the screen or by e-mail. Users have access to Internet or e-mail everywhere, even with their mobile phone. An example of a trigger is when net working capital increases due to the submitted forecasts and exceeds the acceptable bandwidth;

2.   The information must, preferably, be presented in a single and central place for the end-user via a so-called "portal." In this way, the developments in the manager's area of responsibility are instantly clear. From

there on, quick and easy drill-down should be performed to find the cause of the increase of net working capital. After that, actions must be taken to solve the issue before it actually occurs;

3.   Both quantitative and qualitative information must be available. When the net working capital indicator increases due to the introduction of a competitive product and damages the sales of your products, then, for example, the press release information from the competitor is also available as an explanation. The beauty of Internet technology is that different types of information are easy to present together, regardless of where the information is stored.

The information matrix can be used to determine which users need which information delivered and presented and in what way. This should be taken into consideration when disseminating the information.

Integration Services

In the case of huge amounts of data, it is common, for integration purposes, to load this data from operational systems to data warehouses and between applications automatically. When a data warehouse and an ETL tool (Extraction, Transformation and Load) are used it is an advantage to incorporate this into the BI platform. Before data is loaded into a data warehouse it is cleansed, unduplicated and validated to improve and assure the quality of the data. For example, in the case of a mobile telecommunications company all connections must be unique and all data must be associated correctly with each connection, such as personal, billing, payment and contract data. Part of this data will be used in the BI platform and domain-specific applications. This data has to be integrated easily and maintained from the source system or from a central repository. Additionally, if more detail is required in the BI platform this must be readily available to the end-user. For instance, when a number of customers withdraw and defect to the competition: what are their demographic characteristics and in what way are they the same? Action has to be taken before other customers with similar characteristics defect as well.

The openness and integration facilities of the BI platform are very important for setting up new applications. A lot of data is stored in all types of different systems, from "small" databases and spreadsheets to massive, inaccessible (proprietary) databases of ERP systems. As data from different source systems becomes easier to load automatically, the shorter the time for implementation will be and results will be shown quickly to the end-users.

Administrative Services

Maintenance of the BI platform and applications is another relevant component in order to run a complex system used worldwide. Here too, open standards are recommended, as these standards are already being used a lot in the company. The advantage of this is that knowledge is available and it is fairly easy to acquire new employees to assure continuity. Administrative services also include the workflow and control of the management process. This needs to be aligned with the current working method of the organization and not the other way around (i.e., business process redesign in the 80s and 90s in order to use certain ERP systems).

Application Framework

The application framework offers the option to develop applications based on building blocks so that rapid development is possible. These building blocks contain preprogrammed intelligence necessary for an analytic environment. In this way, developing applications from scratch is prevented and applications can be delivered on time and not when the original specifications have become obsolete. Critical business information must easily be available. Examples of applications are mentioned in Figure 4; however, some other examples are: inventory turnover analysis, route profitability, product sales analysis and employee compensation analysis. An application framework is useful for company or industry-specific applications which are not ready-made available or which require a very large investment.

On top of the application framework, different, ready-made applications are available. These can be divided into domain-specific and domain neutral applications.

Domain-Specific

There are, for every domain, applications available in the market such as the ones for financial consolidation or churn analysis. The major advantage of a domain-specific application is the ready-made availability of the accumulated knowledge and experience in it. This shortens the implementation of these applications considerably. Consequently, the danger of separate domain-specific applications is that each has its own definitions; for example, the marketing and sales departments use a different definition of net sales than the people in the finance domain. These applications must be aligned and integrated within the whole framework in order to make management decisions and to set actions. As mentioned earlier, the result of the sales forecast has an impact on the demand planning for the production process, etc.

Domain Neutral

The strategic management of the organization involves the methods used and the management process (Geishecker, 2002). Value-based management has an impact on the entire organization, as all activities must add value to the company. Companies are increasingly focused on profitability by customer and product or service. That is one of the reasons why activity-based management is also used in marketing and supply chain management. As stated earlier, the forecasting process has an impact on all managers with revenue and expenses responsibilities. The readily available, relevant information from people who are close to the business is crucial in order to act fast and stay ahead of the competition. These aspects and automating them are the responsibility of top management, so they increase transparency and their accountability for their activities to all stakeholders.

RESPONSIBILITY

Previous paragraphs have described the use of uniform metrics, a management process and the intelligence systems within a framework. To ensure that users are enabled to work with this framework a company requires organization and procedures to accommodate this. Furthermore, one person should be given ownership and responsibility for the framework. Where that role fits into the company is difficult to answer, as every company is different. From my experience at a number of multinational companies in The Netherlands I saw that the domain neutral applications were initiated and facilitated functionally by the finance domain. Employees from the IT department were available or even added for technical support. The advantage of the financial domain is its broad experience with automation of financial management information and that most applications in the management environment are financially driven. Also, a lot of the methods used, such as value-based management and balanced scorecard, originate from the financial area. The finance domain consists of an internal network within the organization, with local controllers and accountants who are accustomed to working together in the financial reporting process. However, this could not succeed without the support of the IT department. Firstly, this is because current standards (technical and procedural) applied in the organization must be used as much as possible to assure continuity. Secondly, the use of Internet technology and the related security issues is work for specialists. Thirdly, technical people are needed for the development of domain-specific applications, together with people from the domain concerned, based on the company's framework.

Ideally, a separate, organized group of people in a department should be available for the following activities:

- Control of the framework's content based on the information matrix (not to determine the content, as this is done in cooperation with the business users and senior management);
- And to translate this into improvements for current and new solutions;
- To monitor the alignment of the systems used with the management process;
- To accelerate and facilitate the use of applications;
- To take charge with new initiatives;
- To deploy and test scenarios and to conduct complex ad hoc analyses for strategic planning;
- To manage the technical realization and technical control of the BI platform and applications based on company standards;
- To monitor the quality of the metadata, data and performance of the systems used;
- To have a liaison role between business users and the IT department for the management environment.

The following rule of thumb can be applied to this department's reporting within the organization and in the following order: in a business driven commercial company, to the Marketing and Sales Director. If another domain is very important for the business, like manufacturing, and there is a collaborative environment then place it there. In a financially managed company with also a focus on management reporting it is wise to report to the Chief Financial Officer. If IT is the only department with an overview in the whole organization then place it there with a reporting line to the Chief Information Officer (Buytendijk, 2001).

GUIDELINES

From experience and research, I have discovered some useful guidelines on how to start and implement a business performance management framework. These guidelines are as follows:

1. Bring together a limited number (eight to 12) of key users of management information in a workshop and use the described management process to make the following clear:
- How well is the current process compared to the process described in the paragraph *The Management Process*?

- Which reports and analyses are used in the different steps of the management process?
- What is the content of these reports and analyses and how relevant are they? This is used to gain insight into business drivers and metrics.
- Which methods are used enterprise-wide and per domain? Check these according to relevance for business drivers and the most critical metrics.
- Which forward-looking information and metrics are missing?
- How are reports and analyses made and with which systems?
- How is information shared and how do managers collaborate?
- How are the metadata, definitions and data integrated?
- Who is responsible for which systems and which activities are associated?
- What are the company's standards for business intelligence and which of them meet the requirements for the business performance management framework?

It is important to have people participating who are able to look further than their own domain and to realize that the impact of their daily business activities also has an impact on others within the company. If participants are only focused on their own needs then a company-wide view and the creation of alignment is hardly possible. It is advisable to facilitate this workshop with experts in order to prevent people from going into too much detail. By staying focused on the main topics the company's current position becomes clear very quickly. Document this carefully and use this document to find a sponsor from top management: someone who believes in forward-looking intelligence and wants to be able to respond faster in case of events (and feels that this is lacking). This step is also necessary for financing the program and supporting an enterprise-wide implementation.

2. Determine the ultimate goal of the program and then determine the gap with the current situation from Step 1. Construct, with the help of experienced people, the roadmap to execute the program. Divide the program into separately manageable projects and prioritize based on the biggest problems in the organization. For instance, by missing the forecast due to myopia, insufficient insight into the company's own market position and market trends, a lot of companies are afraid to make announcements regarding future results. Therefore, companies themselves do not know how to proceed and are punished by the stock market. This causes problems for financing future growth to sustain or improve their competitive positioning.

3. Ensure the provision of quick and visible results. Start with the 10 to 15 most important metrics for the company. Make sure that the source data is available and use cleansed data so there is no doubt about the quality of the data. Present the metrics to a larger group of key users with a professional tool. Then broaden the scope by number of metrics, end-users and further into all domains. Make use of external experts wherever necessary to acquire knowledge and experience for future projects. I was the external expert for a company due to the people in the company having hardly any experience with a BI platform and business performance management applications. By using a framework and a roadmap it was clear for them (business users, IT department and the external software implementation partner) on how to proceed step-by-step with minimal risks.

4. Have guts and perseverance. The management process is more flexible than the primary process. It is a challenge to support the management process with systems. Operational systems are strict because of the unambiguous primary process, whereas intelligence systems must be very flexible. It is unknown, beforehand, to which questions answers must be given. Use this as a fact when exploring the management process, developing applications and implementing systems. The support of the IT department is key for the technical infrastructure of the framework. The more the framework fits into the current standards and procedures of the IT department the better it is. Nevertheless, flexibility from the IT department is also important because the needs of managers change every day. It is better to be equipped for that than to fight change every day. So make sure that the IT department is aligned as well.

5. Establish a separate department within the organization to secure the maintenance and the use of the framework, as stated in the previous paragraph *Responsibility*.

CONCLUSION

How bright is an organization in anticipating and specifically responding to events which have an immediate impact on profitability and competitive positioning? In this chapter, an approach to this issue is formulated: a business performance management framework. This framework contains methods to derive real insight into the business (drivers) and to get a grip on giant and complex organizations by means of a specific management process. In this process, it is imperative to use uniformly defined metrics and IT systems to supply forward-looking intelligence so people can collaborate for the success of the company. It is essential to root this firmly within the organization in terms of people and procedures to assure alignment and to gain and maintain the required knowledge. There are guidelines provided to start and implement a business performance management framework. With these guidelines, it is possible to start smart and provide results.

REFERENCES

Buytendijk, F. (2001). Research note: SPA-13-8990, Gartner Research.

Geishecker, L. (2002). Research note: COM-18-3797, Gartner Research.

Hyperion Solutions. (2002). *Business Performance Management – Master Deck*.

Mintzberg, H. (1994). *The Rise and Fall of Strategic Planning*. New York: Prentice Hall.

Oakland, J. S. (1993). *Total Quality Management: The Route to Improving Performance*. Oxford: Buttersworth Heinemann.

Porter, M. (1985). *Competitive Advantage*. New York: The Free Press.

Vijverberg, A.M.M. et al. (1993). *Toekomstverkenning in organisaties*. Heerlen: Open Universiteit.

ENDNOTES

[1]   Mr. K. Kramer (2002), CFO Royal Wessanen NV at the Dutch Hyperion user conference.

[2]   Industry analysts are using similar definitions in the same context, e.g., Corporate performance management is the umbrella term that describes the methods, metrics, processes and systems used to monitor and manage business performance from Gartner.

[3]   XBRL is a XML extension and provides a common platform for critical business reporting processes and improves the reliability and ease of communicating financial data among users internal and external to the reporting enterprise (see www.xbrl.org).

Chapter VIII

The Source Map: A Means to Support Collection Activities

Dirk Vriens
University of Nijmegen, The Netherlands

Jan Achterbergh
University of Nijmegen, The Netherlands

ABSTRACT

In the collection stage of the intelligence cycle, one has to determine relevant sources, access them and retrieve data from them. For each data class, many possible sources are available and determining the right ones is often difficult. Moreover, accessing sources and retrieving data may require a lot of effort. In this chapter, we present a tool for supporting the effective and efficient use of sources—the "source map." In essence, a source map links data classes to sources and contains meta data about these links. These meta data indicate the adequacy of sources in terms of ease of access, ease of retrieval, and usefulness of the retrieved data. A source map can support the selection of appropriate sources (given a required data class), and it can support the assessment of the overall adequacy of available sources.

INTRODUCTION

Searching and retrieving data about the environment is an important activity in the intelligence process. This activity—as part of the intelligence cycle—is usually called the "collection stage" (cf., Herring, 1992; Kahaner, 1997; Bernhardt, 1994; Sammon, 1994; Gilad & Gilad, 1988). The collection stage is considered to be the most time-consuming stage (e.g., Chen et al., 2002) and if it is not performed carefully, many difficulties may arise (e.g., too much time spent on search; collection stage leads to irrelevant data; information overload) (cf., for example, Cook & Cook, 2000; Chen et al., 2002; Vriens & Philips, 1999). For successfully carrying out collection activities, knowledge about which sources contain what kind of data, and knowledge about how to approach sources (meta-knowledge regarding the collection of data) would be very helpful. This chapter presents a tool to structure and deal with this metadata: the source map.

An essential question in the collection phase is where to find the requested data both effectively and efficiently. To answer this question, one has to:

1.   identify possible sources;
2.   judge the value of the source (in terms of different criteria, e.g., does it contain relevant data? What are the costs of employing this source? Is it reliable?, etc.);
3.   use the value-judgments to select the appropriate sources.

Many authors discuss Step 1 by pointing to a variety of available sources (cf., Fuld, 1995; Kahaner, 1997; Sammon, 1984). Typical sources include the Internet, online databases, sales representatives, internal or external experts, CEOs, journals, tradeshows, conferences, embassies, etc.

The literature treats the valuation step more implicitly. Most of the time, it discusses distinctions regarding sources, such as open vs. closed sources, internal vs. external sources, or primary vs. secondary sources (see Kahaner, 1997, for a review). These distinctions implicitly refer to different criteria used in the valuation of sources. The distinction open vs. closed sources implicitly refers, for instance, to criteria such as "ease in collection" or "relevance." The distinction primary vs. secondary sources implicitly refers to the criterion "reliability of the data." In our view, it is possible to value sources more precisely when the valuation criteria are stated explicitly and not implicitly in the form of these distinctions.

The selection step is even more elusive in literature (and practice). This step integrates the value-judgments to select a list of appropriate sources for collecting the required data. However, besides, perhaps, traditional decision techniques, few methods seem to be designed for source selection.

In this chapter we propose a tool to structure and support the valuation and selection of sources as part of the collection phase—the "source map." This tool builds on the work of Fuld (1995) on "intelligence maps" and of other authors on "knowledge maps" (e.g., Davenport & Prusak, 1998). The main purpose of the source map is to help in pinning down the appropriate sources quickly. In addition, it can be used for detecting and repairing weaknesses in the available sources.

WHAT IS A SOURCE MAP?

A source map links data (or classes of data) to sources in such a way that the (most) appropriate sources are selected for the collection of the requested data. Table 1 gives the general format of such a map. It facilitates determining what sources to employ to deliver particular data. For instance, data class 1 may stand for "products under development by competitor X" and the column associated with this data class indicates what sources may contain data about it; for instance, a patent-database, economic journals, the Internet site of competitor X, or a scientific conference regarding the technology to make the product.

The map we propose to link sources to data classes is similar to a "knowledge map" (cf., Davenport & Prusak, 1998, pp. 68-88). A knowledge map, however, connects required knowledge to knowledge sources, while a source map links required data classes to data sources.

Table 1. The Source Map Links Data Classes to Sources

		Data classes			
		Data class 1	Data class 2	...	Data class n
Sources	Internet				
	Sales rep's				
	Databases				
	Consultants				
	Experts				
	...				

In this chapter, we treat the source map as a tool for supporting and structuring collection activities, the second phase in the intelligence cycle. We thereby assume that the data (classes) are already defined in the direction phase (the first phase of the cycle).

To determine what sources are (most) appropriate, the source map needs to contain information about criteria for appropriateness and their valuation. The cells in the source map should contain this information. To get this information, it should be clear (1) what the relevant criteria are, (2) how they can be given a value, and (3) how to integrate them into an overall judgment of the appropriateness of the sources. The next two sections deal with these issues.

CRITERIA AND SCORES FOR JUDGING SOURCES

The criteria for assessing the appropriateness of sources link up with the three activities required to deal with sources. These activities are:

1. Accessing the source. Accessing means determining the exact location and approaching the source to prepare retrieval.
2. Retrieving (in interaction with the source) the data from the source.
3. Using the retrieved data in further processing (i.e., for the production of intelligence).

Referring to these activities, the appropriateness of sources depends on four dimensions: (1) ease of access, (2) ease of retrieval, (3) usefulness of the content of the retrieved data and processing ease, and (4) cost-effectiveness. Below, we discuss criteria in these dimensions.

Criteria for Access and Retrieval

To assess the appropriateness of sources regarding access and retrieval, "barriers in employing a source" can function as criteria (cf., Fuld, 1995; Davenport & Prusak, 1998). Below, we present a list of the most relevant barriers. In this list, we also indicate whether the barrier applies to access, retrieval or both.

*   A language barrier. Fuld (1995, p. 203) calls language a major barrier in dealing with (mainly international) intelligence. This is a barrier for access and retrieval.

- A cultural barrier. For instance, Hofstede (1991) points to several dimensions on which cultures differ. When source and collector score differently on these dimensions, it may be more difficult to access the source and interact with it. Not noting a difference in score on Hofstede's dimension "power-distance" (with sources on the high-end of the scale) may lead to problems in approaching the source (e.g., if it is not approached in a manner that is associated to its status—when a title is not used, when a surname is used too quickly, etc.).

Davenport and Prusak point to cultural frictions in transferring knowledge (1998, p. 96 ff.). Lack of trust, different frames of reference, and lack of motivation to cooperate are among these frictions. Although Davenport and Prusak associate these frictions with sharing knowledge, they may also hold for interaction with sources in access as well as retrieval. The cultural barrier applies to access and retrieval.

- An institutional barrier. In some (bureaucratic) organizations, it may be very hard to locate and approach certain people and documents. This barrier mainly applies to accessing the source.
- A personal barrier. Personal characteristics can make it difficult to approach and interact with someone. This barrier applies to both access and retrieval.
- A geographical barrier. Some sources need to be dealt with on location (e.g., a conference, trade-show or even some persons). This can add to the cost of accessing the source. This barrier applies to accessing the source.
- A "technological" barrier. Accessing some sources and retrieving data from them may sometimes be possible only by means of specific information and communications technology requiring specific knowledge or skills. This barrier applies to both access and retrieval.
- A "fee" barrier. For accessing some sources and for retrieving data from them, sometimes a fee is charged.
- A "time" barrier. For some sources, the response time may be very slow—both in access and in retrieval.
- A "clarity" barrier. This barrier refers to the effort one has to take to make sense of the data from the source. Factors that increase this barrier are the use of specific jargon and the lack of (requested) structure in the data. This mainly applies to retrieval.
- A "stability" barrier. This barrier refers to the stability of access to the source (some sources may cease to exist, some are not available at the

expected moment, and others may decide to stop providing their services, etc.). This barrier refers to accessing the source.

Note that this list of barriers is not exhaustive. Rather, it is best seen as an offset for listing the barriers that are relevant in the specific search activities of a particular company.

In the beginning of this section, we referred to the costs of using sources as a separate dimension for judging their appropriateness. The above criteria can be used to express these costs. However, we prefer to deal with the criteria as given instead of using cost estimates that may be derived from them, because (1) it is difficult to translate the criteria into costs and (2) if only cost estimates are used, one loses information about the appropriateness of sources.

To use a barrier as a criterion to assess the appropriateness it can be scored on a five-point Likert scale—where 1 means "very problematic" and 5 means "non-existent."

Criteria for the Use of Data

There are four criteria for assessing the appropriateness of sources regarding the use of the data for the production of intelligence. One of them is a processing criterion and three of them are content criteria.

The processing criterion refers to the ease of processing. This can be determined by the format in which the data are delivered, i.e., does the source deliver the data in a format that can be used directly for the purposes of the collector or does it need reformatting? One may score this criterion on a five-point scale ranging from 1 ("much reformatting needed") to 5 ("right format").

The content criteria are completeness, reliability and timeliness (cf., O'Brien, 1998, for a summary of these criteria). When applied to the value of sources, these criteria mean the following:

- Completeness: the source can deliver all the data required to gain insight into the dataclass for which the source is used. This can, for instance, be measured in terms of the number of times the source was unable to deliver the requested data, and/or the number of aspects of a dataclass for which the source could not provide data.
- Reliability: This refers to the reliability of the data from the source. It can be measured, for instance, in terms of the number of times the data from the source proved to be incorrect.
- Timeliness: the data from the source is up to date. It can be measured in terms of the number of times that the source delivered obsolete data.

In literature, one often finds relevance as an additional criterion to assess the content of data. Relevance then refers to the suitability of the data in gaining insight into the dataclass for which the source was used. However, relevance can be adequately expressed in terms of completeness, reliability and timeliness. Completeness links the data provided by a source to the required data defined by the data class. Given the completeness, the data should further be correct and up to date to be relevant. Relevance, therefore, can be treated as an over-arching concept, referring to the other three content criteria.

The content criteria can, again, be scored on a five-point scale, where 1 means very incomplete, very unreliable, and very obsolete, respectively, and 5 means very reliable, very complete and very timely.

Content of Source Map Cells

The criteria for the appropriateness of sources and their scores should be put in the source map. To this end, each cell in a source map contains the following information (see Figure 1):

1. General information about the source, consisting of the name of the source, the data carrier (human, data or electronic) and (if known) the exact or default location;
2. Scores on the criteria for access, retrieval, content and processing of the (data from the) source;
3. Information about what data could not be delivered if the source was incomplete. This is useful for analyzing the appropriateness of the sources (see next section);
4. Remarks concerning one of the above aspects.

USING THE SOURCE MAP

Once a source map is built—i.e., when it is clear what sources are available, and when the scores of these sources for the criteria discussed in the previous section are given, the source map is ready for use. A source map allows for two different uses; first, to find appropriate sources for a particular data class, and second, to assess the overall adequacy of the sources. For both types of use, it is necessary to compare the sources. In this section, we discuss how to compare sources, and how to use this method for comparison for the two different uses.

Figure 1. Content of Cells in a Source Map (The shaded areas are not applicable.)

	Language barrier	Cultural barrier	Institut. barrier	Personal barrier	Geogr. barrier	Techno- barrier	Time barrier	Fee barrier	Clarity barrier	Stability barrier
Access	1…5									
Retrieval										

Name:
Carrier:
Location:

Content:
Completeness   1…5   If incomplete: what data could not be delivered?
Timeliness: 1…5
Reliability: 1…5

Process/format   1…5

Remarks: …

Comparing Sources

Sources can be compared using a single criterion (e.g., which source scores highest on "completeness"?). It is also possible to integrate the values of (several) individual criteria and compare these integrated scores. To integrate these values into an overall score, we propose the following procedure:

1. Define two classes of criteria: efficiency criteria and effectiveness criteria. The class of efficiency criteria consists of the access criteria, the retrieval criteria and the ease of processing criterion. The class of effectiveness criteria consists of the criteria completeness, reliability and timeliness.

2. Estimate weights for the criteria in the two classes. This leads to nine weight estimates for the access barriers, to seven weight estimates for the retrieval barriers (note: the weights of the overlapping barriers can be the same), to one estimate for the ease of processing criterion and to three weight estimates for the effectiveness criteria.

3. Compute, for each source, the overall scores for the two classes. For efficiency, we suggest taking the weighted average score for the 17 access, retrieval and ease of processing criteria. For effectiveness, too, a weighted average score (for the three criteria) is proposed. Both scores range from 1 (not efficient, not effective) to 5 (very efficient, very effective).

Figure 2. Scores of Five Sources, Regarding their Appropriateness for a Particular Data Class (See text)

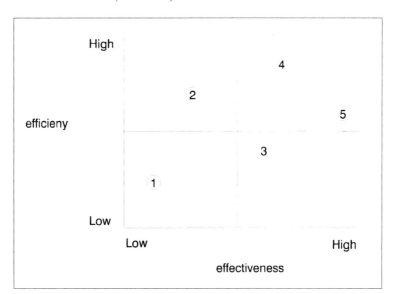

Finding Appropriate Sources

Given a data class, the most straightforward use of the map is to find out what sources are appropriate for a particular data class. In other words, every time an intelligence officer has to find particular data, (s)he can consult the source map to see what sources are available. This results in an inventory of the available sources for a particular data class.

A step beyond merely enumerating available sources is giving a judgment about the appropriateness of these sources in terms of the criteria presented in the previous section. To this end, we use the efficiency and effectiveness scores of the sources. For a particular data class, all the available sources can be plotted regarding these two scores (see Figure 2).

The figure states that source #5 scores best on effectiveness, source #4 best on efficiency and source #1 scores lowest on both classes of criteria.

Figures like the above can help in analyzing the appropriateness of a source for a particular data class. As a general heuristic for ranking the sources, we suggest that sources in the upper-right quadrant should be preferred to those in the lower-right quadrant, and these should be preferred to the ones in the upper-left quadrant. Sources in the lower-left quadrant should probably be discarded.

Sources that come up as appropriate should be checked for completeness. If they are complete, they can be added to the list with preferred sources. If they are incomplete, it is necessary to find out if there are sources that can compensate for this lack. To this end, information about what data the source is unable to deliver (available in the source map—see Figure 1) can be used. This information directs the search for an appropriate compensating source.

For sources that score high on effectiveness but low on efficiency (lower-right quadrant), it should be examined (1) whether the relevance of the data class makes the effort (and costs) worthwhile, and/or (2) whether measures can be taken to make the use of the source more efficient—e.g., efficiency of scale in gathering data (a subscription to an often used online database).

For sources that score in the left two quadrants, it can be established what exactly causes the score. Depending on the outcome of this investigation it may be decided to stop using the source.

It should be noted that overall scores of sources should be used with caution. We want to point out that it is difficult to weigh the criteria. In our experience, and according to many authors in the field of decision-making (see, for instance, Stevenson et al., 1990; Klein et al., 1993), an exact and general weighing scheme is impossible. Weights are highly dependent on specific data classes and circumstances. Even if circumstances do not change, determining a stable set of weight estimations is very time-consuming (or even impossible). Moreover, the values of the scores on the criteria are only estimations and are subject to change and interpretation. However, we feel that if one realizes these shortcomings, the scores can be used to support selecting appropriate sources.

Assessing the Adequacy of Sources

The second way of using the source map is to establish the overall adequacy of the sources. More in particular, the map may help in answering the following questions:

1. Do the sources cover all data classes? This question deals with the completeness of the available sources regarding the data classes. If columns of the source map are empty, some sources are lacking.

2. Do we have adequate sources for the required data classes? An answer to this question reveals whether the data classes are covered by appropriate sources. If some data classes only have sources that have scores in the lower-left quadrant of Figure 2, problems may arise. If a rank-order of the data classes regarding their relevance exists, one can also establish whether the most relevant data classes are covered by appropriate sources.

3.   Do we have enough different sources for the (most important) data classes? This question refers to the flexibility in collecting data. If a source is suddenly unavailable, one needs to have adequate alternatives. It is also useful to have different sources for the purpose of validating the data.

Answers to these questions help intelligence officers to identify weaknesses in the available sources and direct their efforts to repair them.

The case of a business unit of a food producing company illustrates this use of the source map. In this case, the business unit performed intelligence activities to find out in which from ten pre-selected countries it could best locate a new plant. One of the relevant data classes was the prices of raw materials (mostly vegetables) in these countries. For this data class several sources were identified, among which was the intelligence unit of the mother company. It was assumed that this unit would be the most reliable and complete source. The plan was to use other sources as a check for some of the prices. As it turned out, none of the sources could deliver data on all the requested vegetable prices. Relative to the other sources, the internal intelligence unit even scored low on completeness. Moreover, it turned out that the prices of most of the other sources were comparable. However, there was a large difference between these prices and the prices of the intelligence unit. The reason for this is that the intelligence unit used a different (and flawed) method to calculate them. The low score on "relevance" (i.e., incompleteness and unreliability) of the intelligence unit as a source for this data class could be used as an offset for an inquiry into the adequacy and competencies of the unit.

IMPLEMENTING A SOURCE MAP

To build, maintain and use a source map does not require exceptional resources. IT applications for implementing the map range from sophisticated applications to simple solutions. An example of a simple solution is an implementation of the map by means of Microsoft Excel sheets. In the case where we used Excel, both building and maintaining the map were easy. Moreover, the map, thus realized, proved to be easy in helping data collectors to find and judge appropriate sources for a particular data class. Finally, the application supported the assessment of the overall adequacy of the available sources because answers to the assessment questions were readily produced.

It is also possible to use more sophisticated, for instance, Web-based applications of the map. Making the map available via an Intranet, for instance, can enhance its use and maintenance.

In addition to these technological issues, it is important to define and allocate tasks and responsibilities regarding maintenance and use of the map. These tasks should cover checking and updating the map on a regular basis. Finally, data collectors should be motivated to use the map to define their search strategies. In our experience, data collectors see the benefits of a good map, and will be inclined to use and maintain it.

A possible drawback in implementing and using a source map is that the number of data-classes and sources may be relatively large. To tackle this problem, we recommend an "evolutionary" approach: start with a few relevant data classes and build a source map around them. Then, gradually extend the map so that it can be used for more data classes.

CONCLUSION

To produce actionable intelligence, the efficient and effective use of sources is imperative. However, up until now, little attention has been paid to supporting the selection of sources. In this paper, we deal with this omission by presenting the "source map" as a support tool. Source maps can be valuable instruments in the support of collection activities. In our view, they can aid in both the everyday use of sources and in the assessment of the overall adequacy of available sources. Implementing and maintaining a map may require some effort. However, with simple means and an evolutionary approach, functional maps can be built efficiently.

REFERENCES

Bernhardt, D.C., (1994). I want it fast, factual, actionable—Tailoring competitive intelligence to executive needs. *Long Range Planning, 27*(1), 12-24.

Chen, H., Chau, M., & Zeng, D. (2002). CI-spider: A tool for competitive intelligence on the Web. *Decision Support Systems, 34*, 1-17.

Cook, M. & Cook, C. (2000). *Competitive Intelligence*. London: Kogan Page.

Davenport, T.H. & Prusak, L., (1998). *Working Knowledge*. Boston, MA: Harvard Business School Press.

Fuld, L.M. (1995). *The New Competitor Intelligence*. New York: John Wiley & Sons.

Gilad, B. & Gilad, T. (1988). *The Business Intelligence System*. New York: Amacon.

Herring, J.P. (1992). The role of intelligence in formulating strategy. *The Journal of Business Strategy, 13*(5), 54-60.

Hofstede, G.H. (1991). *Culture and organizations—Software of the mind*. London: HarperCollins.

Kahaner, L. (1997). *Competitive Intelligence*. New York: Touchstone.

Klein, G.A., Orasanu, J., Calderwood, R., & Zsambok, C.E. (eds.). (1993). *Decision Making in Action*. Norwood: Ablex.

O'Brien, J. (1998). *Introduction to Information Systems* (2nd edition). New York: McGraw-Hill.

Sammon, W.L. (1986). Assessing the competition: Business intelligence for strategic management. In J.R. Gardner, R. Rachlin, & H.W. Sweeny (Eds.), *Handbook of Strategic Planning* (pp. 4.12-4.19). New York: John Wiley & Sons.

Stevenson, M.K., Busemeyer, J.R., & Naylor, J.C. (1990). Judgement and decision making. In M.D. Dunette & L.M. Hough (Eds.), *Handbook of Industrial and Organizational Psychology* (vol. 1, pp. 283-374). Palo Alto, CA: Consulting Psychologists Press.

Vriens, D. & Philips, E.A. (1999). Business intelligence als informatievoorziening voor de strategievorming. In E.A. Philips & D. Vriens (Eds.), *Business Intelligence*. Deventer: Kluwer.

Chapter IX

Intelligence from Space: Using Geographical Information Systems for Competitive Intelligence

Paul Hendriks
University of Nijmegen, The Netherlands

ABSTRACT

The spatial element, which is omnipresent in data and information relevant to organizations, is much underused in the decision-making processes within organizations. This applies also to decision-making within the domain of Competitive Intelligence. The chapter explores how the CI function may benefit from developing a spatial perspective on its domain and how building, exploring and using this perspective may be supported by a specific class of information systems designed to handle the spatial element in data: Geographical Information Systems (GIS). The chapter argues that the key element for linking GIS to CI involves the identification of situations in which spatial analysis may support organizational decision-making within the CI domain. It presents a three-step procedure for identifying how CI may recognize spatial decision problems that are useful to boost the operation of the CI function. The first step concerns identifying relevant spatial variables, for instance by analyzing economic, demographic or political trends as to their spatial implications. The second step involves using GIS for positioning the organization with respect to the identified variables (present and projected position). The third step amounts to drawing strategic conclusions from Step 2 by assessing how the competition in relationship with the own organization would be positioned along the identified spatial analysis lines.

INTRODUCTION

Recent surveys estimate that more than 80% of information used in businesses contains a location or geographical element, from customer addresses and business locations to trading areas and service delivery routes (Mennecke, 1997). The analysis of geographical information may support decision-making in a variety of business contexts. For instance, it may help understand the range of business applications for geographical information (customer analysis, retail store performance, competitor analysis, locational decision-making, environmental compliance, etc., see Sherwood, 1995). It may also assist in identifying the characteristics of company-specific geographical information, and realize its potential for business purposes. Better use of geographical information via geographical modeling and analysis may help improve strategic, tactical and operational business decisions (Grimshaw, 2000).

The potential benefit for business of analyzing geographical data is reflected in the potential of a specific class of information systems that have been developed to handle spatial data: Geographical Information Systems (GIS). GIS are computer systems that offer facilities to support spatial data collection (e.g., through digitizing or from satellite data), combined spatial and non-spatial—or attribute—data handling, visualization of spatial data (e.g., through mapping) and spatial data analysis (e.g., Longley, Goodchild, & Maguire, 1999a). As Grimshaw (2000) asserts, GIS—when properly selected and applied—makes "terrific business sense" for many companies because it is "an increasingly vital tool for operations and delivery of goods and services." This author recognizes that the potential of GIS to boost business productivity is finally being realized relating to the fact that over the last few years, GIS have become less expensive and easier to use.

Within the domain of business applications of GIS the link between GIS and Competitive Intelligence (CI) has not been explored in the literature. Several authors point at some of the strategic opportunities associated with GIS use (e.g., Goss, 1995; Grimshaw, 2000; Reeve & Petch, 1999). However, these authors do not develop strategy support through CI concepts. CI involves a particular and powerful perspective on strategic issues (see the introductory chapter). Developing the insight as to how CI may benefit from GIS use involves looking at GIS in a specific way. The purpose of this chapter is to develop a perspective on GIS that will help identify the potential value these systems may have for CI professionals. Building such a perspective presumes identifying the relevance of using spatial concepts and insights in the CI domain. The argument developed in the chapter is based on three building blocks: spatial concepts and the particularities of organizational decision-making based on such concepts, facilities of GIS for supporting spatial decision-making, and relevance to CI of spatial decision-making supported through GIS. Because the key activity of CI involves the dedicated analysis of an organization's environment, we will focus on supporting CI through GIS-based spatial analysis and modeling, and pay only limited attention to other GIS functionalities (such as visualization or spatial data handling). The next section positions the argument within the relevant literature. Then, concepts of space and their use in organizational decision-making are explored. Next, GIS and their functionalities are introduced. In the subsequent sections we address the link between CI and GIS-supported spatial decision-making at a general level and by exploring a step-by-step procedure for establishing the value of GIS for CI. Finally, the chapter will look at future developments and areas for further research.

BACKGROUND

In its aim to develop a CI perspective on GIS, the chapter is positioned within the broader literature discussing potentials and pitfalls of using ICT for CI. At present, the role of GIS in this domain has not received systematic attention. The linkage between CI and ICT in general did receive substantial attention from both CI practitioners and scholars. Several authors have established the importance of ICT for CI (e.g., Davenport, 2000; Guimaraes & Armstrong, 1998; Hall, 2000; Hohhof, 1994; Powell & Bradford, 2000).

Particularly, the use of the Internet for CI purposes has received ample attention (e.g., Bergeron & Hiller, 2002; Cronin et al., 1994; Davenport, 2000; Desouza, 2001; Graef, 1998; Nordstrom & Pinkerton, 1999; Pawar & Sharda, 1997; Teo, 2000; Teo & Choo, 2001). Authors also stress the value of several other classes of ICT tools, either within the context of Internet use or not, including intelligent agents or Web robots (Desouza, 2001), data mining (Hall, 2000; Kassler, 1997; Marín-Llanes, Carro-Cartaya, & Espín-Andrade, 2001), neural networks (Aiken, 1999), databases (Rowley, 1992; Tseng, Drenth, & Morris, 1995), and groupware (Gunter, 1999).

GIS does not appear on this list of actual or potential CI applications. Most attention for GIS is directed towards technical and conceptual issues (Longley et al., 1999a), with derived attention for issues of introducing GIS in teaching programs (Benhart, 2000; Kemp, Goodchild, & Dodson, 1992; Zerger, Bishop, Escobar, & Hunter, 2002). If the business potential of GIS is perhaps not the main focus of the GIS literature, this potential has been identified and received ample attention (e.g., Dennis & Carte, 1998; Grimshaw, 2000; Johnson, 1996; Mennecke, 2000; Reeve & Petch, 1999). This recognition also led to the derived attention as to how the business perspective on GIS should be handled in teaching (e.g., Johnson, 1996; Mennecke, 2000). The business value shows what GIS is actually being used for (Goodchild, 1998). Important business users of GIS include owners of large physical distribution networks such as utility companies; for example, gas, phone, electric, water, cable TV companies (Cheng & Chang, 2001; Meyers, 1999; Peng & Huang, 2000) and the telecommunication industry (Fry, 1999). The benefit of using GIS for these types of businesses derives from the fact that the main resource for each company in this class is the spatial network consisting of thousands of miles of wires, and underground pipes with hundreds of thousands of customers, each with a connection to that network. Another typical GIS user is the transportation sector (e.g., Nyerges, Montejano, Oshiro, & Dadswell, 1997; Waters, 1999), including government transportation departments who use GIS, for instance, to store information on the state of pavement on the highway network, maintain an inventory of all highway signs, and analyze data on accidents (i.e., look for "black spots"). This sector also include delivery companies that use GIS technology to keep track of shipments, know where they are, and plan efficient delivery routes. GIS is also being used for siting facilities such as retail shops and warehouses, by analyzing demographic data of customer populations, access routes for customers, delivery routes for suppliers, etc. (Birks, Nasirin, & Zailani, 2003; Vlachopoulou, Silleos, & Manthou, 2001; Weber & Kwan, 2002). Large-scale GIS users also include farmers and foresters who increasingly use detailed maps for planning, analyzing and evaluating land use (e.g., Barrett, Sahay, & Walsham, 2001). Most uses of GIS are of an operational nature aimed at enabling or expediting daily routines (other examples can for instance be found in Dennis & Carte, 1998; Grimshaw, 2000; Harder, 1997; Longley & Clarke, 1995; Swink & Speier, 1999). While several strategic GIS applications have also been documented (e.g., Fung & Remsen, 1997; Grimshaw, 2000; Hendriks, 1998); e.g., related to the marketing and sales domains (e.g., Fung & Remsen, 1997; Goss, 1995; Rowley, 1999), to date no systematic attention for supporting Competitive Intelligence through GIS has been given.

BUSINESS DECISIONS AS SPATIAL ANALYSIS PROBLEMS

The possible value of GIS to CI analysts derives from the possible usefulness of these analysts adopting a spatial perspective in their work. This automatically leads to the question as to what constitutes a spatial perspective. Such a perspective enters into the CI domain when CI analysts conceptualize and treat the problems and challenges they face as spatial problems and challenges. A spatial conceptualization will result from using spatial concepts. The basic spatial category is that of location, referring to where things are, which has two distinct meanings: absolute location ("Where are things in their own right?") and relative location ("Where are things in relationship to others?"). Other spatial categories may be identified in relationship with these two basic spatial concepts. Absolute location, or "site," refers to the position of objects on the Earth's surface. Establishing absolute location presumes the use of some form of georeferencing or coordinate system, either a qualitative system (e.g., postal codes) or a discrete system (e.g., the LatLong system, identifying location in degrees of latitude and longitude). The use of satellites, and particularly the Global Positioning System (GPS), has revolutionized the establishment of absolute location (Lange & Gilbert, 1999). Relative location, or "situation," refers to the notion of spatial relationships. Because of their absolute location, objects maintain relationships or connections with other spatial objects. These relationships include connectivity or topology, which refers to the concept of neighborhood; contiguity, which involves the notions of borders and objects "touching" each other in space; direction, distance and proximity, or spatial closeness; spatial flow or diffusion, which connects notions of space to notions of time; and overlay, which involves overlaps in how two or more spatial objects take up space. Implied in the recognition of both absolute and relative location is the identification of objects whose location is involved. Commonly, four basic types of spatial objects are distinguished: points, lines (or specific collections of points), areas (objects identified by lines beginning and ending in the same point) and surfaces (Martin, 1999). Combinations of these basic classes and their characteristics may produce new types of spatial objects, such as spatial patterns, spatial structures, or spatial networks. For instance, a spatial network such as a road network or a network of pipelines results from understanding points as nodes and lines as connections between nodes, and may be expanded to include areas and surfaces as well. While all the objects in a network are characterized by a specific absolute location, the key to understanding their role in the network is their relative location or topology. Other spatial concepts, such as spatial form or extension, will emerge when looking at the characteristics of spatial objects.

Problems and challenges are not intrinsically spatial or spatial by nature. It is more accurate to say that problems may or may not allow to be treated as spatial. A spatial problem may be defined as any problem for which it may prove useful to use spatial categories for understanding the problem or for instigating relevant actions to deal with the problem. An interesting extension of the notion of a spatial problem comes about when spatial categories are used to address problems that are usually not treated as spatial. The concept of space is then used in a metaphorical sense, transferring spatial concepts to nonspatial domains such as emotion, age, and success (Hernández, 1994, p. 1). This is usually called "spatialization" (see Borner, Chen, & Boyack, 2003; Fabrikant & Buttenfield, 2001; Kuhn, 1992, 1993). An informative example of spatialization can be found in Couclelis (1998). She discusses the concept of an "information landscape" for generating conceptions of complex nonspatial information (see also Chalmers, 1993). An information landscape, which in itself is not inherently spatial, allows introducing and linking basic geographic concepts such as place, way and region. Couclelis argues that once the user of an information system has "seen" the information contained in the system as an information landscape, he or she is better equipped to recognize unity in that information by identifying information elements (tables, documents, etc.) and detecting similarities and disparities between these elements. Spatial relations of proximity and relative position map intuitively into similarity relationships among these elements, while more specifically geographic features (e.g., peaks, valleys, geological strata) may help convey additional information about relative importance, cross-cutting themes, etc. Additionally, the spatialization will elicit certain basic action schemas relevant to the definition of the information space, allowing the user to communicate in an intuitive way with the information system. For instance, Couclelis explores how the concept of the "place" of information in a database leads to database functions such as storing, finding and retrieving particular information and to higher-level functions such as containing, gathering and removing information.

When CI analysts try to identify the spatial relevance for their tasks they enter into the domain of spatial decision-making. While adopting a spatial perspective may prove useful, as we will elaborate below, it will not automatically result in making life easier to the CI analyst. Spatial decision problems are typically complex in nature (e.g., see Dennis & Carte, 1998; Grimshaw, 2001; Jankowski & Nyerges, 2001; Johnson, 1996; Mennecke, 2000; Swink & Speier, 1999). Here we will not elaborate on all possible sources of complexity that enter the stage when CI tasks are conceptualized as spatial tasks. Instead we will focus on the key issue of adopting a spatial perspective, with its associated challenges and problems, which involves creating and dressing up a spatial worldview through spatial analysis. What is spatial or geographical analysis? Answering this question is not unproblematic. The general definition that spatial analysis is any analysis that uses spatial concepts (e.g., see Maguire, 1995) is hardly if at all more informative than the definition of spatial concepts we gave above. Also defining the concept of analysis as the production of spatial information and specifying it into such operations as structuring, evaluation or simplification of data (e.g., Uran, 2002) does not help much. To make it more informative we need insight into different forms that spatial analysis can take. Two classes of distinctions have been proposed that may be used to that purpose: deductive distinctions starting from a logical ordering principle and descriptive distinctions starting from types of content of the analysis models. Within the first class several distinctions have been used: the degree of formalization in the models, the form of the data they use or produce, different geographical data types, the distinction between static and dynamic models, or model structure, etc. (for an overview see Wegener, 2000). These approaches, which categorize spatial analysis models by deducing classes from a categorization principle, have the advantage of being general and encompassing. The drawback of using these generic classification schemes of spatial analysis models is that it involves the inevitable drawback of lack in information value. They convey little of how spatial analysis may help understand new terrains, such as options for decision support in the CI domain. The second class of categorizations takes a more content-oriented approach. For instance, Van Herwijnen (1999) distinguishes between transformation models (changing one map into another, e.g., by reclassification or filtering), aggregation models (transforming one map into one value, e.g., by aggregating value maps), combination models (combining alternative maps into one map, e.g., by overlaying different maps), and combined aggregation models (combining two or more alternatives into one value, e.g., by combining several best alternative maps). A much-used distinction, which also focuses on the content of the models, is offered by Berry (1987): reclassifying maps, overlaying maps, measuring distance and connectivity and characterizing neighborhoods. Also, descriptive classification of spatial analysis models has been pursued by looking at the application of these models; e.g., by distinguishing application fields: environmental sciences, social sciences, etc. (see Wegener, 2000). Descriptive categorizations identify and specify individual types of spatial analysis. They are richer in information value but lack the rigidity of a logical deduction, with the associated problems of haphazardness and lack of generality.

In dealing with this "embarras du choix" between rigid but information-poor and information-rich but haphazard classification approaches we propose to work along two lines simultaneously. The first line consists of using a general definition of spatial analysis as the backdrop against which it may be assessed whether an operation on data relevant to the CI function qualifies as spatial analysis. This first line does not guide a CI professional in selecting an appropriate spatial analysis type in an active way, but allows to conceive of possible spatial analysis types, to assess whether an analysis type once identified may be called spatial and therefore to establish whether it makes sense to consider if dealing with the problem may be supported through the analysis functionalities of GIS. Based on the definition of spatiality and spatialization offered above, spatial analysis is defined by the fact that it derives insight into phenomena by inspecting and detecting aspects of considering where the phenomena are located (either literally or metaphorically; either in the sense of absolute location or relative location). Both the input and output sides of these analyses will consist of objects with combined attribute and location data. Four types of spatial analyses can then be discerned: (1) from attribute to attribute: forms of analysis leading to new attribute data of existing spatial objects, while not affecting the location data of these data (e.g., map reclassification; characterization of the known catchment area of a service); (2) from location to attribute: forms of analysis providing insight into attribute properties of known spatial objects (e.g., characterization of known spatial patterns, or comparison of routes through networks); (3) from attribute to location: forms of analysis aimed at the detection and characterization of spatial objects by analyzing attribute data of phenomena with a location footprint (e.g., identification of the catchment area of a service); (4) from location to location: forms of analysis aimed at detecting new spatial characteristics of existing spatial objects or aimed at detecting new spatial objects by examining their spatial properties alone or in conjunction with associated attribute data (e.g., detection of spatial patterns or network routes). A further distinction can be made by separating the location elements in these analysis types into using or producing data as to position or spatial relationships.

The second line consists of offering examples of spatial analyses that may prove relevant to CI. As to the second line we propose that an informative approach comes about when identifying types of spatial analysis through types of spatial decision problems. Such spatial decision problems will consist of the combinations of spatial modeling and analysis steps we described above in combination with a decision problem. For the purpose of identifying types of spatial decision problems we have examined the descriptions of case studies and other descriptions of actual or possible use of spatial analysis in business situations described in the literature (as reported in Fung & Remsen, 1997; *GIS for business: Discovering the missing piece in your business strategy*, 1995; Grimshaw, 2000; Harder, 1997; Hernandez, 1999; Longley & Clarke, 1995; Longley, Goodchild, & Maguire, 1999b; Mennecke, 1997) and by visiting the Internet sites of GIS vendors offering case descriptions. Based on the review we selected those spatial decision problems that involve an element of looking outside the realm of the own internal organization (e.g., customers, possible alliance partners, mergers, acquisitions, competitors) as this is a necessary condition for the decision problem to become relevant to CI. On the basis of this analysis we identified four classes of spatial decision problems potentially relevant to CI. It should be stressed that this is not an exhaustive list, but a list of analysis options that may serve as eye-openers for applying or expanding the list in the CI domain.

Firstly, the segmentation of customer markets and redefinition of sales territories defines a possibly relevant domain of spatial analysis (e.g., Birkin, Clarke, & Clarke, 1999; Fung & Remsen, 1997; Harder, 1997). An example that illustrates the type of spatial analysis involved is presented by Harder (1997). He describes the case of an ink producing company interested in realigning the sales territories assigned to representatives of the firm. The company experienced many problems with its current sales territory definition, including too much time spent on travel by representatives and customers complaining that their next-door neighbors received better advice from different reps than had visited them. Multiple spatial criteria linked to attributes of customers as well as the workforce are involved in the decision problem of conceiving of a better sales territory definition. These include routing, geo-demographical data of customers, specific abilities and competencies of sales reps, etc. Spatial analysis can integrate data on these different criteria by creating profiles of different classes of customers, mapping classes of customers based on their profile by geocoding the accounts, plotting current sales reps visits on top of the customer map, and analyzing possible gains in travel time by calculating aggregated routing data (time and distance) after reshuffling identical customer types among sales reps.

Secondly, spatial analysis may concern the identity characterization of customers, trade areas, catchment areas or other relevant spatial objects (e.g., Birkin et al., 1999; Fung & Remsen, 1997; Grimshaw, 2000; Harder, 1997; Mennecke, 1997). An important data source for performing these types of analysis are demographic data with a spatial footprint (e.g., aggregate demographics of postcode zones) that present the spatial analyst with interesting opportunities (e.g., Batey & Brown, 1995; Birkin, 1995; Gatrell & Senior, 1999; Openshaw, 1995) as well as risks (see Curry, 1999; Goss, 1995). Within the marketing literature many examples have been reported that fall within this category (see references above). Spatial analysis and modeling can support strategic planning in marketing organizations. Combinatory analysis of spatial and attribute data allows a business planner to identify and locate residences with incomes greater than a defined floor, within a specific age range, and distributed around a retail outlet within a given driven time threshold. The locations of these potential customers are then used for direct micro-marketing campaigns, which are utilized by mailing materials to those residences that exhibit aggregate characteristics as defined prior to query for those potential consumers. Spatial analysis also empowers a planner to better understand the spatial distribution of a given market by locating existing customers' residences for a given facility. This process can be carried out for a series of outlets, after which the relative strength of customer clusters within each district can be determined (a trade area is defined by purchasing behaviors and the series of customers' residential locations). One example documented in the literature concerns Levi Strauss, the clothing manufacturer and retailer (see Sherwood, 1995). This firm uses GIS to analyze geo-demographic data to fine-tune product marketing and product mix at store level. Other popular examples concern the use of GIS by supermarkets to adapt the range of goods they offer per outlet to the demographics of their local clientele (Hernandez, 1999; Hernandez, Byrom, Bennison, & Hooper, 2001; Jones & Biasiotto, 1999).

Thirdly, well-known forms of spatial analysis involve site suitability assessment and associated decision problems of location and allocation, such as sales force allocation, which involve a combination of the spatial analysis types running under the first two classes of spatial decision problems. This type of analysis may either support the selection of possible sites for locating a new facility, or may help establish which current locations are the best candidates for closure in case of a declining market (e.g., see Fung & Remsen, 1997; Grimshaw, 2000; Harder, 1997). For an example of the second type, consider the site suitability analysis performed by a home electronics rental company as described by Clarke and Clarke (1995). The company in question was facing market declines for its products and had to close down several of its stores. GIS can be used to predict how many customers may be expected to open an account at a shop if it is positioned at a specific location, by analyzing and combining demographic data, routing data, and other location-related information. Therefore, GIS can also be used to make an estimate of the loss of clientele when existing shops are closed. The authors show that the predictions of the impact of closing down particular locations by GIS-based analysis proved far more accurate than those made by the organization's management.

Fourthly, spatial analysis may concern estimating or calculating the likelihood of events. For instance, Sherwood (1995) describes how insurance companies use insight into the spatial variation of risks to offer particular insurance products to identified customers or to adapt the conditions of existing insurances. The calculation of risk may, for instance, use information as to the closeness of particular properties to woods that in dry periods present fire hazards, combined with climate data and information on how forest fires developed in the past.

GIS AND THEIR FUNCTIONALITIES

The next step in our argument is to introduce GIS into the picture. To be able to assess their value for supporting spatial analysis, the question has to be asked as to what GIS is. What does a GIS look like, i.e., how would I know one if I saw one? This question can be asked and answered in several different ways (Goodchild, 1998). GIS as a computer application includes specific hardware, dataware, software, and orgware. The GIS software is typically sold by specialized software developers (Hartung & MacPherson, 2000; Hartung & Macpherson, 2001). GIS hardware is mostly like that of any other computer, with some specific peripherals such as big printers or plotters for printing maps, and devices to input data from maps to GIS, such as digitizers, scanners or GPS recorders. As to their functionality it should be noted that GIS is used as an umbrella term covering various types of technology, ranging from relatively simple mapping facilities to advanced environments supporting spatial analysis. A commonly used distinction, based on different types of users, may help illustrate the broadness of the term (ESRI, 1996):

- *View GIS* or *Consumer GIS:* a system offering map presentation facilities for data stored in a standard database system; aimed at users with average spatial knowledge;
- *Desktop Mapping:* a system with more advanced computer cartography functions, can be used for producing customized thematic maps; for instance, available as an extension to a spreadsheet; users typically need more advanced cartographic knowledge;
- *Desktop GIS:* a multifunctional system offering more advanced spatial analysis functionality, limited by the size of the database they can handle; requires experienced GIS users with dedicated spatial knowledge concerning the application domain;
- *Workstation GIS* or *Professional GIS:* a multifunctional system, with functionalities dedicated to their specific application domain, usually in the form of a distributed system with facilities for handling very large databases and extensive data management or analysis functionality (used, for instance, by utility companies or roadmap producers); requires experienced GIS users in a professional organizational setting.

While a broad variety of different types of GIS exist, they all draw their operability from three classes of functionalities: spatial data storage and management, visualization facilities, especially in the form of maps, and spatial analysis functions (Aronoff, 1993; Hendriks & Ottens, 1997; Longley et al., 1999a). What distinguishes GIS from other computer applications is that these functionalities all concern aspects of working with spatial data. Different GIS differ in the degree to which they have fully developed functionalities in all three classes. For our purpose, particularly the third class is relevant: that of spatial analysis or spatial modeling functions. Several authors discuss the connections between GIS and spatial analysis (e.g., Chou, 1996; Fotheringham, 2000b; Fotheringham & Rogerson, 1994; Getis, 2000; Goodchild, 2000; Goodchild, Parks, & Steyaert, 1993; Goodchild, Steyaert, & Parks, 1996; Hendriks & Ottens, 1997; Longley, 2001; Longley & Batty, 1996). Using GIS, particularly most proprietary GIS, for spatial analysis is certainly not unproblematic as it is not a law of the Medes and Persians that GIS use will expedite or improve spatial modeling (e.g., Fotheringham, 2000a). GIS may offer support for spatial decision-making but they are no substitutes for human spatial insight. GIS do not offer an appropriate spatial analysis with the push of one button. GIS is best understood as a toolbox of spatial data-related operations that may be combined in multiple ways, guided by the analysis needs of the GIS user. Learning to use GIS does not in the first place involve learning to find the tools and applying them in a given situation. First and foremost it involves developing an understanding of what a spatial perspective on reality involves and gaining a thorough understanding of issues of spatiality and spatialization. A meaningful use of GIS can only result as an extension of such an understanding. This explains the considerable amount of attention that is given to issues of introducing GIS as part of curricula in spatial sciences (geography, geometry, spatial planning, etc.), instead of teaching GIS as a technical toolbox in its own right (e.g., Benhart, 2000; Forer & Unwin, 1999; Goodchild, 1998; Johnson, 1996; Kemp & Goodchild, 1998; Kemp et al., 1992; Mennecke, 2000; Zerger et al., 2002).

To give an idea of the type of support GIS may offer we will give a short overview of possible classes of GIS functions linked to the four types of spatial analysis presented above. It should be stressed that one particular type of operation offered by GIS may prove useful in more than one class of analysis models. In the first class, analysis models are represented that lead to new attribute data of existing spatial objects, while not affecting the location data of these data (working from attribute to attribute data). GIS functions to support such analyses concern classification and retrieval. As an example consider a shop that is interested in how the demography in its existing service area is developing and is expected to develop, for instance, because it wants to explain changes in its sales volumes and assess possibilities for adapting its range of goods. GIS allows defining this neighborhood as a window around a target (the shop) and analyzing prevailing demographic properties of residents within the window by connecting the spatial object with external attribute data as are available for postcode zones. Also, overlay operations, which are commonly present in GIS, may be used to implement this type of analysis if the spatial objects to be overlaid in several maps are the same objects. These operations involve putting one map on top of another to construct a third map out of the combination of the spatial objects present on the two base maps. An example of overlay analysis that fits within this class of spatial analysis is the cross tabulation of two variables represented on two maps (e.g., private-public ownership and land use classes of lots) resulting in a characterization of the areal units on the map in a third map (e.g., conveying an insight into the connections between ownership and land use of lots).

Secondly, forms of analysis can be distinguished that provide insight into attribute properties of known spatial objects (working from location to attribute data). Examples of GIS functions that may support this type of analysis include interpolation (e.g., estimating the unknown attribute value of a location by combining known data of nearby locations; e.g., estimate the chance of precipitation at a given location where an open air facility is to be located by combining data of nearby climate stations), aspect (calculating the direction a slope faces, e.g., assessing whether a particular location is likely to run the risk of pollution in the case of a toxic spillover because of how the downhill path runs from the spillover location; this operation may, for instance, be used for risk calculation of certain areas based on the nearby location of potentially dangerous activities as the basis for accepting, modifying or rejecting insurances).

The third class of spatial analysis models concerns the forms of analysis aimed at the detection and subsequent characterization of spatial objects by analyzing attribute data of phenomena with a location footprint (working from attribute towards location data). GIS may, for instance, offer facilities to perform neighborhood operations aimed at defining what the neighborhood of a specific target is and examining the characteristics of that neighborhood. This type of operation is called for if a shop does not know what its actual service area is, or if it is interested in exploring which areas could be interesting as possible service areas because of the demographic properties associated with them. GIS functions useful for supporting these types of analysis include search (e.g., defining new spatial objects as those that share particular attributes such as a combination of demographic data of residential areas), and contour generation (e.g., drawing lines around areas that are considered sufficiently homogenous based on the spatial distribution of a continuous phenomenon such as income or average age in postcode areas).

The fourth class concerns forms of analysis aimed at detecting new spatial characteristics of existing spatial objects or aimed at detecting new spatial objects by examining their spatial properties alone or in conjunction with associated attribute data (working from location to location data). Functions typically represented in GIS that support this type of analysis concern overlay operations. If the maps to be overlaid are based on the vector data model the overlay operation may take three possible forms: polygon-on-polygon overlay (detecting how the areas in two zoning systems overlap), point-in-polygon overlay (detecting which points, e.g., wells or landmarks, represented in one map are contained within an area represented in another map, e.g., land use zones), line-in-polygon overlay (detecting which lines, e.g., rivers or roads, represented in one map dissect an area represented in another map, e.g., cities). Other examples within this class involve connectivity functions offered by GIS aimed at establishing whether known spatial objects are connected, or constructing new spatial objects by connecting existing ones. Examples of connectivity functions include the use of proximity (e.g., using address information to determine how close residents are to a service such as an ambulance post or community service as the possible basis for defining the catchment areas of these services), contiguity measures (combining adjacent areas when they share a common attribute, e.g., defining the catchment areas of services by linking postcode zones with minimum distance to the same service point), networks (e.g., calculation of an optimal route for an ambulance or fire engine through a street network using traffic information), intervisibility (e.g., performing an intervisibility analysis to assess in which residential areas and on which highways a shop and its signposts can be seen).

USING GIS FOR
COMPETITIVE INTELLIGENCE

This brings us to the central question addressed in the chapter: Which perspective on GIS is necessary to identify the potential of these systems to support CI analysts? We have prepared an answer to this question by gathering and sketching the main building blocks of such a perspective. Linking GIS to CI calls for a relevant spatial perspective on the CI domain. The question therefore is what is "relevant" and what is "spatial." The latter question we answered in the third section: spatial refers to a specific conceptualization of phenomena using spatial concepts, which are concepts that directly or indirectly relate to issues of location: recognizing where phenomena are, either in an absolute or relative sense. The former question we responded to by interpreting "relevant" as "useful to support the decision-making aspects of the tasks implied in the CI function." Following this argument, the linking pin between CI and GIS lies in the examination as to whether and when CI can be usefully perceived as spatial decision-making. The role of GIS comes into the picture as these systems may offer functionalities to support such spatial decisions, as we explored in the previous section.

An elaboration of this argument calls for an elaboration of the CI concept. There is no standard, accepted definition of Competitive Intelligence (e.g., see Kahaner, 1996; Pollard, 1999). One possible way of defining CI is to see Competitive Intelligence as the discipline of breaking down the matrix of a market, and of providing targeted intelligence on an organization's competitive landscape (Blagg, 2002). It is then seen as the continuous investigation of a market landscape providing intelligence on strategic issues that will arise in the short to medium-term affecting an organization's competitiveness or market position. CI involves gathering and use of data by a company for the purpose of learning about its competition in a given market. A typical trait of CI is that it aims to put a company in the shoes of its competitors for the purpose of projecting or conjecturing their strategic position and options. CI aims to develop a specific window on the world outside the own company, while not forgetting about the own company. Its aim is to best understand competitor action, strategy and future plans. CI "is not generating answers, it is generating opportunity for dialogue" (Fahey, 1999). CI therefore involves looking at the present and prospective strategic situations of the own company in conjunction with the present and prospective strategic situations of the competition, while not forgetting other strategic forces, particularly the customer. An elaboration of the CI tasks is typically given in the CI cycle of planning and direction, collection, analysis, and distribution (see the introductory chapter). Within this cycle we choose to focus on the analysis stage for two related reasons. Firstly, the analysis stage can be looked upon as the key activity in the operational tasks of CI professionals, involving the identification and resolution of the fundamental CI decisions. Secondly, the role of GIS as decision support systems depends first and foremost on their facilities for supporting spatial analysis and spatial modeling, which implies that a focus on the analysis stage will allow GIS to show their true colors.

The linking pin between CI and GIS is defined by the types of spatial or spatialized problems that describe relevant aspects of the object of CI research for which GIS may offer support. We described classes of such problems above: the segmentation of customer markets and redefinition of sales territories; identity characterization of customers, trade areas, catchment areas or other relevant spatial objects; combination of the previous classes in such problems as sales force allocation; site suitability assessment and associated decision problems of location and allocation; likelihood of events calculation. The question then is how a CI professional may find use of any of these classes of spatial problems for identifying and assessing strategic options or choices for the company. Answering this question can be described as a three-step procedure. Firstly, the CI analyst will have to identify which spatial variables are relevant or can be made relevant for understanding how the present and future positions of the company vis-à-vis its competitors can be captured. Questions that the CI analyst is going to ask to identify such variables include:

Is the location of customers, if we can find out what it is, something useful for distinguishing ourselves? Can developments and trends on any relevant field be translated into spatial or spatialized objects and representations? Secondly, the CI analyst may use GIS to map and analyze the present and future positions of the own company and its competitors on the basis of the variables identified in the first step. Thirdly, the CI analysts will have to translate the spatial analysis and mapping outcomes into the identification of strategic chances and threats of the company, by integrating the four resulting pictures of Step 2: the current situation of the own company, the projected situation of the own company, the current situation of the competition, and the projected situation of the competition. GIS will play a major role only in Step 2. Step 1 involves looking at elements of the CI domain through the lens of spatiality or spatialization and serves as a necessary preparatory step for allowing GIS to contribute in a sensible way. Step 3 is typically the trade of CI in which adopting the spatial perspective is to show its value.

Each of these steps will now be elaborated.

STEP 1: IDENTIFYING SPATIAL VARIABLES

The task of CI involves developing an insight into how the competitive environment of the company may develop in the future, and how these developments may be influenced. Two dimensions are therefore present in the task of the CI function: the time dimension and the business object dimension. In addressing and combining these two dimensions, the CI analyst may choose between two different starting points, leading to two different routes for identifying relevant spatial variables. The first route concerns starting from the business object dimension and introducing the time dimension in elaborating this dimension. This involves identifying the various business objects in the strategic domain and examining whether looking at these objects from a spatial point-of-view may produce information that is relevant to CI (including the identification of the time dimension). The second starting point would be to look at developments and trends that occur outside the company and see how they may be made relevant to the business. This route is opposite to the first in that it starts in the time dimension and works towards the business object dimension. We will look at both routes in some more detail.

As to the first route a possible point of departure is given by Harvard Business School Professor Michael Porter's well-known competitive forces model (Porter, 1980). Porter identifies five forces that drive competition within an industry:

1.   The threat of entry by new competitors;
2.   The intensity of rivalry among existing competitors;
3.   Pressure from substitute products;
4.   The bargaining power of buyers;
5.   The bargaining power of suppliers.

The role of suppliers and even some competitors has changed substantially over the last decades, particularly through digitalization, globalization and deregulation. These have led, among other things, to the emergence and development of virtual organizations, strategic alliances and partnerships. If the situation allows or calls for it, companies appear to be able to transform both suppliers and previous competitors into strategic partners. While such partners could be included both in Porter's classes 1, 2 and 5, we argue that to sharpen the analysis it is better to treat them as a class of their own. Therefore, elaborating Porter's competitive forces framework in the following six classes of objects of CI interest:

1.   Customers and their characteristics such as demography;
2.   Possibly new competitors and their characteristics, such as the nature of their product or service;
3.   Existing competitors and their characteristics, such as their competencies;
4.   Substitute products and their characteristics, such as quality, price;
5.   Suppliers, their characteristics and the characteristics of their supplies that are the raw materials of the products and services of the own company;
6.   (Possible) alliance partners and their characteristics, such as organizational culture and proven trustworthiness.

We will present two examples to explain the type of consideration as to these classes of objects that is needed to produce useful spatial indicators. The first example concerns conceiving of the products of the company and its possible substitutes as objects with spatial connotations (Class Four in the enumeration). This involves considering the characteristics of these products as spatial dimensions. Take, for example, a car manufacturer. This company could aim at spatializing what the distinguishing features of its cars and their competition are in relationship with the type of customer that buys the different types. Possibly interesting dimensions may be the traditional variables of price and quality, but also such distinguishing variables as sportiveness, degree of retro or progressive radiation, or degree of family style. This spatialization operation will be useful if it makes sense to think of these variables as dimensions to position the different cars in their own right or compared to other cars on all dimensions combined. This implies that their usefulness derives from the possibility of mapping the various cars along the distinguished dimensions and detecting spatial-like patterns in their arrangement in this n-dimensional space based on the relative location of the individual cars, the neighboring effects that appear and possibilities to detect elements of contiguity. To make the spatialization useful for CI purposes, it should be possible and sensible to speculate or project what future developments as to these variables may be. It should not only be possible to assess the values for the specified variables in the present situation, but also to guide the company's vision as to how its competitive landscape will develop into future. In the example: the introduction of such dimensions as sportsmanlike and retro radiation is useful to the degree that these dimensions may be expected to make a difference in future markets.

The second example concerns retail chains that derive an essential part of their customer appeal from accessibility, such as green warehouses, large do-it-yourself (DIY) shops or fast food chains. Let's take the example of a green warehouse. The raison d'être of such a shop is that it offers a broad selection of gardening-related products under one roof at a reasonable price, in combination with appropriate advice. Green warehouses distinguish them-selves from more traditional gardening outlets such as commercial nursery gardens by offering a broader range of goods, often invading the domain of DIY-shops and even gift shops. Particularly because their assortment includes bulky items such as trees and plants, accessibility and adequate parking facilities are essential for green warehouses. Because of the importance of these spatial variables characterizing green warehouses, these shops will benefit largely from knowing the spatial behavior of their own clientele as well as the clientele of their competitors. The example therefore concerns Class One in the list above: the spatial characteristics of their present or potential customers. Their geo-demographics define an important class of useful spatial variables. Also data on travel behavior, including mode of transportation, routing data, combinations in multipurpose trips, etc. may be an invaluable source of information for guiding company projections and decisions. Based on informa-tion on present travel behavior and associated spatial variables, reliable predictions can be made as to how all variables identified will behave in various what-if scenarios.

The second route for generating relevant spatial criteria involves the detection of trends that co-produce the competitive environment of the organization and the analysis of these trends to detect relevant spatial variables. Several classes of such trends can be discerned:

1.   Technological trends that may involve opportunities for the production and delivery of new products or services or changes in the production processes of existing products and services; for instance, these trends may change patterns of delivery (e.g., the Internet) and travel options and routes for customers;

2.   Demographic trends, particularly concerning relevant characteristics of current or possible customers; for instance, if the popularity of ecological products is associated with the population distribution on such variables as age and degree of education, it may be interesting to establish whether regional variations can be detected in demographic trends with regard to these variables to target new markets;

3.   Societal-cultural trends; for instance, trends towards individualization that are countered by the inclination to reinforce norms and values above the individual level; these trends will affect ideas as to what constitutes "Corporate Social Responsibility" and "Responsible Entrepreneurship"; the emergence and conceptual development of such concepts may be scanned for spatial connotations, such as care for the local community or the preference for local alliance partners;

4.   Political trends, such as the swing towards sharing of particular responsibilities between central and local government, industries and individuals; if a spatial element can be recognized in these responsibilities, it may induce idea generation of the directions an organization may take;

5.   Ecological trends, such as a shift of attention from issues of global heating to the associated but more focused issues of water management; for companies operating in domains that are related to these issues, the problems and solutions associated with managing water supplies may be analyzed from the perspective of recognizable regional components, both at a local and a global scale;

6.   Economic trends, such as globalization issues, related issues of regional specialization (e.g., the formation of specific knowledge regions) and the shift of driving competitive forces away from flexibility towards innovativeness with its associated focus on knowledge as a competitive force; if, for instance, trends towards regional specialization are noticeable in different but related types of industry, it may be interesting to explore whether developments in that direction may provide new opportunities for the own industry as well.

Next to the smaller examples presented above a somewhat more elaborate example may serve to explain the type of exploration and analysis involved in identifying potentially useful spatial indicators following route two. Consider the case of an environmental consultancy firm specialized in civil engineering related projects. The spatial component of such a firm is important in practically every project the firm engages in. How serious, for instance, ground pollution in a specific location is, always depends on the presence or absence of related activities or phenomena in the vicinity (e.g., ground water). Insight into spatial characteristics and relations is therefore a crucial element in the knowledge of the environmental engineers employed by the firm. The importance of the spatial element in their object of study is also reflected by the fact that most of the information systems used for supporting the primary process typically involve spatial data. This will hold true for the extensive databases with environmental data, and also for the automated programs running advanced explanation, exploration or simulation models. Also, most reports produced by these firms include maps presenting the research outcomes. Instead of looking at its present operations through the lens of spatial concepts, as the examples above do, this firm could use the importance of space to reconsider how applying spatial concepts to these trends may sharpen insight into trends in its environment. Particularly, combining political, ecological, societal-cultural and technological trends offers starting points for this operation. Based on its competencies developed in previous projects the consultancy firm may examine how it can proactively look for new application areas of existing services and products. If, based on its developing norms and values, society allows or expects firms to take responsibility in signaling and solving ecology-related problems (e.g., calculation of specific environmental disaster likelihood), it may offer examples of their expertise to authorities instead of waiting to ask for tenders for projects specified beforehand by the authorities. It may look for shifts in ecological priorities at the level of society to see which evolving themes the company does not currently put in the foreground may generate new business in the future. For instance, it could use its knowledge of ground pollution related to such issues as ground water levels, water pipes and drainage pipe networks, to shift its products toward the market of water management products with a distinct spatial accent.

STEP 2: SPATIAL POSITIONING OF THE ORGANIZATION THROUGH GIS

The next step in linking CI and GIS brings GIS into the picture. It concerns spatially analyzing the position of the company in the present and projected situation, which involves making sense of the data on the variables that were identified in Step One. We will discuss the role of GIS by looking at its potential in the three examples described in the previous section.

The first example concerns the case of a car manufacturer mapping car types on several product dimensions, such as price and sportiveness. In this case GIS may perform both visualization and analysis functions. As every dimension can be entered as a spatial dimension, standard maps can be drawn of any combination of two dimensions, which allows visually inspecting the emergence of spatial patterns. Using three-dimensional models such as the Triangulated Irregular Networks (TIN) or Digital Elevation Model (DEM, see Hutchinson, 1999 #131], the visualizations may be made more encompassing, but perhaps also more complex to read. The resulting picture has to be inspected as a mountain landscape in which peaks and valleys take on meaning through the combined scores on the used dimensions. Overlaying operations may be used to combine a larger selection of dimensions into one overall either two-dimensional or three-dimensional map that may then be plotted for visual inspection. Combining descriptions of the present situation with future projections may enhance these combinations of two, three or more dimensions. Every new projection will add a dimension to the map, using the different ways in which time may be represented in GIS (see Peuquet, 1999). In the analysis realm GIS may assist in detecting proper ways of distinguishing how individual types of cars form groups (using contiguity measures and spatial clustering techniques). Demographic data of customers may play a key role in this operation. Through GIS the CI analyst may construct customer profiles and use these profiles to construct and label the clusters of car types.

In the case of considering location choices of a retail chain, the second example, the typical and well-documented GIS functionalities for performing a site suitability analysis and supporting location choice come into the picture: creating maps of areas with the appropriate size, closeness to relevant census tracts, closeness to infrastructures such as highways, and overlaying these maps to combine suitability criteria, etc. (see description and references above). GIS analysis can generate sales predictions of alternative locations by using geo-demographics of the trade areas that are constructed through a network analysis of travel times and routes. Because the accessibility criterion is of central importance to these chains, the GIS analysis can be expanded to include the effects of projected changes in the infrastructure around alternative locations to see what effects these will have.

The third example concerns an environmental consultancy firm exploring ways to use the spatial element in its products to see how recognizable trends offer chances for new business. This firm may use GIS to define its new products, e.g., producing spatial water management advice as an outgrowth of existing ground pollution studies. It may use GIS to target the types of customers that these new products may be sold to, and to identify whether its existing sales territory delineation is adequate for serving these new classes of customers. It may use relevant spatial data of the competition it has at its disposal to detect contiguities or overlaps in sales territories along with other spatial contingencies as elements for preparing cooperation with those competitors that trend analysis has designated as potential future partners.

STEP 3: RECOGNIZING STRATEGIC IMPLICATIONS

The final step concerns the translation of the emerging picture into strategic implications. This presumes bringing the competition into the picture. The third step in the procedure we describe has the purpose of completing the 2-by-2 matrix of the current and projected situations of the own organization as well as these situations of its competition. The spatial concepts that emerged in the first two steps and their processing through GIS play a key role in defining the cells in this matrix. While this third step is crucial if the whole procedure of using GIS is indeed to lead to increased business intelligence, the spatial element is not all that different from the first and second step. The spatial analysis in the third is mostly a straightforward extension of the analysis in the second step, applied on the combination of the own company and the competition. Therefore we pay less attention to an elaboration of this third step. Again we will use the three examples presented in the previous sections to explore briefly the nature of the tasks involved.

In the first example, mapping car brands, the extension of the second step involves bringing in data of car types of the competition. The extended analysis may involve looking for white spots in the resulting maps to see where combinations of scores on the dimensions do not lead to clusters of existing or projected car types or brands. This may be the basis for constructing new projections. It may also involve identifying the types of customers that would be most interesting from the perspective of taking away business from the competition, and based on the geo-demographic data of these customers in combination with information on trends of the associated demographic classes, may inspire targeting the areas with an above average representation of these customers as well as aligning future car development projects along the associated demographic trends. The spatial clustering operation might also be used as the starting point for pinpointing detailed car development projects along identified dimensions with the competition as potential project partners.

In the second case, supporting location choices of retail chains, the spatial analysis takes on a full CI character only if it examines the competition as an integrated element in the picture. This implies that locating new outlets should not just be considered from the perspective of locating that outlet and allocating customers to it, but also from the perspective of assessing how much business would be taken away from existing outlets and projected new outlets of the competition, and how an optimization of generated revenues can be effected through an intelligent spatial organization of the own chain in relationship to others. It would also involve looking for those combinations where new outlets would involve a minimal amount of cannibalization of the chain's own existing or projected outlets.

The extension that is involved in the case of the environmental consultancy firm, the third example, taking the third step in the procedure of linking GIS and CI that we outlined, is of a similar nature to the second example. The same types of analyses that we described above would also have to be performed for actual or potential competitors to assess which will lead to an optimal expansion or shift in services and products offered.

FUTURE TRENDS AND RESEARCH

Looking at GIS from a CI perspective has shown that GIS introduction and use may enhance the CI function significantly. At the same time, the conclusion should be that the current conceptions and functionalities of GIS are not attuned to the requirements of CI. A common criticism of GIS is that it lacks analytical power (e.g., see Brown, 2000; Clarke & Clarke, 1995; Frank, 2000; Goodchild, 2000). These systems, so the critics say, offer broad toolbox functionality but leave it to the well-informed user to combine functionalities for analysis purposes, leading to the risk of abuse by the less-informed user. For enhancing the use of GIS as CI support systems, specific expansion of their functionality seems required. Particularly useful extensions for the CI professional would include fuzzy querying capabilities, flexible query result inspection facilities (e.g., using hyperlinks), specific tools for storing and using meta-information about GIS usage, support for constructing and using spatial mental models, tools for stimulating conflict and dealing with conflicting spatial information interpretations, and a wider spread of standard decision support functionalities such as shared graphics and multi-user access to databases. In other words, when looking from GIS to CI, one will detect several functionalities that may prove very propitious to CI. Also, when looking from CI to GIS, clear lacunas become apparent, since potentially useful functions (such as data sharing facilities) are not attuned to the specific requirements of CI, or because CI-specific functions (such as support for the construction of mental models of a firm) are largely lacking. These assertions call for an extension of the GIS concepts and functions dedicated to CI.

The other side of the picture is that in their present perspective on the world the CI professionals hardly use geographical concepts. The aim of this chapter is to illustrate that adopting a spatial perspective through the use of spatial concepts and spatial modeling offers interesting options to give the work in the CI domain a whole set of new options, many of which lie beyond the horizon of the options identified in the chapter. What is needed first and foremost are CI professionals developing their own understanding of space in their domain. It seems more adequate and realistic to assert that CI professionals should introduce spatial elements in their present world perspective, than to call for the development of a completely new perspective on their work. Additional research is needed to establish how this shift in perspective in CI professionals conceiving of their tasks is best effectuated.

Future research is therefore needed along the two lines identified, and connecting these two lines. Exploring how extensions of GIS functionality for enhancing their usefulness to the CI function is best approached by involving CI professionals in these efforts. Thinking in GIS terms may help them understand the possible value of thinking in spatial terms. GIS, with its graphical appeal, and its strong database facilities may serve as a vehicle for introducing CI professionals into the world of spatial thinking and enhancing their "spatial intelligence." It may, in its slipstream, also assist in pinpointing the shortcomings of GIS if these systems are to be used as dedicated tools for CI support, and identifying possible interfaces for hooking current CI analysis approaches into a GIS environment.

CONCLUSION

"Space, the final frontier." The opening sentences of the renowned TV serial Star Trek also apply to the topic of this chapter: using spatial concepts to provide inspiration to the CI function of a company. The mission of the starship Enterprise and its crew that the series features is "to explore strange new worlds. To seek out new life and new civilizations. To boldly go where no man has gone before." This is exactly the appeal that space offers to the CI function of enterprises: its task is to explore the organization's future with respect to its competitors and customers by looking at the present situation in new ways, beyond the imagination of the current daily routines. Perhaps the challenges that space holds for CI are not as physical as the challenges that Captain Spock of the Starship Enterprise and his crew were facing. The prime challenge involved in the CI function exploring space as its own final frontier is of a conceptual nature. GIS may provide important support in the efforts of meeting these challenges, as we explored in the chapter. It would be inappropriate to say that GIS plays second fiddle. GIS is not just a toolbox that, when used properly, may expedite visualization of spatial data and spatial modeling. It may also serve as an eye-opener as to how concepts of space may lead to new perspectives on relevant objects and developments in the CI realm. Through the use of GIS, CI professionals may explore what challenges a spatial conception of the firm's competitive environment holds. GIS may thus play a role at the outset of conjecturing or inventing possibly useful and inspiring applications of spatial concepts to CI task elements. Which spatial concepts may help make sense of technological, economic or other trends? How can concepts of location, spatial pattern, way, route, spatial form, etc., be of help in coming to grips with potentials and risks associated with forces shaping the competitive landscape of the organization, such as customers, substitute products, and possible alliance partners? Toying with GIS may provide the inspiration to CI analysts for answering such questions. GIS may also play a role at making spatial conceptions pay off, once these are sketched. GIS may provide the means to analyze maps of present and future products of the organization and its competitors along multiple descriptive dimensions of these products couched in spatial terms. Through GIS the detection and analysis of geo-demographics of customers, or site suitability analysis of outlets with respect to locations of the competition, come to the desktop of the CI analyst. Concepts of space in close unison with the functionalities of GIS may provide an organization with the mental direction to boldly go where no enterprise has gone before.

REFERENCES

Aiken, M. (1999). Competitive intelligence through neural networks. *Competitive Intelligence Review, 10*(1), 49-53.

Aronoff, S. (1993). *Geographic information systems: A management perspective.* Ottawa: WDL Publications.

Barrett, M., Sahay, S., & Walsham, G. (2001). Information technology and social transformation: GIS for forestry management in India. *Information Society, 17*(1), 5-20.

Batey, P. & Brown, P. (1995). From human ecology to customer targeting: The evolution of geodemographics. In P. Longley & G. Clarke (Eds.), *GIS for Business and Service Planning* (pp. 77-103). Cambridge: GeoInfomation International.

Benhart, J. (2000). An approach to teaching applied GIS: Implementation for local organizations. *Journal of Geography, 99*(6), 245-252.

Bergeron, P. & Hiller, C. A. (2002). Competitive intelligence. *Annual Review of Information Science and Technology, 36*, 353-390.

Berry, J. K. (1987). Fundamental operations in computer assisted map analysis. *International Journal of Geographic Information Systems, 1*(2), 119-136.

Birkin, M. (1995). Customer targeting, geodemographics and lifestyle approaches. In P. Longley & G. Clarke (Eds.), *GIS for Business and Service Planning* (pp. 104-149). Cambridge: GeoInfomation International.

Birkin, M., Clarke, G. P., & Clarke, M. (1999). *GIS for Business and Service Planning* (No. 0-471-32182-6). Chichester, UK: John Wiley & Sons.

Birks, D. F., Nasirin, S., & Zailani, S. H. M. (2003). Factors influencing GIS project implementation failure in the UK retailing industry. *International Journal of Information Management, 23*(1), 73-82.

Blagg, M. (2002). Know your market. *Critical Eye, 1*(2), 39-40.

Borner, K., Chen, C. M., & Boyack, K. W. (2003). Visualizing knowledge domains. *Annual Review of Information Science and Technology, 37*, 179-255.

Brown, L. A. (2000). The GIS/SA interface for substantive research(ers): A critical need. *Journal of Geographical Systems, 2*(1), 43-47.

Chalmers, M. (1993). Using a landscape metaphor to represent a corpus of documents. In A. U. Frank & I. Campari (Eds.), *Spatial Information Theory: A Theoretical Basis for GIS* (vol. 716, pp. 377-390). Berlin: Springer.

Cheng, M. Y. & Chang, G. L. (2001). Automating utility route design and planning through GIS. *Automation in Construction, 10*(4), 507-516.

Chou, Y. H. (1996). *Exploring Spatial Analysis in GIS.* Santa Fe, NM: OnWord Press.

Clarke, G. & Clarke, M. (1995). The development and benefits of customized spatial decision support systems. In P. Longley & G. Clarke (Eds.), *GIS for Business and Service Planning* (pp. 227-246). Cambridge, MA: GeoInfomation International.

Couclelis, H. (1998). Worlds of information: the geographic metaphor in the visualization of complex information. *Cartography and Geographic Information Systems, 25*(4), 209-220.

Cronin, B., Overfelt, K., Fouchereaux, K., Manzvanzvike, T., Cha, M., & Sona, E. (1994). The Internet and competitive intelligence—A survey of current practice. *International Journal of Information Management, 14*(3), 204-222.

Curry, M. R. (1999). *Rethinking Privacy in a Geocoded World* (No. 0-471-32182-6). Chicester, UK: John Wiley & Sons.

Davenport, E. (2000). Social intelligence in the age of networks. *Journal of Information Science, 26*(3), 145-152.

Dennis, A. R. & Carte, T. A. (1998). Using geographical information systems for decision making: Extending cognitive fit theory to map-based presentations. *Information Systems Research, 9*(2), 194-203.

Desouza, K. C. (2001). Intelligent agents for competitive intelligence: Survey of applications. *Competitive Intelligence Review, 12*(4), 57-63.

ESRI. (1996). Enterprise GIS in the 90s. *Arc News, 18*(2), 38-40.

Fabrikant, S. I. & Buttenfield, B. P. (2001). Formalizing semantic spaces for information access. *Annals of the Association of American Geographers, 91*(2), 263-280.

Fahey, L. (1999). *Competitors*. New York: John Wiley & Sons.

Forer, P. & Unwin, D. (1999). *Enabling Progress in GIS and Education* (No. 0-471-32182-6). Chicester, UK: John Wiley & Sons.

Fotheringham, A. S. (2000a). GIS-based spatial modelling: A step forwards or a step backwards. In A. S. Fotheringham (Ed.), *Spatial Models and GIS: New and Potential Models* (Vol. 7, GisData series, pp. 21-30). London: Taylor and Francis.

Fotheringham, A. S. (2000b). *Spatial models and GIS: New and potential models*. London: Taylor and Francis.

Fotheringham, A. S. & Rogerson, P. A. (1994). *Spatial Analysis and GIS*. London: Taylor & Francis.

Frank, A. U. (2000). Geographic Information Science: New methods and technology. *Journal of Geographical Systems, 2*(1), 99-105.

Fry, C. (1999). *GIS in telecommunications* (No. 0-471-32182-6). Chicester, UK: John Wiley & Sons.

Fung, D. S. & Remsen, A. P. (1997). Geographic information systems technology for business applications. *Journal of Applied Business Research, 13*(3), 17-24.

Gatrell, A. & Senior, M. (1999). *Health and Health Care Applications* (No. 0-471-32182-6). Chicester, UK: John Wiley & Sons.

Getis, A. (2000). Spatial analysis and GIS: An introduction. *Journal of Geographical Systems, 2*(1), 1-3.

GIS for Business: Discovering the Missing Piece in your Business Strategy. (1995). Cambridge: GeoInformation International.

Goodchild, M. F. (1998). What is GIS? In K. K. Kemp & M. F. Goodchild (Eds.), *The NCGIA GIS Core Curriculum for Technical Programs.* Santa Barbara, CA: National Center of Geographic Information and Analysis.

Goodchild, M. F. (2000). The current status of GIS and spatial analysis. *Journal of Geographical Systems, 2*(1), 5-10.

Goodchild, M. F., Parks, B. O., & Steyaert, L. T. (1993). *Environmental modeling with GIS.* New York: Oxford University Press.

Goodchild, M. F., Steyaert, L. T., & Parks, B. O. (1996). *GIS and environmental modeling: Progress and research issues.*

Goss, J. (1995). We know who you are and we know where you live—The instrumental rationality of geodemographic systems. *Economic Geography, 71*(2), 171-188.

Graef, J. L. (1998). Using the internet for competitive intelligence: A survey report. *Competitive Intelligence Review, 8*(4), 41-47.

Grimshaw, D. J. (2000). *Bringing Geographical Information Systems into Business* (2nd ed.). New York: John Wiley & Sons.

Grimshaw, D. J. (2001). Harnessing the power of geographical knowledge: The potential for data integration in an SME. *International Journal of Information Management, 21*(3), 183-191.

Guimaraes, T. & Armstrong, C. (1998). Exploring the relations between competitive intelligence, IS support, and business change. *Competitive Intelligence Review, 9*(3), 45-54.

Gunter, K. (1999). A comparison of two case studies illustrating the use of a collaborative information system to support competitive advantage. *International Journal of Technology Management, 18*(5-8), 549-561.

Hall, H. (2000). Online information sources: Tools of business intelligence. *Journal of Information Science, 26*(3), 139-143.

Harder, C. (1997). *ArcView GIS means business.* Redlands: Environmental Systems Research Institute.

Hartung, V. & MacPherson, A. (2000). Innovation and collaboration in the geographic information systems (GIS) industry: Evidence from Canada and the United States. *R&D Management, 30*(3), 225-234.

Hartung, V. & Macpherson, A. (2001). Location and the innovation performance of commercial GIS companies. *Growth and Change, 32*(1), 3-22.

Hendriks, P. H. J. (1998). Information strategies for Geographical Information Systems. *International Journal of Geographical Information Science, 12*(6), 621-639.

Hendriks, P. H. J. & Ottens, H. F. L. (1997). *Geografische Informatie Systemen in ruimtelijk onderzoek [Geographical Information Systems in spatial research]*. Assen: Van Gorcum.

Hernández, D. (1994). *Qualitative Representation of Spatial Knowledge* (Vol. 804). Berlin: Springer.

Hernandez, T. (1999). *Explaining Retail GIS: The Adoption, Use and Development of GIS by Retail Organisations in The Netherlands, the UK and Canada*. Utrecht: Koninklijk Nederlands Aardrijkskundig Genootschap Amsterdam: Vakgroep Ruimtelijke Economie Vrije Universiteit Amsterdam.

Hernandez, T., Byrom, J., Bennison, D., & Hooper, P. (2001). The use of geographical data and information in retail locational planning. *Journal of Targeting, Measurement and Analysis for Marketing, 9*(3), 219-229.

Herwijnen, M. v. (1999). *Spatial Decision Support for Environmental Management*. Utrecht: Elinkwijk.

Hohhof, B. (1994). Developing information-systems for competitive intelligence support. *Library Trends, 43*(2), 226-238.

Jankowski, P. & Nyerges, T. (2001). GIS-supported collaborative decision making: Results of an experiment. *Annals of the Association of American Geographers, 91*(1), 48-70.

Johnson, M. L. (1996). GIS in business: Issues to consider in curriculum decision- making. *Journal of Geography, 95*(3), 98-105.

Jones, K. & Biasiotto, M. (1999). Internet retailing: Current hype or future reality. *The International Review of Retail, Distribution and Consumer Research, 9*(1), 69-99.

Kahaner, L. (1996). *Competitive Intelligence: From Black Ops to Boardrooms—How Businesses Gather, Analyze, and Use Information to Succeed in the Global Market Place*. New York: Simon & Schuster.

Kassler, H. S. (1997). Mining the Internet for competitive intelligence: How to track and sift for golden nuggets. *Online: The Magazine of Online Information Systems, 21*(5), 34-45.

Kemp, K. K. & Goodchild, M. F. (1998). *The NCGIA GIS core curriculum for technical programs.* Santa Barbara: National Center for Geographic Information and Analysis.

Kemp, K. K., Goodchild, M. F., & Dodson, R. F. (1992). Teaching GIS in geography. *Professional Geographer, 44*(2), 181-191.

Kuhn, W. (1992). *Paradigms of GIS Use.* Paper presented at the 5th International Symposium on Spatial Data Handling, Columbia.

Kuhn, W. (1993). Metaphors create theories for users. In A. U. Frank & I. Campari (Eds.), *Spatial Information Theory: A Theoretical Basis for GIS* (vol. 716, pp. 366-376). Berlin: Springer.

Lange, A. & Gilbert, C. (1999). Using GPS for GIS data capture. In P. A. Longley, M. F. Goodchild, & D. J. Maguire (Eds.), *Geographical Information Systems* (vol. 1, pp. 467-476). Chicester, UK: John Wiley & Sons.

Longley, P. & Clarke, G. (1995). *GIS for Business and Service Planning.* Cambridge, MA: GeoInformation International.

Longley, P. A. (2001). *Geographic Information Systems and Science.* Chicester, UK: John Wiley & Sons.

Longley, P. A. & Batty, M. (1996). *Spatial Analysis: Modelling in a GIS Environment.* Cambridge: GeoInformation International.

Longley, P. A., Goodchild, M. F., & Maguire, D. J. (1999a). *Geographical Information Systems* (vol. 1). Chicester, UK: John Wiley & Sons.

Longley, P. A., Goodchild, M. F., & Maguire, D. J. (1999b). *Geographical Information Systems* (vol. 2). Chicester, UK: John Wiley & Sons.

Maguire, D. J. (1995). Implementing spatial analysis and GIS applications for business and service planning. In P. Longley & G. Clarke (Eds.), *GIS for Business and Service Planning* (pp. 171-191). Cambridge: GeoInfomation International.

Marín-Llanes, L., Carro-Cartaya, J., & Espín-Andrade, R. (2001). Information analysis techniques for the competitive intelligence process. *Competitive Intelligence Review, 12*(1), 32-40.

Martin, D. J. (1999). Spatial representation: The social scientist's perspective. In P. A. Longley, M. F. Goodchild, & D. J. Maguire (Eds.), *Geographical Information Systems* (vol. 1, pp. 71-80). Chicester, UK: John Wiley & Sons.

Mennecke, B. E. (1997). Understanding the role of geographic information technologies in business: Applications and research directions. *Journal of Geographic Information and Decision Analysis, 1*(1), 44-68.

Mennecke, B. E. (2000). Teaching spatial analysis in business: An examination of the use of geographic information systems in a decision support systems course. *Journal of Computer Information Systems, 40*(3), 24-31.

Meyers, J. (1999). *GIS in the Utilities* (No. 0-471-32182-6). Chicester, UK: John Wiley & Sons.

Nordstrom, R. D. & Pinkerton, R. L. (1999). Taking advantage of Internet sources to build a Competitive Intelligence system. *Competitive Intelligence Review, 10*(1), 54-61.

Nyerges, T. L., Montejano, R., Oshiro, C., & Dadswell, M. (1997). Group-based geographic information systems for transportation improvement site selection. *Transportation Research Part C-Emerging Technologies, 5*(6), 349-369.

Openshaw, S. (1995). Marketing spatial analysis: A review of prospects and technologies relevant to marketing. In P. Longley & G. Clarke (Eds.), *GIS for Business and Service Planning* (pp. 150-166). Cambridge: GeoInfomation International.

Pawar, B. S. & Sharda, R. (1997). Obtaining business intelligence on the Internet. *Long Range Planning, 30*(1), 110-121.

Peng, Z. R. & Huang, R. H. (2000). Design and development of interactive trip planning for web- based transit information systems. *Transportation Research Part C-Emerging Technologies, 8*(1-6), 409-425.

Peuquet, D. J. (1999). *Time in GIS and Geographical Databases* (No. 0-471-32182-6). Chicester, UK: John Wiley & Sons.

Pollard, A. (1999). *Competitor Intelligence.* London: Financial Times Publishing.

Porter, M. E. (1980). *Competitive Strategy: Techniques for Analyzing Industries and Competitors.* New York: Free Press/Collier Macmillan.

Powell, J. H. & Bradford, J. P. (2000). Targeting intelligence gathering in a dynamic competitive environment. *International Journal of Information Management, 20*(3), 181-195.

Reeve, D. E. & Petch, J. R. (1999). *GIS, Organisations and People: A Socio-Technical Approach.* London: Taylor & Francis.

Rowley, J. (1999). Loyalty, the Internet and the weather: the changing nature of marketing information systems? *Management Decision, 37*(6), 514-518.

Rowley, J. E. (1992). Current-awareness or competitive intelligence—A review of the options. *Aslib Proceedings, 44*(11-12), 367-372.

Sherwood, N. (1995). Business geographics—A U.S. perspective. In P. Longley & G. Clarke (Eds.), *GIS for Business and Service Planning* (pp. 250-270). Cambridge: GeoInfomation International.

Swink, M. & Speier, C. (1999). Presenting geographic information: Effects of data aggregation, dispersion, and users' spatial orientation. *Decision Sciences, 30*(1), 169-195.

Teo, T. S. H. (2000). Using the Internet for competitive intelligence in Singapore. *Competitive Intelligence Review, 11*(2), 61-70.

Teo, T. S. H. & Choo, W. Y. (2001). Assessing the impact of using the Internet for competitive intelligence. *Information & Management, 39*(1), 67-83.

Tseng, G., Drenth, H., & Morris, A. (1995). The selection of online databases for UK company information. *Journal of Librarianship and Information Science, 27*(3), 159-170.

Uran, O. (2002). *Spatial Decision Support Systems for Coastal Zone and Water Management*. Enschede: PrintPartners Ipskamp.

Vlachopoulou, M., Silleos, G., & Manthou, V. (2001). Geographic information systems in warehouse site selection decisions. *International Journal of Production Economics, 71*(1-3), 205-212.

Waters, N. (1999). *Transportation GIS: GIS-T* (No. 0-471-32182-6). Chicester, UK: John Wiley & Sons.

Weber, J. & Kwan, M. P. (2002). Bringing time back in: a study on the influence of travel time variations and facility opening hours on individual accessibility. *Professional Geographer, 54*(2), 226-240.

Wegener, M. (2000). Spatial models and GIS. In A. S. Fotheringham (Ed.), *Spatial Models and GIS: New and Potential Models* (Vol. 7, pp. 3-20). London: Taylor and Francis.

Zerger, A., Bishop, I. D., Escobar, F., & Hunter, G. J. (2002). A self-learning multimedia approach for enriching GIS education. *Journal of Geography in Higher Education, 26*(1), 67-80.

Chapter X

Building a Competitive Intelligence System: An Infrastructural Approach

Egbert Philips
University of Nijmegen, The Netherlands

ABSTRACT

Competitive intelligence is understood as the process of acquiring environmental data and transforming them into strategic relevant intelligence. To realize the activities in the four stages of the intelligence process (directing, collecting, analyzing and distributing), a so-called intelligence infrastructure is needed. This infrastructure consists of all the requirements (division of tasks and responsibilities, human resources, and ICT) to perform the intelligence activities. In this chapter we propose an infrastructural approach to designing and implementing a competitive intelligence system. In the infrastructural approach, it is acknowledged that ICT solutions are only a part of the total infrastructure, realizing the

CI activities. Moreover, the infrastructural approach is characterized by a specific view on the development process. The different elements of the infrastructure are simultaneously developed and the design of the process is actually executed by the future users. The goal of this participative design process is to create user commitment by taking the interests and needs of the potential users into account. This commitment is supposed to be a necessary prerequisite for a successful implementation of a CI infrastructure. In this chapter, a case is described to illuminate how an infrastructural approach with respect to CI works.

INTRODUCTION

Competitive intelligence is understood as the process of acquiring environmental data and transforming them into strategic relevant intelligence (Philips & Vriens, 1999). The main contribution of competitive intelligence is to enable organizations to operate proactively in a complex and turbulent business environment. To realize this contribution, both quantitative and qualitative data are required. Quantitative data refer, for instance, to market share, financial figures, or growth percentages. Qualitative data cannot be captured in figures. They include, for instance, movements of competitors, their marketing approach, their organization, or possible future developments. The competitive intelligence process should collect both kinds of data and transform them into strategic intelligence.

As many authors point out, the process of collecting and producing intelligence is often described as a cycle of four interrelated stages: the direction stage (defining the required strategic information); the collection stage (searching the information); the analysis stage (analyzing the strategic relevance of the collected information); and the dissemination stage (where the intelligence is forwarded to the strategic decision makers). See, for instance, Kahaner (1997), Bernhardt (1994), or Fuld (1995) for similar descriptions of the intelligence process.

To realize the activities in these four stages, a so-called intelligence infrastructure is needed. This infrastructure consists of all the requirements (in terms of a division of tasks and responsibilities; of human resources and of ICT) to perform the intelligence activities. During the last decades, many organizations have tried to implement an intelligence infrastructure—e.g., in the form of "intelligence units," equipped with CI staff and necessary ICT tools. At the same time, the role of ICT (as a part of the intelligence infrastructure) has been growing rapidly. For instance, much attention has been paid to the use of Internet applications for search activities (cf., Cook & Cook, 2000). Still more attention, however, seems to be paid to so-called "business intelligence tools" which should be understood as a collection of tools regarding data warehouses, data mining and OLAP (Online Analytical Processing) (Cook & Cook, 2000; Hannig, 2002). Business intelligence software is often used as a label to indicate the whole field of competitive intelligence.

Due to these developments regarding ICT, there tends to be an overemphasis on the role of ICT as a part of the whole intelligence infrastructure. In their efforts to implement the intelligence infrastructure, organizations often use an "ICT-driven" approach. This means that they take a specific ICT tool (e.g., a data warehouse with analysis tools) as the starting point for organizing the whole CI process. This approach may lead to the problem that the software tools are not used properly and do not generate the added value expected from them. In this approach, a competitive intelligence system is just a collection of software tools.

To avoid such problems, we propose an infrastructural approach to designing and implementing a competitive intelligence system. In the infrastructural approach, it is acknowledged that ICT solutions are only a part of the total infrastructure realizing the CI activities. The approach takes the CI process and its goals as a starting point. This CI process functions as a concept for building and implementing a CI infrastructure, constituted by organizational, human, and ICT elements. In this approach the use of ICT tools is (1) determined against the background of the goals of the CI process and (2) integrated into the total infrastructure. In this approach, a competitive intelligence system is a system of interrelated elements of the intelligence infrastructure realizing the goals of the intelligence process.

In this chapter we discuss the application of the infrastructural approach to design and implement a competitive intelligence system. The approach was applied in a large international firm in vegetables seeds, which will be called GEMODI. The chapter describes how the infrastructural approach was employed at GEMODI to arrive at a CI infrastructure, supported by a Lotus Notes database tool.

To discuss the application of the infrastructural approach, the chapter is organized as follows. We first introduce GEMODI and the background of the project. Next, we elaborate on the general concept of the intelligence infrastructure. We then describe the step-by-step procedure we followed to define the infrastructure and present the resulting intelligence infrastructure. In the last section we will show how an ICT tool (a Lotus Notes application) was developed to support the intelligence activities.

THE GEMODI CASE

GEMODI is a globally operating company in developing and marketing vegetables seeds. GEMODI operates in a highly competitive environment. Because of its aim to improve its marketing policy and tactical marketing operations by a more effective and efficient use of (locally available) competitor intelligence, GEMODI started a Competitor Intelligence Project. The goal of this project was to design and implement a CI system. This system should systematize and give concrete form to the process of competitor tracking and analysis. Finally the process had to be supported by "a systematic competitor tracking and analysis tool." The aim of this tool is to structure, analyze and transform data and information into actionable intelligence on current and future competitor moves. The emphasis in this project was on the development of qualitative data instead of quantitative data. Quantitative data refer to market shares, financial figures, or growth percentages. Qualitative data are not expressed in figures and reflect, for example, developments of competitors, data about innovations, marketing approaches, or the organization of work of competitors. In fact, qualitative data are all data that are not easy to capture by figures. Sometimes they refer to rumors, sometimes to perceived developments. In the GEMODI case, qualitative data were perceived to be very important—so an important goal of the European GEMODI organization was to involve its people in all 20 participating countries to produce qualitative intelligence about its competitors. This process should result in intelligence that is supposed to contribute to an improvement of the marketing plans, competitive strategies, product plans, developmental plans, and sales strategies. The development of a CI infrastructure should secure the production of the required intelligence.

THE CONCEPT OF INFRASTRUCTURE

As mentioned in the introduction, an infrastructural development approach can be distinguished from an ICT-oriented development approach. In an ICT-oriented development approach of CI, the realization of an ICT tool is the central aim. This approach often leads to problems because the organization of activities with respect to the functioning of the ICT tool (filling and using) is not adequately realized. As a consequence, the tools are not properly used and, therefore, investments are destroyed. The main reason for these failures is a lack of understanding of the needs of the users and an inappropriate concept of the user context at the beginning of the project. Users are not conceptualized as people with specific interests. Information needs and motivations are not taken into account properly. As a result, only when the tool is realized, one starts worrying about motivating people to use and contribute to the system. Most of the time, this is far too late and the system developed implodes. One can imagine easily what might happen if users cannot fulfill their information needs with the database. In such a case they will not use it. As a consequence, they will not contribute to the filling of the database as well. This may lead to more problems: if the database is not properly filled with data, it is not useful to other users, who, as a result, will not contribute to the system. A self-amplifying process has started that, in the end, leads to total failure of the system developed.

The opposite of an ICT-driven development approach is an infrastructural approach. In the infrastructural approach, this motivational and acceptance problem of the ICT tool does not appear. In the infrastructural approach a set of different measures is directed at the realization of the CI process. ICT is just one element of the infrastructure. As a consequence, the ICT tool is not the point of reference for the development of a CI system. Instead, the CI process itself is the starting point for organizing and implementing competitive intelligence. This CI process, therefore, is conceptualized as a joint process of parties who all have their own interests. By contributing to the CI process they want to realize their personal interest.

In the GEMODI case it would have been tempting to start the project with an ICT-driven approach. Because of the functionalities and possibilities of different ICT platforms, firms can easily imagine how they can benefit from these products. But this is a mistake many companies make. They start thinking with the opportunities of the platforms and ICT tools instead of "at the beginning." This "beginning" should be the goal organizations want to realize with the intelligence to be produced, the process in which the desired intelligence should be produced, and finally, the organizational context in which intelligence becomes possible to be produced.

In an infrastructural development approach (see also Frid, 1999) one starts with worrying about the organizational context in which the CI process has to be realized. It is this context (the personal skills of people, the division of CI activities in the organization, the division of responsibilities with respect to CI) that determines if people are going to use the tool. Information requirements and personal interests are taken into account in the development of the CI process. As a result, the ICT tools to be developed are carefully anchored in the organization. Motivation to contribution and acceptance of the ICT tool are secured.

The core of the infrastructural approach (see also Frid, 1999) is a proportional attention for the different elements which constitute the infrastructure. The elements that should constitute the CI System are the CI process, the organization of the activities which should realize the CI process, the knowledge and skills required to make it possible for employees to execute the required activities, and finally, a tool to support the execution of these activities. Moreover, the infrastructural development approach is characterized by a specific view on the development process. The different elements of the infrastructure are simultaneously developed and the design of the process is actually executed by the future users. In the next section we will pay attention to the development characteristics of the infrastructural approach.

Figure 1 illuminates the infrastructural approach of designing a CI system. The process to be realized is only a concept. It is an idea in the mind of the designer and becomes emergent if it can be separated into activities which are realized by people "in reality." To make this process emergent there should be a 'shared' notion of the CI process by the people who have to make the process happen. If this condition is realized the process can be divided into activities. An organization of CI tasks and responsibilities consists of groups of activities (Layer 2 in Illustration 1). These tasks and responsibilities have to be executed

Figure 1. The CI-Infrastructure

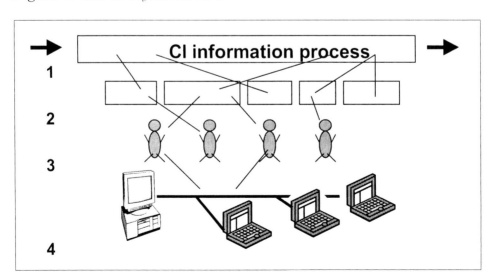

by people. Therefore, these organizational tasks have to be appointed to people and these people have to be motivated to perform these tasks as well as possible (Layer 3 in Figure 1). Finally, tools are available, and maybe tools have to be designed, to support people in executing their tasks. At this level (Layer 4 in Figure 1) requirements are set for the selection and development of supporting ICT tools.

The infrastructure that constitutes the CI system consists of a set of people and tools which are related in a specific way and in this relationship together realize the CI process. To develop such a system the designer uses organizational (Layer 2), human resource (Layer 3) and ICT (Layer 4) measures. These measures are all necessary to realize the system in an appropriate way. Central and crucial in this infrastructural way of thinking is not conceptualizing the ICT tool as the center of the universe and creating a context which stimulates the functioning of the tool. It is thinking the other way around. Starting at the business perspective, the focus is at the process which should be kept 'going' by realizing all kinds of measures.

DEVELOPMENT OF THE GEMODI COMPETITIVE INTELLIGENCE SYSTEM

According to the infrastructural approach explained in the previous paragraph, the development of the GEMODI CIS should have started with a description of the CI process involved. Such a description would allow us to identify activities to be executed and accordingly to construct an organization of these activities. This would make it possible to assign the activities to people. However, this is not a proper way and, therefore, is not suggested by the infrastructural approach. In fact, the suggested approach creates an essential problem. This is the problem of the identity of the designer. Who is designing the process? And who should be involved in this designing process because of commitment and implementation reasons?

In the traditional "design table" approach there is the "designer" designing the process involved. In most cases this is a consultant or an organizations specialist. Theoretically the designer can be everybody. This designer, as an observer, will make a design of the CI process involved. In such an approach a design is like a blueprint. As the blueprint is finished the next stage of implementation and realization is started. For commitment and implementation reasons this "design table approach" is not an adequate method. It creates a distance between the designer and the user or executor of the process and the resulting tools. This distance enlarges the chance that users will not support the designed process. Potential users of the system should, therefore, be involved in the designing of the process. Thereby it is made possible for them to bring in their interests and needs in an early stage. If we involve the group of potential users in this early stage they become, together with the "consultant or organizations specialist," the designers of the CI process. This will make them co-authors of both the process and the resulting tool, and generates commitment. This commitment is based on the one hand on the possibility to bring in their personal needs and interests. On the other hand it is also based on the psychological feeling of being the co-designer of the process. As a result of this alternative "development approach," the resulting designed process is part of the mind of a set of important organization members, instead of in the head of one single external observer. This creates an enormous advantage in latter stages of the development and implementation process. As might be clear by now, this kind of development (a development approach) is quite different from the traditional "design table approach" mentioned earlier.

But how can we, in fact, realize the development approach? Which steps do we have to take in what sequence? Let's define a step approach by explaining the three elements on which the development approach used in the GEMODI CIS project is based. The first is a project organization constituted by a representative user group. The second element consists of a pilot approach. And the third and final element is the framework used for going through the pilot. We will explain each element now.

The Representative User Group

Crucial in the development approach is not designing the process, organization and resulting tool on the design table, but involves the future users in this process. Therefore, we choose first to form a representative user group (it is not possible to involve all potential users!) The criteria for representation are three-fold: each participating country needs to be represented in the pilot organization. Furthermore, each type of function (from sales representative next to a general manager of the operating company) needs to be represented. Finally it is important to have a representation according to future CI functions. The chosen members of the pilot group need to have the capabilities to function as a CI champion in their local organizations. This means that the chosen local representatives are meant to be the future CI coordinators for their countries. The principal of the project, who eventually is supported by an organizations specialist, is meant to be the central coordinator. As a result the first version of the CI organization already exists at the beginning of the project. And it is this organization itself who is designing the process, improving the CI organization and designing the tools.

The Pilot Project

The second element of the development approach refers to the activities to be executed by the representative user group. In fact, with their installation, they are responsible for the designing of the process and the resulting process. But how are we going to deal with this problem? What means do they have? The second element of the development approach is a framework which serves as a means to give structure to the discussions about the design. Structure is given by a pilot approach. This approach is based on the insight that if we want to design a process for continuously monitoring and analyzing our competitors, we can learn about this design by simply going through one simple case: the pilot. If we want to know how a process of competitive intelligence is executed we simply can produce a lot of knowledge by doing one specific case and reflect on the activities we are executing. In the case of the GEMODI project we chose one relevant competitor to go through the intelligence process. In this process we designed the CI process and generalized it. From this design we derived the functional requirements to the organization and the supporting tools.

Framework for Activities in the Pilot

The third element is a framework for going through the pilot project process. If we are choosing one unique case as an object to learn about the CI process in general, we do need a tool which tells us what activities to execute in the pilot project. As a framework in the GEMODI project we used the BI cycle (Kahaner, 1997; Philips & Vriens, 1999). For the selected pilot competitor we went through all four stages of the BI cycle: the direction stage, the collection stage, the analysis stage and the distribution and usage stage.

The development approach based on the three elements explained above is to be executed by the following concrete steps:

Step 1. Installation CI workforce—Representative user group

Step 2. Selection of pilot competitor

Step 3. Workshop 1—Definition of point of reference for BI Cycle

Step 4. Workshop 2—Direction phase, definition of information needs

Step 5. Organization of search activities

Step 6. Workshop 3—Analysis phase

Figure 2. The BI Cycle

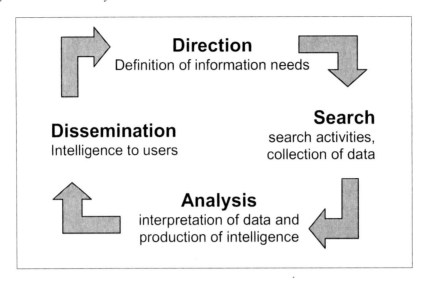

Step 7. Workshop 4—Usage phase
Step 8. Presentation designed CI process
Step 9. Evaluation process and feedback of functional requirements
Step 10. Building of the ICT tool
Step 11. Training and Implementation

We will now first elucidate some essential steps that will not be clear by now. After selecting the pilot competitor we need to produce intelligence about this competitor by going through the BI cycle. First, we have to define what information needs we have with respect to the competitor. Hereafter we have to define how we are going to realize these needs by the collection of data. Third, we have to analyze data, and finally we have to distribute and use the results of the analysis. The assumption is that we simply can generalize the needs and tools produced in the pilot process to other competitors.

In the second workshop (Step 4) we define what needs we have with respect to the competitor. But how are we doing this in a representative user group? The framework we used for this exercise is based on systems theory. By defining the system (the GEMODI company) we create a shared point of reference for defining the environment (first workshop, Step 3), relevant competitors and the relevant information needs with respect to these competitors. In the workshop of Step 3, therefore, we play a game directed at the collective production of a company profile. This profile consists of six important elements: the mission of the company, the competences of the company, the environment of the company, its products and services, and its organization and its financials. This company profile is filled for the GEMODI company in a game that was directed at the solution of a strategic problem. By filling this company profile, a shared point of reference is created in which all individual interests of the members of the representative user group are taken into account. From the resulting point of reference it is possible to define what we need to know from our competitor (Step 4). It is important that all individual needs of the members of the user group will be taken into account. This is very important because the assumption is that most data about competitors are available somewhere within the GEMODI organization or are easily accessible by people within the GEMODI organization. Most of the time, however, the data stay with these people who do not use it or do not see the relevance of it. The starting point, therefore, is that in the GEMODI organization people sometimes ask for competitor data and sometimes are a source for this data. The process and tool to be developed should facilitate the exchange process between demand and provision of data. This process will only keep running, as it is in the interests of the people involved. In other words, employees only contribute to the process if they can gain from it. And the only way they can gain from the process is if in their exchange of data their specific individual needs are taken into account. This is exactly the reason why a representative user group is defining the information needs with respect to the competitor intelligence process; because, as a result, the individual needs from the main providers of crucial competitor data are taken into accent. This means that a permanent process of exchanging interest by data interchange will be facilitated. This durable exchanging process is the motor of the CI process.

In the following steps of the project the next phases of the BI cycle are executed with respect to the selected competitor. In the search phase search activities are executed and knowledge about search strategies is shared. In the third workshop the resulting data is analyzed. In this analysis, session requirements are defined with respect to the way the process and tool to be developed can support the analysis activities. In the last workshop (which is about usage of the resulting knowledge) the resulting intelligence is transformed into organization actions.

In fact, at the end of the Workshops 1 to 4 a CI process exists and a primitive initial CI organization is apparent. If we evaluate the elements of an infrastructure, which are the shared conception of a process, the division of tasks and responsibilities, the development of essential knowledge and the availability of supporting tools, we can conclude that by the end of Workshop

4 a primitive CI organization exists. Consider that there are templates of information needs developed, there is an initial division of CI tasks with respect to the search activities, knowledge about the execution of the process is developed, and there are some primitive tools for supporting the process available. Therefore, we can only conclude that the beginning of a professional CI infrastructure is apparent. The development approach is, therefore, characterized as "designing in development" instead of a "design table approach."

A CI INFRASTRUCTURE

The policy processes the CI infrastructure aims to support function as a steering point of reference. At the central level these processes are the business planning process, but also the process of marketing planning and product planning. These processes determine when what kind of intelligence is needed. The lead-time of the intelligence processes, and therefore the intelligence cycle, is constituted by the time planning of these business processes. If a marketing manager needs specific competitor intelligence to support his or her marketing plan, this actual intelligence needs to be available in the beginning of this marketing planning process and not afterwards. If we know this time schedule we can plan the filling of the templates representing the intelligence needs of the marketing manager (most of them are part of the business environment category of the GEMODI profile). These templates can concern all competitors involved, but it is also possible to plan the competitors involved in the intelligence process on a yearly basis. At the beginning of the CI process the competitors involved in the CI process of that specific year are identified. By this structure, business processes are structurally coupled to the intelligence processes. In this process, specific choices are made with respect to the competitors involved in the intelligence process of that year. Most companies plan the monitoring and analyzing of their competitors in time. By, for example, dealing with three major competitors each year, a competitor knowledge basis is built that is actualized on a three year basis. Of course, actual developments can be an argument for monitoring a competitor each year or for changing the originally planned process.

Of course, the planning and communication of the coupling of the business processes with the intelligence processes needs to be coordinated. A central role in the CI organization, therefore, is reserved for the so-called CI coordinators. In fact, the CI organization exists of the whole organization structured by a network of CI coordinators (see Figure 3). The role of the CI coordinators is crucial. They coordinate the communication between the business process at their specific management level (central holding level, divisional level or decentralized level). They plan the execution of the BI cycle and initiate activities by sending templates to the people involved in the execution of the intelligence cycles. They coordinate and facilitate the process of searching and analysis. In the end, they validate the intelligence produced collectively and make it available for the rest of the organization. They are the intermediate between the business process and the intelligence process. They plan the deliverables of the process and both identify and facilitate the people involved in the execution of the intelligence process. They are pretty autonomous in planning this process. The members of the representative user group were selected to be the local CI coordinators for their specific countries. In the GEMODI case, the decentralized CI coordinators were steered by the central CI coordinator in their task of supporting the central CI processes. But, of course, they also have their own CI priorities in supporting their local business processes. They are autonomous in organizing the execution of the CI activities but are also autonomous in defining their local CI policy. An example for the autonomous organization of CI activities in the GEMODI case was illustrated by the difference between, for example, involved countries such as Belgium and Turkey. In Turkey the organization was quite different from the Belgium organization. Sales representatives were not employees of the company as they were in Belgium. As a result, the CI coordinator for Turkey did not always involve these sales reps in the CI process because they possibly were working for competitors too. Another difference with respect to these two local areas is the geographical characteristics. If we consider Turkey to be a huge country and Belgium a relatively small one, we can imagine that collective analysis activities are executed in a totally different manner. In Turkey a small elite group executes the analysis at the head office. In Belgium all sales reps come together twice a year at a central place to analyze their competitor data. By organizing a network of central and local CI coordinators different motors of a durable CI process are shaped. With the business processes of the different business levels as a starting point, coordinators are starting CI processes which amplify and support each other. By this structure different motors are shaped behind the building of a competitor knowledge base.

A major task and responsibility of the local CI coordinator (who normally executes another task, such as sales rep, marketing manager, or product manager) is motivating the people involved in the local CI process to deliver their contribution to the CI process. The chance of a successfully operating CI

Figure 3. The CI Organization

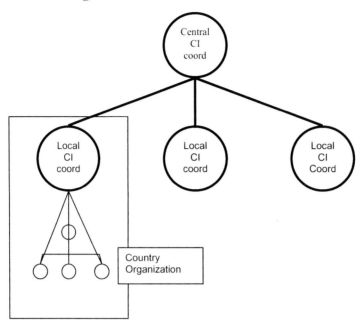

coordinator depends on different human resource measures. First, the chance of obtaining their contribution is increased if the people involved can realize their personal interests by the CI process. We discussed this topic earlier. Secondly, there are other different measures which can be used to increase the chance of obtaining the desired contribution. The people involved need to be conditioned, motivated and eventually sanctioned to deliver their contribution. Conditioning can be realized by integrating the CI tasks in the job descriptions of the people involved. For example, a sales rep's function can be extended by the task of filling in a competitor paragraph after visiting key customers. These people can be motivated to perform this task well if their bosses evaluate them on the performances they deliver on these tasks. Part of the review conversation should be the evaluation of the contribution to the collective CI process. Finally, if people do not contribute to the CI process while they are supposed to do so, they can be sanctioned. This means that consequences are attached to not contributing to the CIS process. An example of a very clear and evident sanction is not receiving the annual wage raise.

ICT: CIS LOTUS NOTES DATABASE

Crucial in the infrastructural approach of developing a competitor intelligence system is that the ICT tools are supportive tools to be designed when process, division of tasks and responsibilities and human capabilities are designed. The ICT tools to be designed only serve to support the process already designed on paper by the project team. A goal of the ICT tools is to make it easier for the people involved to deliver their contributions and execute their activities. The support an ICT tool can deliver concerns in the GEMODI case the central storage and availability of data, the communication with the central database from local stations, the availability of the data on each point in time and the sharing of knowledge by the possibility to make remarks on certain data.

We already stated earlier that it is very important that a change of interest facilitates the process of competitor monitoring and analysis. This change of interest is realized by the parties concerned that sometimes are user, but sometimes are also source in the competitive intelligence process. The basic fundament that serves as a motor for the intelligence process is the prerequisite that individuals only contribute to the process (and therefore the system) if they have something to gain from it. And they have something to gain from the process if they get something useful in return for their contribution. To design this motor of the intelligence process it is important to design a system that delivers operationally useful data for all people concerned who are supposed to contribute. This was the reason, in the first place, why a representative user group was established in the designing process. If we take a look at the database tool to support the competitive intelligence process, as a consequence, data are available that support all different individuals in the execution of their functions. For example, a marketing manager of a certain product is supported by templates about the image of the competitor (see Figure 4), the marketing tools competitors are using, the staff they have organized, etc. Because different functions imply different data needs, using the information needs profiler with the representative user group covers the whole spectrum of data needs. Each category of the profiler is translated in data templates that reflect the data needs of certain functions (see range of templates resulting in Figure 4).

If we look at the left site of the screenshot in Figure 4, we see the navigation system of CIS. In this navigation scheme the three levels of supporting the execution of functions become clear. The data level (the spectrum of data needs that is covered) is behind the topic "Views". In the CIS database there are

Figure 4. Screenshot of CIS—Competitor Image

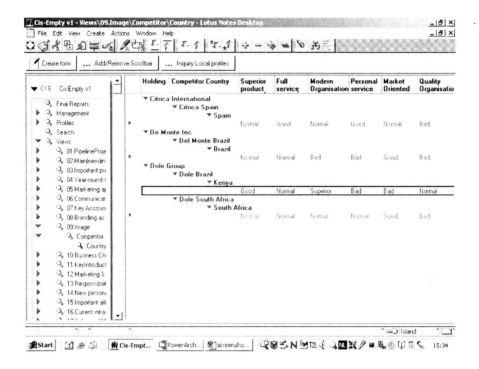

twenty customized templates to support people in the execution of their tasks with specific competitor data. Behind Topic 2, "Profiles", the information level of the CIS database is hidden. Here interpretations and conclusions of people in the organization about data collected by others is stored and made available. In the end the "knowledge level" of the database is hidden behind the topic "final reports". Here the final profiles of competitors are stored.

The aim of the database is not to make all knowledge available with the gatekeepers of the organization explicit. The Lotus Notes CIS database facilitates the disclosure of knowledge available about competitors somewhere in the organization. According to a set of specified templates this knowledge covers all relevant functional areas. Sources are directed to fill the templates and in return are provided with the intelligence they need to execute their functions better. In a template, implicit knowledge can be disclosed by answering key questions with key answers structured to relevant themes. The items, theme, keyword, competitor, product and, for example, relevant country disclose this knowledge. Because the source of the knowledge is always announced in the form, users of this data are always capable of disclosing the

Figure 5. Screenshot of CIS—'Form; Author of Data Always Specified'

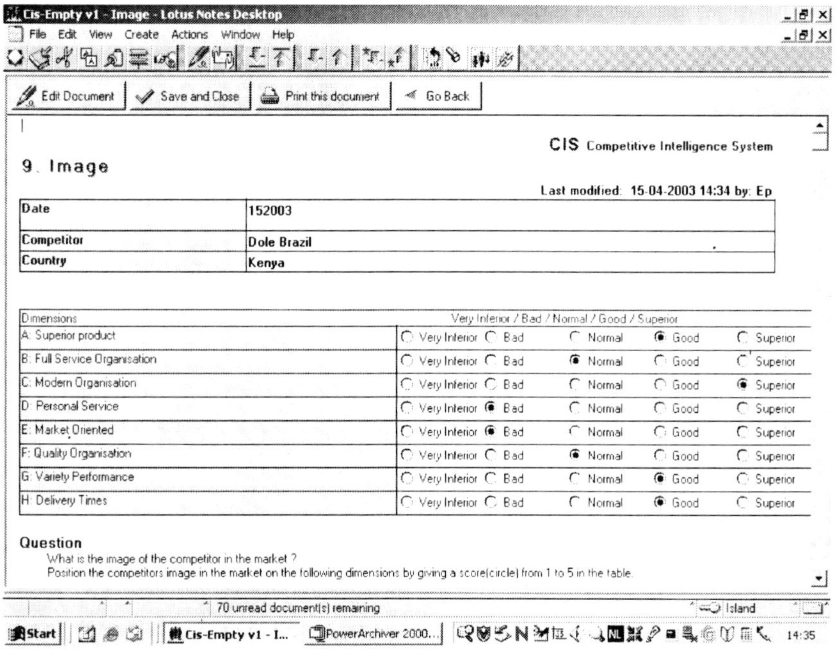

tacit knowledge remaining behind the filled templates (see, for example, Figure 5).

As mentioned earlier, not only data are important, but also the attached interpretations of people. Intelligence is produced amongst others by adding value to data through interpreting. This interpreting is facilitated by the CIS database by providing the user with the possibility to view data in a structured way. A sales manager in the GEMODI is, for example, responsible for the strategy and results in a certain country. Therefore, he wants to make data available selected by country. A product manager, on the contrary, wants to view data not by country but by product. In the navigation scheme this structured way of disclosing data is supported.

If a specific view is selected users become sources by the possibility to add their comments, interpretations and conclusions to the database. These interpretations can be filled in a conclusion form (Figure 6) that serves as a supporting file to generate draft profiles of competitors (per product or per country). Of course, it is possible to have a discussion about the validity of these interpretations. However, we think this discussion is not that appropriate. It is

Figure 6. Screenshot of CIS—'Interpretations are Added to the Database'

more valuable to an organization to identify trends, occurrences, and speculations while keeping in mind that these data sometimes are only speculations and inferences. We do not think it to be wise to invest far too much in validation and keep data hidden before validation has taken place. We think so because with the identification of these data validation becomes possible in the first place. Secondly, all users know the status of the data within the CIS database. They can comment on it, and accordingly, by a forum of different organizational specialists, the data become more and more validated.

As stated earlier the conclusion forms can be fed back to the themes the conclusions are drawn about. By this mechanism the CIS database supports a business analyst with an automatic tool to generate a draft profile of a competitor. Of course not only business analysts can make use of this tool, but product and marketing managers (responsible for a competitor with respect to a certain product or a certain country) as well. This draft profile is a big form where all conclusions and interpretations are ordered in a matrix to both relevant business topics as to a relevant part of competitor profile.

By using the draft profile again value can be added in the competitor intelligence information process. The interpretations and conclusions made

Figure 7. Screenshot of CIS—Final Profiles from Competitors

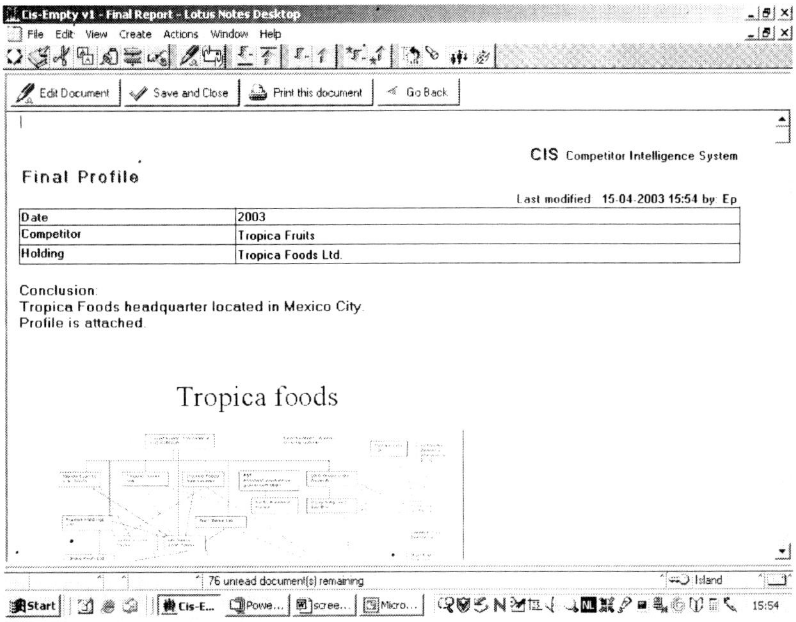

about the data filled in by all kinds of specialists and validated by their comments again serve as a base to add value by drawing inferences. By combining the conclusions and interpretations in the draft profile conclusions can be drawn and presuppositions can be made about the strategy of a competitor. For example: by combining the conclusions about the development of certain competences, the new products they are working on and their way of marketing, very interesting insights about the strategy of a competitor might appear. The business analyst using the draft profile makes these combinations. By doing so, he or she again adds value to the intelligence process and makes this value available to others in the organization by publishing the results in the CIS database. The results of the analysis of the business analyst are profiles of competitors (see Figure 7).

The result of the GEMODI project is a professional competitor watch process which delivers the intelligence to make better plans. Because of the infrastructural approach the database tool used is carefully anchored in the organization. The other organizational measures secure an appropriate realization of the process. By these measures a culture change has taken place. All positions are involved in collecting and using competitor data that generated a far more competitive attitude. Because all individuals (both at central and local level) profit from the CIS process they keep contributing to the process.

CONCLUSION

ICT-driven approaches to the development of CI often fail. In this chapter, as an alternative, an infrastructural approach to the development of a CI process is illuminated.

The infrastructural approach differs in many respects to an ICT-driven approach. Except for the fact that an infrastructural approach acknowledges that ICT is only a tool that supports a process to be executed more efficiently, it is argued that motivational and acceptation aspects need to be taken into account in the development process. An appropriate CI process needs to be carefully anchored in the organization. The interests of users, therefore, are of crucial importance for the acceptance of the system to be implemented. In the development process, for this reason, the future users are involved in an appropriate way in a very early stage. By this involvement they become co-designers of the system, which creates the necessary commitment.

By demonstrating the GEMODI case it became clear how an infrastructural approach could be used in practice. As a result of this approach in the GEMODI case a much more environmental-oriented organization developed. By the collective collection and analysis of competitor data in a shared process, employees were not only provided with data necessary to perform their functions, they were also involved in a process of sharing and delivering data and knowledge to other users in the organization. By this collective exchange process, as an important side effect, a change in organization culture arises. Instead of being internally oriented and protective, most users developed an external market orientation and became much more open to the sharing of information. Of course this change in attitude, again, amplified the process of collectively collecting, analyzing, sharing and using competitor data.

REFERENCES

Bernhardt, D.C. (1994). 'I want it fast, factual, actionable'—Tailoring competitive intelligence to executive needs. *Long Range Planning, 27*(1), 12-24.

Cook, M. & Cook, C. (2000). *Competitive Intelligence. Create an Intelligent Organization and Compete to Win.* London: Kogan Page.

Frid, R.J. (1999). *Infrastructure for Knowledge Management*. Lincoln: Writers Club Press.

Fuld, L.M. (1995) *The New Competitor Intelligence: The Complete Resource for Finding, Analyzing, and Using Information about your Competitors*. New York: John Wiley & Sons.

Hannig, U. (2002). *Knowledge Management and Business Intelligence*. Berlin: Springer.

Kahaner, L. (1997). *Competitive Intelligence*. New York: Touchstone/ Simon & Schuster.

Philips, E.A. & Vriens, D. (1999). *Business Intelligence*. Deventer: Kluwer Bedrijfsinformatie.

Chapter XI

It's All in the Game: How to Use Simulation-Games for Competitive Intelligence and How to Support Them by ICT

Jan Achterbergh
University of Nijmegen, The Netherlands

Dirk Vriens
University of Nijmegen, The Netherlands

ABSTRACT

In this chapter, we explore the role of simulation games for intelligence activities. Although games have been used in intelligence activities, the contribution of building and using simulation games to Competitive Intelligence has, to our knowledge, not been examined thoroughly. In this chapter we fill this gap by explaining the building and using stages of simulation gaming and by discussing the contribution of these stages to directing, collecting, analyzing and disseminating Competitive Intelligence. Moreover, we discuss the role of ICT to enhance the contribution of simulation games to competitive intelligence.

INTRODUCTION

As many authors on competitive intelligence point out, organizations need to collect and process information about the environment to (re)formulate their strategy. Moreover, the pressure to produce timely, accurate, actionable and strategically relevant information is growing because the complexity and dynamics of the environment is increasing rapidly (cf., Kahaner, 1997; Fuld, 1995; Cook & Cook, 2000 for similar arguments). Hence, organizations are trying to structure their competitive intelligence process—the process by means of which strategically relevant information about the environment is delivered.

In the literature on Competitive Intelligence (CI), this process is usually broken up into four stages: direction, collection, analysis, and dissemination (cf. Sammon, 1986; Bernhardt, 1994; Fuld et al., 2002; Kahaner, 1997; Vriens & Philips, 1999). In the direction stage, CI professionals establish what data are relevant for the purpose of strategic decision-making. In the collection stage, relevant data sources are determined and data are collected from them. In the analysis stage, collected data are transformed into competitive intelligence that can be used by strategic decision-makers. In the dissemination stage, the competitive intelligence resulting from analysis is disseminated over strategic decision-makers so that they can incorporate it in the process of (re)formulating their strategies (for a more thorough treatment of the process of competitive intelligence, see Chapter I of this book).

If CI is to deliver its contribution to the process of strategy formulation, a pro-active mode of intelligence gathering seems most appropriate (cf., Ellis, 1993; Hannon, 1997; Tessun, 1997). In a pro-active mode, intelligence practitioners try to anticipate environmental developments that may have a strategic impact and assess their consequences. Pro-active intelligence requires, in our view, a deep insight into the "organization in its environment." For instance, directing the search for information requires an insight into strategic problems the organization in focus has to cope with and environmental factors having an impact on these problems. To direct the search for data, CI professionals need to construct models of these strategic problems and environmental factors. Analyzing collected information and transforming it into intelligence builds on these constructed models and requires an insight into possible effects of a multitude of states of affairs and events in the environment of the organization, on both parties relevant to and the organization in focus itself.

Not only do CI practitioners need a model of the "organization in its environment," it is also important that this model is shared among the different parties involved in the intelligence process. The model should be shared among CI professionals so that they have a common orientation towards performing their CI activities. Moreover, it should be shared among CI professionals and strategic decision-makers for several reasons. Among these are: (1) improving the understanding of CI professionals of strategic problems, (2) grounding the model in the strategic orientation of the organization, (3) facilitating the dissemination of the intelligence, (4) ensuring commitment of strategic decision makers to using the intelligence, and (5) improving the process of monitoring and maintaining the model itself.

Sharing the model among the relevant parties in the organization requires high quality communication (both regarding content and process) between these parties. In this chapter, we examine the potential of (ICT-enabled) simulation games to support this communication process. As Geurts et al. (2000) assert, simulation games may be a valuable tool contributing to improving the quality of the communication. The element of simulation requires participants to interactively model the organization in its environment, systematically analyzing relevant variables, parties, processes and their relations. The element of gaming allows participants to interactively experiment with the model in a relatively safe environment. Together, the simulation and the gaming elements can improve both the content and the process of communication required for pro-active competitive intelligence. Although the use of games in supporting intelligence activities has been reported (e.g., Allgaier & Powell, 1998; Clark, 1998; Fuld, 1998), the link between the different stages of simulation games to CI has not been treated thoroughly. In this chapter, we will examine this link.

To deliver its contribution to the intelligence process, simulation games may be supported by ICT in various ways (e.g., by groupware of various Web-based applications). The role of ICT to enable simulation games is also discussed in this chapter.

To explore the contribution of simulation games to improving the quality of the communication required for the CI process and the possibilities for enabling this contribution by ICT, we first discuss the process of competitive intelligence and its required communication. Simulation games are at issue are then discussed. In particular, we define simulation games as practicing tools for improving communications about complex problems (e.g., problems related to competitive intelligence as a process). Moreover, we discuss the stages of building and using simulation games and list the particular functional contribution of these phases to the improvement of communication about complex problems. This is followed by linking previous chapter discussions and specifying a model describing the possible contribution of simulation games to improving the quality of communications required for the CI process. We then highlight the possible contribution of ICT to simulation games improving the quality of communications needed to carry out CI processes. Finally, we conclude the chapter with a summary of the findings.

COMPETITIVE INTELLIGENCE

By competitive intelligence as a product, we understand it to mean information about the environment of organizations required for strategic decision-making (see also Chapter I of this book for a full treatment of CI as a product). Competitive Intelligence is produced in a process consisting of four stages: directing, collecting, analysis, and dissemination. To be able to assess the possible contribution of simulation games to support the required communication in the CI stages, we discuss these stages and their communicative requirements in this section.

In the direction stage, the environmental information needed for strategic decisions has to be identified. In other words, the strategic information requirements have to be specified. The result of this stage is a list of relevant data (classes) about which information has to be gathered to monitor and/or (re)formulate the strategy of the organization. A crucial issue in the direction stage is to determine the relevance of these data (classes). In order to determine this relevance, directing officers need to be aware of, have knowledge about, and insight into the decisions and underlying problems strategic decision-makers have to deal with. They have to build and maintain a model of the organization in its environment to be able to create the required awareness, knowledge and insight. Moreover, they should use this model to define which environmental factors have an impact on the organization and are, therefore, worth monitoring. Building and using these models places high demands on the communication and cooperation between CI direction officers and strategic decision-makers in the direction phase. During the direction stage, ideally, CI professionals (and strategic decision-makers) are engaged in a continuous process of communication in which they build and maintain a model of the organization in its environment and in which they use this model to derive relevant data classes about which environmental information should be gathered. This communication requires that CI directing officers and decision-makers have a shared language to conceptualize strategic problems and environmental factors relevant to make decisions dealing with these problems.

During the collection stage, sources are identified and data is retrieved from these sources. To this end, one needs to be aware of the availability of sources and of the suitability of the available sources for the efficient retrieval of data. Although a part of data collecting activities may be automated (e.g., by alerting services or online databases), knowledge about what the most appropriate sources are for a particular data class and how to approach them requires experience and the exchange of this experience. Hence, communication among those involved in search activities is important.

During analysis, CI professionals need to determine whether the collected data are significant for strategic purposes. In the analysis stage, the collected data are transformed into intelligence usable by strategic decision-makers. This presupposes that—just like in the directing phase—CI analysts are knowledgeable of the problems strategic decision-makers have to deal with. To this purpose, CI analysts need an underlying model of the organization in its environment—preferably the same model they produced during the direction stage. Moreover, they need continuous feedback about the intelligence they produce in the analysis stage.

In the dissemination stage, the intelligence produced in the analysis stage is forwarded to strategic decision-makers. This entails the selection of (content and format) of the way the intelligence is presented and the actual communication of the intelligence. During this stage of intelligence, practitioners may also receive feedback on the presented intelligence. To disseminate the products of the analysis process, CI officers and strategic decision-makers, again, need a shared language to speak about the developments in the organization's environment in relation to the strategic decision-making process. Moreover, CI officers need to be aware of the formats of the intelligence that are convenient for the strategic decision-makers. If CI officers and strategic decision-makers are both involved in developing and using the model of the organization in its environment, they may have already created a shared language in which they can express strategic problems and the impact of certain environmental trends on the organization. Jointly building and maintaining such models, then, greatly

Table 1. CI-Stages and Required Knowledge

	Description	*Required Knowledge*
Directing	Determine strategic information requirements	Model of organization in its environment How to use the model to derive required information
Collecting	Identify sources and retrieve data from them	How to select sources How to approach sources
Analysis	Transform data into intelligence	Model of organization in its environment How to use the model to assess the impact of specific constellations of environmental variables
Dissemination	Forward intelligence to strategic decision makers	Selection of presentation format and content of intelligence

enhances the understanding (and hence) dissemination of intelligence. Table 1 provides an overview of the four CI stages and their required knowledge.

In our view, the creation of the required knowledge in the stages is dependent on a high quality communication process involving CI professionals and strategic decision-makers. In this communication process feedback is given about the required knowledge in the stages (e.g., about the quality of the model of the organization in its environment) and about the products of the stages (e.g., the information requirements in the first stage). For this communication process to succeed, all participants need to have a shared language to be able to articulate the specific requirements, problems and issues of a stage (e.g., a shared language to build and maintain a model of the organization in its environment, or a shared language to use this model for the assessment of the impact of environmental events).

SIMULATION GAMES

To define what a simulation game entails we turn to the work of Geurts, de Caluwé, and Stoppelenburg (2000). From an overview of the existing literature, these authors derive three perspectives relevant for defining a simulation game.

The first perspective is the *essence* of gaming that, according to Geurts et al. (2000, p. 27) consists of "people in models." By this somewhat cryptic description they understand that simulation games involve: (1) models, i.e., representations to provide insight into complex wholes enabling the analysis of relationships between structure and behavior, and (2) people who from their own perspective interactively participate in and contribute to the simulation that is an organizational prototype.

The second perspective is the *function* of simulation games. This function consists of "practicing communication." By means of simulation games participants learn from each other and from the model that provides a hybrid language for the complex problems the simulation game is about. Moreover, the game/ simulation functions as an exercise providing a safe environment for communicating about problems by experimenting with and analyzing different interventions under varying circumstances.

The third perspective is the *form* of the simulation game that is described as "orchestrated complexity." Simulation games are organized procedures consisting of particular building blocks (see Duke, 1974, for the "complete" set of 12 building blocks) allowing for the differentiation between the game package and its use, and the repeated, controlled, and documented application of the game.

Using these three perspectives, we define a simulation game as an organized procedure involving particular building blocks allowing participants to improve communication about complex problems by providing a safe and controlled environment to experiment with different interventions under varying circumstances by means of models representing these complex problems.

For the purpose of this chapter, it is relevant to distinguish between the *building* and *usage* stage of simulation games, for each of these phases may in its own way contribute to improving communication in the CI process.

Building a Simulation Game

Building a simulation game involves three interdependent stages, (1) building the model, (2) transforming the model into a simulation game, and (3) specifying relevant simulation game scenarios.

Model-Building

During the *model-building* stage, the simulation game constructors construct a simulation model of the problem they want to incorporate in the game. To this purpose, they start by defining the central problem they want to tackle by means of the simulation-game. This problem constitutes the core of the goal of the simulation game. For instance, the central problem the game should address is the improvement of communication between CI officers and strategic decision-makers about CI required for selecting the organization's product market technology (PMT) portfolio. Given the definition of the central problem of the game, the game constructors translate this problem in terms of a simulation model.

To this purpose, they should proceed by identifying "real" systems, parties or actors involved in the problem that can become either players or exogenous forces influencing the course of the game (e.g., the organization in focus, its competitors, legislators, etc.).

Moreover, they should define variables relevant for modeling the problem in focus. Some of these variables count as "essential game variables." These are the variables used to establish game results (e.g., profit margin, market share). Other variables count as "playing variables" (e.g., number and type of products in the PMT portfolio). These variables both influence the essential game variables and may be influenced by the operations of the players of the game.

In addition to the variables, the game constructors should select "driving" parameters influencing the behavior of the selected essential game variables or playing variables. The values of these driving parameters influence the behavior of the selected parameters and the players of the game cannot influence them. Examples of such parameters are macro-economic parameters such as investment climate, inflation, or national spending on consumer goods.

Given the selection of the variables and parameters, the game constructors should define operations (interventions) admitted in the game. Operations change the value of playing variables. Given the change of the value of a playing variable and the values of the driving parameters, the value of other playing or essential game variables may also change. To be able to specify how an operation changes the value of essential game variables given the value of the driving parameters, the game constructors should define the relations between operations on playing variables, the values of the parameters, and the value of the variables in terms of transformation tables or functions.

Finally, the model should be tested for consistency and realism. The result of model building is a tested simulation model of the problem the simulation game is about.

Transformation

In the transformation phase, the constructors *transform* the simulation model into a game/simulation. To transform the simulation model into a simulation game, the constructors should start by defining the goal of the simulation game in terms of objectives. It is useful to make a distinction here between out-game and in-game objectives. Out-game objectives are objectives the constructors want to realize by means of the game (for instance, improving communication about a particular complex problem). In-game objectives are objectives the players should realize while playing the game. These in-game objectives are measured in terms of the essential game variables (for instance, market share for a particular product).

Given the definition of the out- and in-game objectives, the game actors and their roles should be defined by selecting as actors "real" systems involved in the problem. Moreover, the in-game objectives should be defined in terms of "open" or "closed" targets for these actors. For instance, realize a larger market share for a particular product than your competitors is an example of an "open" target. Realize a market share of 80% is an example of a "closed" target. To make the game actors into real actors influencing the course of the play admitted operations should be allocated to them. If more than one individual player plays a game actor (e.g., four people play an organization that is an actor in the play), then individual playing roles should be defined.

Once game actors and roles are defined, the game constructors should define the game steps, specifying the sequence of operations in consecutive game turns. Moreover, rules and procedures for implementing these operations should be laid down. In addition, constructors should specify the physical appearance and paraphernalia (e.g., gaming documentation forms, meeting rooms, playing cards, etc.) of the game and the conditions for playing the game.

The result of the transformation stage is the untested simulation game. During the transformation stage, the constructors may be required to go back to the model building stage, for instance, because it may turn out that given the simulation model, the actual game becomes too complicated to play.

Scenario Building

To construct a playable game, the constructors should finally define scenarios for the simulation game. To this purpose, they should start by further specifying the out- and in-game objectives; for instance, improving communication about CI required for composing the PMT portfolio under different economic circumstances (growing or slacking economy) or improving communication about CI required for rolling out a relatively small PMT portfolio or rolling in a relatively large PMT portfolio.

Given this further specification, the constructors can define the "possible worlds" fitting these objectives by specifying the initial values of both the variables and the parameters and by defining "game events" (i.e., "unexpected" autonomous changes in values of either variables or parameters). For instance, in the scenario of rolling out a relatively small PMT portfolio, the essential game variables "number of product in the portfolio" and "market share per product" get a relatively small initial value. In the scenario of a growing economy, macro-economic parameters such as "inflation" and "consumer spending" get values to simulate the growing economy.

Once the scenarios have been built according to the out- and in-game objectives, the game simulation can be tested for realism and playability. The result of the scenario-building stage is a set of tested relevant playable scenarios.

Using the Simulation Game

The use of a simulation game involves four stages: (1) preparation, (2) introduction, (3) gaming, and (4) analysis and feedback.

Preparation

To prepare playing the simulation game, the facilitators should start by specifying the out-game objectives of the simulation game session. Given these objectives, they can select the relevant scenario, the relevant participants/teams involved in the simulation game, the roles of these participants, and the physical requirements for playing the simulation game.

Introduction

In the introduction stage, the facilitator introduces the participants to the learning objectives, the goals, scenarios, roles, rules and setting of the simulation game session. The facilitator also takes actions to ensure the involvement and commitment of participants (anticipating uncertainty of the participants, difference in learning styles and possible resistance).

Gaming

During this stage, the actual game/simulation is played. Participants play their roles and try to reach the goals of the game/simulation according to the rules of the game. While playing the game, participants are taking actions that influence the values of the relevant variables, given a certain scenario.

In addition, while participants are playing, the facilitator may intervene to increase the pressure, give feedback or motivate the participants to alter their behavior to improve the game.

Analysis and Feedback

Analysis and feedback can focus on several aspects of the game/simulation. First it may be directed at the results of the game—i.e., at the effect of (playing within) a certain scenario on the relevant variables. This analysis aims at the learning objectives of the game. Second, the analysis may be directed at the suitability of the game itself—i.e., whether it is properly built and used.   .

The analyses from simulation games may feed back into building them. In this way, building instructs simulation game usage, and simulation game usage instructs building. For instance, analysis of a simulation game may hint at problems with the model underpinning the simulation element of the game, may bring to light shortcomings in the gaming element of the simulation, or suggest additional scenarios for the simulation game. In this way, a simulation game can become an ongoing process of improving the simulation game and thereby improving the quality of the communication about the complex problem the simulation game is about.

Both the building and the usage phases of simulation games can contribute to improving communication about complex problems. To discuss this possible contribution in a more differentiated way, it is useful to identify the (desired) effects practicing communication by simulation game can serve and to analyze how building and using a simulation game may contribute to realizing these effects.

On the basis of their analysis of the existing literature, Geurts et al. (2000, p. 29ff) mention five organizationally relevant desired effects or functions, as they call them, of simulation game: increasing awareness and motivation, training skills, improving knowledge and insight, improving communication and cooperation, and integration of learning experiences. Each of these desired effects, in its own way, contributes to improving the content and/or the process of communication about complex problems.

By increasing awareness and motivation, Geurts et al. mean that a simulation/game can help to gain a preliminary understanding of a problem, its consequences and the effects of particular ways of dealing with it. This understanding may also motivate participants to think about the problem and about particular ways to solve it.

A simulation game invokes certain new skills for dealing with a problem. As Geurts et al. put it: "participants are stimulated to find new lines of behavior and put these into practice" (p. 30).

By means of a simulation/game, participants can actively examine the specific consequences of certain lines of action regarding a certain problematic situation. It thus improves knowledge and insight into a certain problem and into the effects of certain ways of dealing with it.

In a simulation/game, participants work together on problematic situations—i.e., they need to communicate and cooperate to explore possible courses of actions. A simulation/game can therefore be seen as a means to diagnose and improve the communication and cooperation regarding dealing with complex problems.

A simulation/game can be used to integrate learning experiences of the participants regarding the complex problem at hand. A simulation/game provides a dynamic background against which knowledge and insights may be ordered.

In Table 2 we list possible contributions of simulation games to improving communication about complex problems.

Table 2.   Contributions of Gaming to Improving the Quality of Communication

		Increasing awareness and motivation	Training skills	Increasing knowledge and insight	Improving communication and co-operation	Integration of learning experiences
Building the simulation-game	Model-building / Transforming model into game / Scenario definition	Model building may increase awareness of the importance of knowledge and communication. Motivating dealing with the problem	Training in structuring complex problems in terms of simulations. Training in making understandable complex models and making them transferable to other people	Increasing knowledge about the problem under consideration (what is the problem, why is it a problem). Increasing knowledge about relevant variables, parameters, events, and relations related to the problem	If participative methods for model-building, transformation, and scenario definition are used, chances are created to improve communication and co-operation between parties dealing with the simulated problem	Participative building allows for pooling knowledge and creating a shared language improving discussions between parties dealing with the simulated problem
Using the simulation-game	Preparation / Introduction / Playing the simulation-game / Analysis and feedback	Awareness of differences between points of departure, differences between events; Differences between 'lines' of interventions and their effects. Motivation providing a sense of control and security needed to deal with problems. Focus is on habitualisation and tacit knowledge	Quickly picking up relevant aspects of a complex problem situation. Operationally dealing with complex problems in different circumstances. Dealing with unexpected events and interventions	Knowledge and insight in (constellations of related) variables causing certain effects given certain starting conditions, events and interventions. Focus is on analysis and explicit knowledge	Teams of players playing against or with each other need to co-operate and communicate. And get feedback on communication and co-operation and the results. Improvements can be monitored by playing the game more than once	Shared understanding and awareness of the dynamics of the complex problem given different conditions events and interactions

SIMULATION GAMES FOR COMPETITIVE INTELLIGENCE

To explore how simulation games can contribute to improving communication about the required knowledge related to stages in the CI process, we are now in a position to bring together the results from earlier sections. We had listed the required knowledge for the different stages of the CI process and we derived an overview of the particular contribution of building and using simulation games to improving the quality of communication about complex problems.

In the present section, we first present an example of a simulation/game useful in the context of CI. Next to illustrating a CI game, the example also provides a background to explore how the contributions of building and using simulation games can contribute to improving communication about the required knowledge related to the stages of the CI process.

A Strategic/CI Simulation Game: The Product-Market-Technology Portfolio

Important strategic decisions focus on the composition of the "product market technology (PMT) portfolio" for a certain period. This portfolio consists of all the products (for certain markets, produced using a certain technology) of an organization at a given point in time. Strategic decision-makers should deal with questions regarding its composition in the future. Key questions are: do we need to change the current portfolio and if so—what is the nature of these changes? This decision-making requires strategic knowledge and information about the environment—particularly about the moves of competitors and environmental trends and developments. To focus the required intelligence activities, a game may be designed and used in which this process of decision-making regarding the PMT portfolio of an organization is in focus and a competitor is simulated.

The goal of such a game would be to formulate an adequate PMT portfolio for a certain period of time. Variables to determine the adequacy of this portfolio may be the impact of the portfolio (in terms of profitability, market share, brand-impact, etc.) and feasibility of the PMTs (in terms of costs and the effort to make them fit into the current organization, means of production, culture, etc.). These variables are the essential game variables.

Another set of variables consists of the parameters influencing the game. Among these may be internal parameters like available budget, available capacity (staff, competencies, machines, ICT, etc.), and the mission of the organization. External parameters may be the macro-economic circumstances, labor market, capital market, technological developments, moves of competitors, customer trends, etc. During the game, the players cannot change the value of these parameters. However, the game may be designed in such a way that developments in the external parameters may alter the value of the internal parameters—and influence the course of the game. Such developments may be modeled by autonomous external events.

The game may simulate the discussion of two groups of strategic decision-makers: one group deciding about the PMT portfolio of the own organization and another group working on a PMT portfolio of the most important competitor. Both groups may consist of participants playing different roles in the discussion: marketing managers, production managers, financial experts, etc. During the game the groups may perform one or more of the following operations: (1) add a new item to the PMT portfolio, (2) remove an item from the portfolio, (3) acquire a piece of information about the environment and (4) share a piece of information with the environment.

The game may be designed in such a way that both groups may acquire environmental information by only "one piece of information" per time-unit (e.g., a statement about an environmental parameter) and that the total number of information elements that can be acquired is limited. In this way, the information-gathering behavior can be monitored.

The game can also provide one or more occasions where players from different groups meet each other (e.g., on a trade show, or on a golf-court). The goal of these occasions is to try to find out about the portfolio of the competitor—and, at the same time, hold back essential information as much as possible. Many more features may be added to the game—but a complete description is beyond the scope of this chapter.

Contribution of Simulation/Games to the CI stages

Simulation/games may contribute to the knowledge required in the intelligence stages. In general, building and using a simulation game may lead to an insight into (1) the definition of information requirements, (2) the definition and use of information sources, (3) the analysis and use of information to strategic decision-making (for instance, in how it leads to a PMT portfolio), and (4) in the dissemination of the information and intelligence, given the different values of the parameters. In this section, we elaborate on these contributions.

Contribution of Gaming to the Direction Stage

During the building stage, a model of the organization in its environment in terms of relevant parties, variables, parameters, and variables relevant for strategic decision-making is built and tested. Such a model is relevant for the direction stage because it can guide identifying relevant environmental data classes. If, for example, CI professionals and game constructors work together to build a realistic game for generating a PMT portfolio, they should decide on the essential game variables, the playing variables and on the environmental parameters that may affect these variables. They should also decide on the initial values of these variables and parameters. A realistic choice (e.g., a relevant technological or customer trend, a relevant mission statement, relevant macro-economic circumstances) is impossible without a valid model of the organization in its environment. Building a game may be a trigger to improve current models for identifying relevant environmental (values of) variables and parameters.

In the building stage, a number of different scenarios (the specific initial values of the variables and parameters) are defined, each of which is the starting point of playing a game. During the game (for each scenario), knowledge is created about the impact of certain (initial) values of these variables and parameters in the context of making certain strategic decisions (e.g., formulating a PMT portfolio). For instance, it may turn out that certain initial parameter values have a high impact on organizational or competitor behavior. This knowledge may again be used in directing the intelligence activities—specific environmental parameters or variables may be monitored closely because some of their values may have a high impact on the organization. Playing a certain scenario can also reveal that some data classes gain in importance to make a certain strategic decision, while others cease to be of value. This knowledge can also be used to direct intelligence activities when a certain scenario comes into being.

Contribution of Gaming to Collection

During the building stage of a game for competitive intelligence, the model of the organization in its environment should be consulted to identify possible sources for collecting information about the environment. These sources could be made available to the players during a game. While a game is played, participants may create knowledge about the usefulness of these specific sources. In particular, it may turn out that the use and perceived relevance of specific sources depends on the different scenarios.

Contribution of Gaming to Analysis

The building stage results in a tested model of the organization in its environment in terms of relevant parties, variables, parameters and their relations. It thus provides a model for analyzing collected information about the environment as well. If the model is a realistic one, it may serve as a background for interpreting changes in value of the variables and parameters in the "real world." The value of this model increases when different scenarios are tested during playing the game. During a simulation game, one may find out that specific constellations of parameter values have a certain effect on the organization. This knowledge should be used to interpret the values of the actual parameters.

Contribution of Gaming to Dissemination

One of the purposes of simulation games is to provide an insight into and support for communication and cooperation practices. Communication and cooperation are important issues for disseminating and using the intelligence in strategic decision-making. It is often claimed that adequate communication and cooperation between intelligence professionals and strategic decision-makers is the key to ensure that intelligence is distributed correctly and used. Building a simulation game may provide several possible settings for the communication about intelligence and cooperation between CI professionals and strategic decision-makers (ranging from a "passive" mode, in which intelligence professionals give an update on their output once in a while, to a "collaborative" mode, in which both groups cooperate intensely and produce the intelligence together). During the building stage, one may thus gain insight into the different forms of communication and cooperation. While using the simulation game (in different scenarios) knowledge may be created about the adequacy of these settings (under different scenarios). This may help in designing an adequate setting for communication and cooperation.

Moreover, when both CI professionals and strategic decision-makers participate in (building or playing) the game, building or playing the game itself realizes cooperation and communication about relevant knowledge for competitive intelligence purposes (e.g., the models, possible scenarios, etc.). It helps to create a shared language to facilitate (current and future) intelligence matters.

Table 3 summarizes the different contributions of a simulation/game to the intelligence stages. Dependent on the design of the specific game, it may also lead to specific intelligence. The specific game of the previous section may, for

Table 3. Simulation Games Contributing to the Acquisition of Knowledge for the CI Stages

	Directing	Collecting	Analysis	Dissemination
Building the simulation-game	Building a model of the environment of the organization in focus in terms of parties, variables, and variables relevant for strategic decision-making that can guide identifying relevant knowledge domains and data-classes	Identifying possible sources for collecting information about the environment	Providing a model for analyzing information about the environment. The model, used in the direction stage can be used for analysis purposes as well	Providing different settings for distributing environmental information and its use in strategic decisions
Using the simulation-game	Identifying knowledge domains and data-classes for making particular strategic decisions in different scenarios	Gaining knowledge about the usefulness of specific sources in different scenarios.	Gaining knowledge of the adequacy of the model for analysis purposes in different scenarios	Gaining knowledge about the adequacy of different settings for the distribution of the intelligence and its use (in different scenarios)

instance, give valuable insights in how an organization sees the strengths and weaknesses of a relevant competitor (given different scenarios).

Simulation/gaming can be regarded as a means to support generating relevant knowledge for intelligence activities. In the next section, we discuss how ICT may support the building and using stages of gaming in order to create, store, share and apply required knowledge for the competitive intelligence stages.

ENABLING SIMULATION GAMES FOR CI BY ICT

The role of ICT to support simulation games for competitive intelligence falls into two broad categories: (1) ICT for supporting building and using a simulation/game and (2) ICT for making the results of the game available for the 'real' intelligence activities.

In the building stage, ICT (e.g., the Internet) can be used to collect intelligence to construct a realistic game. In fact, the same ICT tools normally employed in intelligence activities may be used. Moreover, ICT can greatly enhance the communication and cooperation needed to construct and test a realistic model of the organization in its environment. For instance, Intranet applications and GroupWare can aid in online construction and testing of the model. ICT applications can also support the choice of parameters and relevant values of the parameters for the specific scenarios used in the game. For instance, system-dynamic software can help in building a model of the causal relations between the essential game variables and the parameters. It can also help in determining specific effects of parameter values on essential game variables.

ICT can support the stage of using the game as well. ICT can help the participants to monitor the environment, to store the results of the game and to support the communication and cooperation needed during the game. To store the results of the game, a "scenario database" can be made and updated. In this database, all the relevant outcomes of playing the game in different scenarios should be stored. This information is relevant for the participants playing the game as it provides a log of the results of the current scenario. An insight into the results of playing the different scenarios is also relevant for the "real" intelligence activities (see below). ICT can also serve to generate a virtual game setting—i.e., simulate a part of the environment participants use to play the game (e.g., a virtual stock market, or a virtual trade show). In a similar vein, ICT can be used to generate autonomous environmental events and forward information about it to the participants. Another way of using ICT during the game is to provide a 'decision support system' participants may apply to calculate the consequences of their decisions.

Table 4 lists possible uses of ICT to support creating, sharing and storing knowledge for the CI stages.

The second function of ICT regarding simulation games for competitive intelligence is to store the resulting knowledge from the simulation game and make this knowledge available to intelligence professionals. To this end, the model that was built and tested and resulted in several playable scenarios should be stored and used in the intelligence activities. A model of the organization in its environment is the essential model for directing and analyzing activities. During the game it can be tested in a "safe environment"—and this may lead to valuable information about its use in real intelligence activities. Therefore, it is essential to store the model and provide easy access to it (and to the arguments leading to the choice of certain essential game variables, parameters and their initial values). Likewise, the information resulting from playing different scenarios should be stored (see the scenario database mentioned earlier) and made available for intelligence purposes.

Table 4. Examples of ICT Applications Supporting Simulation/Gaming to Arrive at Knowledge for CI (The table builds on the contributions given in Table 3.)

	Directing	Collecting	Analysis	Dissemination
Building the simulation-game	To build a model of the environment of the organization, forms of groupware may be used. To identify relevant (values of) variables and parameters, DSS or System dynamics software may be used. ICT can also provide a 'virtual setting for gaming'	To identify possible sources for collecting information about the environment and to find relevant parameters, variables and their values ICT-applications for monitoring the environment may be used (Internet, on-line databases, etc.)	Providing a model for analyzing information about the environment. The model, used in the direction stage can be used for analysis purposes as well -- for ICT use see directing	Different forms of ICT may be part of the different settings for distributing environmental information and its use in strategic decisions (e.g., e-mail; electronic conferencing, dedicated software). The adequacy of the different forms may be tested during the game
Using the simulation-game	To identify knowledge domains and data-classes for making particular strategic decisions in different scenarios, participants may use groupware to support thier communication and co-operation. DSS or SD-software may be used to determine the effect of values of variables in order to direct the search activities ICT can be used to generate information about autonomous events to the participants	During the game the participants may use specific software to monitor the 'game-environment'. And during the game, ICT can be used to store the results about the usefulness of specific sources in different scenarios	ICT should be used to store knowledge about the adequacy of the model for analysis purposes in different scenarios. Groupware can be used to support the communication and co-operation during strategic discussions and the meaning of environmental information. DSS or SD-software may be used to determine the effect of values of variables in order to make strategic decisions. Through ICT common analysis tools can be made available (e.g., an automated SWOT)	To store the knowledge about the adequacy of different settings for the distribution of the intelligence and its use (in different scenarios) ICT can be used

CONCLUSION

The purpose of this chapter was to explore the relevance of simulation/gaming for competitive intelligence and to examine the role of ICT to support simulation/gaming for competitive intelligence. Simulation/gaming can be a valuable tool for arriving at knowledge required in intelligence activities. Its main contribution is to build and test different scenarios regarding the impact of the environment on the organization. During building and testing these scenarios, awareness, knowledge and insight may be gained about the underlying model of the organization in its environment and about the impact of different values of environmental parameters on relevant organizational variables. Moreover, building and testing different scenarios may also enhance the communication and cooperation needed for intelligence activities. ICT can support delivering the contributions of simulation/games to competitive intelligence in various ways. In this chapter, we discussed some possibilities to support the building and using stages and to facilitate the dissemination and use of the knowledge resulting from the game to intelligence activities.

In our view, simulation/games can be an important tool to support intelligence activities. However, one should be aware of the effort it takes to build and use a simulation/game. At the same time, if a simulation/game is properly designed, the knowledge gained from it may well be *the* knowledge used in the direction stage (and for a great part in the analysis stage). In addition, if properly enhanced by ICT—simulation games may well be one of the most important tools to direct intelligence activities.

REFERENCES

Allgaier, C. & Powell, T. (1998). Enhancing sales and marketing effectiveness through competitive intelligence. *Competitive Intelligence Review, 9*(2), 29-41.

Bernhardt, D.C. (1994). 'I want it fast, factual, actionable'—Tailoring competitive intelligence to executive needs. *Long Range Planning, 27*(1), 12-24.

Clark, B. (1998). Managing competitive interactions. *Marketing Management, 7*(4), 9-20.

Cook, M. & Cook, C. (2000). *Competitive Intelligence*. London: Kogan Page.

Duke, R.D. (1974). *Gaming, the Future's Language*. Beverly Hills, CA: Sage Publications.

Ellis, R.J. (1993). Proactive competitive intelligence: Using competitor scenarios to exploit new opportunities. *Competitive Intelligence Review, 4*, 13-24.

Fuld & Company. (2002). *Intelligence Software Report 2002*. Retrieved at: http://www.fuld.com.

Fuld, L.M. (1995). *The New Competitor Intelligence*. Chichester, UK: John Wiley & Sons.

Fuld, L.M. (1998). *The Fuld War Room: The Ultimate in Competitive Intelligence.* Cambridge, MA: Fuld & Company.

Geurts, J., Caluwé, L. de, & Stoppelenburg, A. (2000). *Changing the Organization with Gaming/Simulations.* Den Haag: Elsevier.

Hannon, J.M. (1997). Leveraging HRM to enrich competitive intelligence. *Human Resource Management, 36*(4), 409-422.

Kahaner, L. (1997). *Competitive Intelligence.* New York: Touchstone.

Sammon, W.L. (1986). Assessing the competition: Business intelligence for strategic management. In J.R. Gardner, R. Rachlin, & H.W. Sweeney (Eds.), *Handbook of Strategic Planning.* New York: John Wiley & Sons.

Tessun, F. (1997). Scenario analysis and early warning systems at Daimler-Benz aerospace. *Competitive Intelligence Review, 8*(4), 30-40.

Vriens, D. & Philips, E.A. (1999). Business intelligence als informatievoorziening voor de strategievorming. In E.A. Philips & D. Vriens (Eds.), *Business Intelligence.* Deventer.

Chapter XII

Using Groupware to Build a Scenario-Based Early Warning System

Theo van Mullekom
University of Nijmegen, The Netherlands

Jac A. M. Vennix
University of Nijmegen, The Netherlands

ABSTRACT

Scenario analysis has been used as a technique to support strategy formulation for several decades. During scenario analyses, the effects of different possible futures (scenarios) on the performance of an organization are assessed. Moreover, actions are formulated to deal with these effects. This analysis may help organizations to prepare themselves to take effective actions when one of these futures manifests itself. A scenario approach to strategy formulation depends on intelligence gathering: one should (1) have relevant environmental information to build effective scenarios, and once a set of scenarios has been defined, one should (2) continuously monitor the environment to determine in what direction the future is moving. The usefulness of scenario analysis to focus intelligence activities—specifically the direction and analysis stages of the intelligence cycle—has been noted by several authors (e.g., Ellis, 1993; Tessun, 1997). In this chapter we will focus on scenario analysis as a tool to support the direction stage. In particular, scenario analysis may lead to a set of relevant early warning variables. Specific attention will be paid to the role of ICT tools (specifically groupware tools) to support the construction of scenarios and to derive a set of relevant early warning indicators.

INTRODUCTION

Without timely, accurate and actionable information about the environment of an organization, formulating, monitoring and reformulating strategies would be very hard. The process of gathering and analyzing environmental information is often referred to as competitive intelligence (cf., Kahaner, 1997; Cook & Cook, 2000; Fleisher & Blenkhorn, 2001). Competitive intelligence is usually described as a process consisting of four stages (cf., Sammon, 1986; Vriens & Philips, 1999; Kahaner, 1997). In the direction stage the information about the environment needed for strategy formulation is determined. In the collection stage the sources containing the required information are determined and the information is collected from these sources. In the analysis stage, the information is analyzed to determine its strategic value. If the information is of strategic significance, it is forwarded to strategic decision-makers in the dissemination stage. Although this process has always been important, due to several developments (e.g., globalization, increased speed of business, rapid technological development, political changes, increased competition; cf., Kahaner, 1997; Cook & Cook, 2000) the need to structure this information process is increasing. Many organizations have, for instance, built so-called intelligence units institutionalizing the process (e.g., Prescott & Fleisher, 1991). And, to support intelligence activities, a large set of tools and techniques has been developed (for overviews see Kahaner, 1997; Fuld, 1995; Powell & Algaier, 1998).

An important distinction regarding intelligence activities is that between a reactive and a pro-active mode of intelligence gathering (e.g., Hannon, 1997; Vriens & Philips, 1999; Gilad & Gilad, 1988). In a reactive mode, intelligence activities start after some (strategic) problem occurs (e.g., the emergence of a new competitor, the launch of a new product, or the introduction of a new technology). Strategic decision-making based on this kind of intelligence can only react to developments. As Simon (1993, p. 134) states, this may not be enough, because, in his view "[…] survival and success in an uncertain, rapidly evolving world [requires] (1) anticipating the shape of an uncertain future, (2) generating alternatives for operating effectively in changed environments, and (3) implementing new plans rapidly". In a pro-active mode, intelligence activities should help to anticipate developments having a strategic impact and they should help to generate suitable plans for dealing with them. Pro-active intelligence is desirable, but far more demanding than reactive intelligence. In a pro-active mode, CI professionals should be able to determine the strategic relevance of environmental developments before they actually occur. To do this, they need to build and maintain (implicitly or explicitly) a model of "the organization in its environment." This model is used to project possible environmental developments and to analyze their strategic impact. Based on this analysis, CI professionals can identify early warning indicators for crucial environmental developments, so that, if they occur, plans for dealing with them can be implemented before they can do any harm to the organization.

To support CI professionals in their pro-active intelligence activities, scenario techniques have been proposed and used (cf., Ellis, 1993; Tessun, 1997; Powell & Algaier, 1998; Cook & Cook, 2000). Scenarios are descriptions of possible futures based on different values of environmental parameters for an organization (cf., Van der Heijden, 1996). Based on these descriptions, plans can be delineated to deal with a specific possible future. Once a scenario (is about to) manifest(s) itself, actions can be taken. Scenario techniques have been used in many organizations. Shell, for instance, was able to survive the 1973 oil crisis reasonably well because of its use of scenarios. According to Tessun (1997), large companies like BASF, Boeing or Daimler Aerospace use scenarios to support their strategic decision-making. Scenario analysis is important for CI because it can support the direction *and* analysis stage. It can support the direction stage because it can help to identify a set of "early warning variables." Specific values of these variables indicate the possibility of the emergence of a certain scenario—and thus serve as early warning signs for a scenario. For intelligence activities, then, it is crucial that these variables are monitored. Scenario analysis also supports the analysis stage. Specific values of the early warning variables are examined against the background of the formulated scenarios. Ellis (1993) and Tessun (1997) give accounts of using scenarios to create an early warning system to be used in intelligence activities.

The contribution of scenario analysis to competitive intelligence may be enhanced by the use of ICT. ICT can, for instance, help to (1) facilitate the process of building and maintaining scenarios and deriving early warning variables, (2) link the early warning variables to internal and external information sources (e.g., a data warehouse, an online database, or the Internet), (3) support the analysis, and (4) disseminate knowledge about scenarios and early warning variables throughout the organization. In our view, ICT not only speeds up the process of scenario analysis for competitive intelligence, but some forms of ICT can even help to arrive at scenarios at a higher level of quality. In particular, we believe that a specific type of groupware will greatly enhance the contribution of scenario analysis to CI (see for instance also McGrath & Hollingshead, 1994). The main purpose of this chapter is to describe the role of groupware to facilitate the process of building scenarios and deriving early warning variables on the basis of these scenarios. In this way, we examine the role of ICT to support scenario analysis as a tool for directing intelligence activities.

The framework of this chapter is as follows. We first discuss the use of scenarios to derive early warning indicators. Next, we discuss the potential of ICT to support scenario analysis for CI purposes, and finally we focus on the use of groupware to build scenarios and formulate relevant environmental variables.

SCENARIOS

As stated in the introduction, survival in a rapidly evolving world depends on the ability to anticipate an uncertain future and to generate (and test) alternatives to deal with it. Pro-active strategy formulation should deal with this anticipation and generation. However, precisely because of its uncertainty, anticipating the shape of an uncertain future [as Simon (1993) puts it] is a difficult activity. To support strategic decision-makers, scenario analysis has been proposed as a technique. Scenario analysis is a method that can be helpful in exploring uncertainties in the future. In scenario analysis possible images of the future environment are generated, which are analyzed for their consequences for the organization. It is not the goal of the method to predict the future. The main objective is (by means of the several scenarios) to change and/ or enrich existing mental models and to structure a strategic conversation in order to be better prepared for the future. Scenario-building is not about strategy as a product, but about the process of strategy formulation (see for instance Van der Heijden, 1996).

During the past several decades, scenario analysis has received a lot of attention as an aid in the process of strategy formulation. Kahn and Wiener were among the first to give a definition of the concept of scenario: "Scenarios are hypothetical sequences of events constructed for the purpose of focusing attention on causal processes and decision-points. They answer two kinds of questions: (1) Precisely how might some hypothetical situation come about, step by step?, and (2) What alternatives exist, for each actor, at each step, for preventing, diverting, or facilitating the process?" (Kahn & Wiener, 1967, p. 6).

In this definition of Kahn and Wiener a scenario is a hypothetical sequence of events leading to a possible future. By taking into account several scenarios, several possible futures may be envisaged. An important aspect of scenario analysis is that more than one possible future is constructed. Practice shows that many organizations have a narrow perspective when formulating their strategy. Often, strategic decision-makers take only one possible future as a point of reference, and for this future they formulate only one strategic course of action. However, because of the contingency of the future, it seems to be safer to take into account and analyze more than one possible future. Experience also shows that strategic decision-makers find it hard to think about how the future environment might evolve. People are inclined to think in terms of what they want, and thus neglect thinking about less desirable possible futures (e.g., worst-case scenarios). Both problems (taking into account only one possible future or only desirable possible futures) can be mitigated by means of scenarios.

A second important element in the definition of Kahn and Wiener is that scenarios explicitly generate possible strategic courses of action to deal with the various futures indicated. Scenario-building is not only constructing future images of the environment. It also aims at looking at the strategic opportunities and threats regarding these futures and the actions to deal with them.

A third important element in the definition of Kahn and Wiener is the focus on causal processes. Scenarios should not only provide an image of what the future might look like. They should also indicate how the present might evolve into different possible futures. So-called causal diagrams can be used for this. In a causal diagram the most important variables and the causal relations are depicted.

The objective of scenario analysis is to start a continuous strategic dialogue within the organization (Van der Heijden, 1996). In this dialogue possible futures and actions to deal with these futures are constructed and analyzed. In this way, this strategic dialogue enables organizations to be prepared for the future—and take necessary actions in time.

There are different approaches and techniques for building and analyzing scenarios (see for instance Fahey & Randall, 1998; Von Reibnitz, 1998; Ringland, 1998; Van der Heijden, 1996). This chapter deals with a method for scenario-building developed and applied at the Nijmegen School of Management during the past few years. One of the most important characteristics of this method of scenario-building is that it emphasizes the interactive process. Managers from an organization go through the process of building and analyzing the scenarios together, enabled by facilitators, in order to form a *shared* view on possible futures and strategic courses of action to deal with them (see for instance De Geus, 1988; Vennix, 1996; Wack, 1985).

The scenario-building process consists of the following seven steps.

Step 1: Stating the Strategy of the Organization

The process starts with a description of the current long-term strategy of the organization (its mission, objectives and actions to realize these objectives). Although it may be tempting to question this strategy, this is not the intention of this step. The goal of this step is to establish a shared point of departure for the rest of the process.

Step 2: Making an Inventory of Trends and Developments

After the analysis of the current strategy of the organization, the group makes a broad inventory of trends and developments relevant for the future viability of the organization. Often these trends and developments are subdivided into different categories: societal trends, economic trends, political trends, technological trends, and ecological trends. Van der Heijden (1996) calls this the "September formula."

Next to collecting ideas in the categories mentioned above, it is useful trying to identify so-called "weak signals" (see for instance Ansoff, 1975). Weak signals are indicators for trends that do not play a significant role right now, but which might become very important in the future. By paying attention explicitly to these kinds of weak signals in an early stage, an organization trains for identifying possible strategic challenges before they are a fact. History gives some famous examples of the importance of identifying weak signals. Just prior to the breakthrough of personal computers as being a part of everyday life, IBM's CEO, Thomas Watson, is assumed to have said that there was "a worldwide need for five to six computers." And in 1995 Bill Gates stated that the Internet was just hype.

Step 3: Identifying "Driving Forces"

To make the step from trends and developments towards scenarios, an intermediate step is necessary. Trends are more or less stable developments on a specific dimension. For instance, "economic growth" is a development on the dimension "economic development." If it is uncertain in which direction on the dimension a trend will develop and if trends in any of these directions have a large impact on the performance of the organization, then the dimension is of importance in giving shape to the future. The two environmental developments with the highest degree of uncertainty and impact are used as so-called "driving forces." They define the scenarios. It is the goal of this step to identify those driving forces. Figure 1 gives an example of two driving forces ("economic development" and the "political development of Europe" with their respective trends "economic growth" and "economic decline," and "European integration" and "European disintegration") and the four scenarios based on them. In this way four quadrants can be discerned. Each quadrant defines a scenario describing a possible (relevant, yet uncertain) future environment of the organization (Schwartz, 1991).

Step 4: Indicators and Steering Variables

To be able to judge whether a specific scenario is favorable or unfavorable for an organization we use indicators. These indicators show the state of affairs of the organization or its immediate environment (i.e., the transactional environment; see for instance Van der Heijden, 1996). They are important because

Figure 1. Example of Two Driving Forces and Four Scenarios

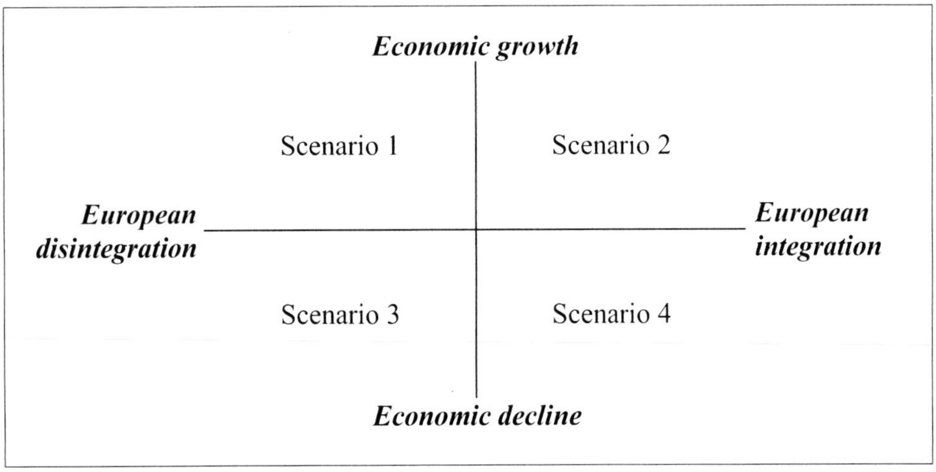

they can function as signals when something goes wrong, resulting in the need for the organization to take action. Examples related to the four scenarios in Figure 1 could be the market share of the organization, the number of foreign companies on the domestic market, or the amount of legislation coming from the European Union.

Next to indicators it is also useful to identify steering variables. Steering variables enable organizations to intervene in the immediate environment, with the purpose to change the values of (some of) the indicators towards the desired direction. Examples are the number of employees in a company and the price of the product the company sells.

Step 5: Writing Scenarios

In this step, the indicators are used to describe the effect of a certain scenario on the organization. To this end, the participants try to envisage how a specific scenario affects the organization by linking the different positions on the driving forces to the indicators. Next to this, participants should also try to describe how each scenario came into being. So, not only the end states (the specific possible futures and their effect on the indicators), but also their development should be described. The participants should draw up logical and plausible lines of reasoning of how the present may develop into the various possible futures. In this way, participants construct scenario stories (see for instance Schwartz, 1991; Van der Heijden, 1996).

An important aid during this step is the so-called causal diagram, well-known in the field of system dynamics (see for instance Forrester, 1969, 1973, 1980; Richardson, 1991; Sterman, 2000). The objective of a causal diagram is to depict a situation from a "systems point of view," thus making explicit connections between various parts or aspects of the system. Causal diagrams consist of variables and connections between those variables that cause the variables to increase or decrease. There are two sorts of causal relations: positive and negative. In the case of a positive causal relation two variables change into the same direction. That is, an increase of variable A (the cause) results in an increase of variable B (the effect), and a decrease of variable A leads to a decrease of variable B. A negative causal relation on the other hand means that two variables do not change into the same direction. In that case an increase of variable A will lead to a decrease of variable B, and vice versa (cf., Vennix, 1996).

To build a causal diagram (or diagrams) for the purpose of scenario-building, one can start with the causal paths from the driving forces to the indicators. Next, more indicators can be added. The diagram can be expanded until one has a more or less complete picture of the indicators and driving forces and the way they are causally connected. Figure 2 contains an example of a (preliminary) causal diagram. Ideally, this diagram contains the causal logic underlying all scenarios. In the example, four scenarios can be discerned: the four possible futures emerging given the combinations of the two positions on the two driving forces (European political development and economic development).

With the aid of this causal diagram the specific possible futures (in terms of the different directions on the driving forces) and their effects on the indicators can be described and analyzed. Moreover, these diagrams assist in making the scenario stories, thus enhancing their logic and plausibility.

Step 6: Inventory of Scenario-Consequences

The result of the previous step is an insight into the different possible futures and their effect on the organization and its immediate environment in terms of the indicators. This may be summarized in tables like Table 1. The rows of the table refer to the indicators. In the columns the four scenarios are given. In the

Figure 2. Example of a Causal Diagram for Scenario-Building

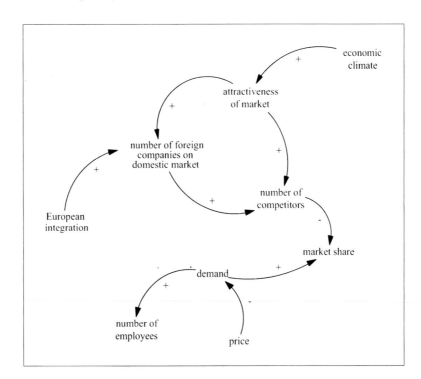

cells of the table the indicators are scored given a certain scenario. An indicator is given a positive score if it has a positive outcome, given a scenario. In the example, the value on the first indicator has the most positive effect when Scenario 2 will emerge. Next to scoring indicators by means of a plus or a minus, other ways are possible, for instance giving a verbal expression of what an indicator might do in a certain scenario.

The inventory of the effects of each scenario on the indicators gives an insight into how favorable or unfavorable the scenarios are for the organization and its immediate environment and is a starting point for generating actions to deal with each of these futures—the next step.

Step 7: Generating Actions to Deal with Possible Futures

The aim of this step is to generate, for each possible future, a set of actions that counter their negative effects and/or take advantage of their opportunities. To this end the organization should have defined several steering variables (Step 3), by means of which it can exercise some control over the environment. To analyze the consequences of different actions (i.e., different positions on the steering variables), it is useful to use the causal diagram of Step 5. For each scenario, the effect of certain combinations of steering variables on the indicators may be investigated. In the example, the management team may try to alter the price of a product to investigate its consequences on relevant indicators given a specific scenario. This analysis enables scenario-builders to formulate a list of actions for each possible future. These lists may be used to analyze the robustness of the current strategy (as formulated in Step 1). They

Table 1. Example of Scoring Indicators in Scenarios

	Scenario 1	Scenario 2	Scenario 3	Scenario 4
Number of foreign companies on domestic market	--	++	--	+/-
Market share	economic growth and less foreign competitors on the domestic market: market share will rise (considerably)	economic growth is positive for market share, but might suffer under the increase in the number of foreign competitors on the domestic market		
...				

may be used to establish (1) whether changes are needed when a specific scenario manifests itself, and, if they are needed, (2) what changes are required to deal with this future.

Scenarios and CI: Early Warning Variables

The process of scenario-building, as described by Steps 1 to 7, may lead to a shared view of several possible futures (as combinations of the positions on the driving forces and their impact on the indicators). It may also lead to a common understanding of the kind of actions an organization can take to counter the negative effects of the scenarios or to take advantage of their opportunities. However, to use this knowledge, it is necessary to collect and analyze information about the environment. More specifically, the following data classes should be monitored:

1.   Data that indicate whether a specific development on the driving forces occurs. This requires that one defines data classes, indicating specific directions. For instance, if economic development is a relevant driving force, data classes should be defined to indicate both trends (e.g., indicators for economic decline and growth: GNP, stock indices, interest rate, inflation rate, etc.). If the values of these indicators are below or above a certain value for a specific amount of time, they may indicate (the start of) a specific trend.
2.   Data about the trends on dimensions with a high impact and with low (perceived) uncertainty. It may be that developments occur that influence the certainty of a specific trend. In such a case, scenarios may be rebuilt and analyzed regarding their consequences.
3.   Data that indicate the performance of the immediate environment or the organization itself. Values on these indicators can be used to predict the manifestation of a specific scenario. They can also be used to validate the causal model underlying the scenario analysis.
4.   Data that indicate whether the actions, as delineated in Step Seven, can still be performed to deal with specific scenarios. These data concern the requirements for taking actions (e.g., price strategies may be dependent on governmental regulations, and it may be that in the near future the freedom to price products is bound by such regulations).

In intelligence activities connected to scenario analysis, the above data classes (the early warning variables) should be identified, monitored and analyzed. The identification may be the last step in the scenario-building process. This defines an early warning system based on scenarios. The scenario-building process described in this chapter ends with listing a set of early warning indicators. It thus links scenarios to the direction stage of the intelligence activities. In further steps the sources should be identified, and data should be collected and analyzed against the background of the scenarios. In this chapter, however, we focus on the link between scenario-building and directing intelligence activities. In the following section, we show how interactive scenario-building (and directing intelligence activities by scenarios) can be supported by ICT, thus contributing to the discussion of using ICT for directing intelligence activities.

ICT TO SUPPORT INTERACTIVE SCENARIO-BUILDING

The process of building scenarios and directing intelligence activities based on these scenarios as sketched in the previous section may be enhanced by ICT. In this section we will discuss how specific forms of ICT (Groupware) can support scenario-building.

In the literature a variety of names is being used for computer systems to support communication and decision-making in groups. Examples include:

- GDSS (Group Decision Support Systems)
- GCSS (Group Communication Support Systems)
- GNSS (Group Negotiation Support Systems)
- EMS (Electronic Meeting Systems) (cf., Jessup & Valacich, 1993)

A more generic term, which we will use throughout this chapter, is Groupware. There are several commercial groupware packages. One of these is called GroupSystems (developed at the University of Arizona, cf., Nunamaker et al., 1991). Most of these software packages contain a number of features with which particular cognitive group tasks can be supported. Typical cognitive group tasks include: generating information (e.g., brainstorming), prioritizing, making a choice (e.g., through voting), evaluating information, etc. (cf., McGrath, 1984). GroupSystems, for example, includes the following features:

- Brainstorming tools
- Voting systems
- Multi-criteria analysis
- Plotting graphs

As can be seen from the previous section on the methodology of developing scenarios, a facilitator guides the process of interactive scenario construction. Typically the facilitator confronts the management team with a number of cognitive tasks aimed at eliciting relevant information from group members and at making choices.

As stated, in an interactive scenario construction process the first task is to state the current strategy of the organization. To this end, the group can use a discussion facility of GroupSystems. During such a session, the members of the management team first state, individually, on the computer a number of strategies and submit these (via the network) to the computers of the other participants. The group can discuss online the submitted strategies (i.e., comment on the contributions of the members and react on the comments). Eventually, a number of strategies are identified as the current strategy of the organization.

The second task in interactive scenario construction for a group is to come up with a number of trends. In GroupSystems this process is supported by the so-called categorizer: a kind of electronic brainstorming which allows the typing in of ideas by group members and sorting these after collecting all the ideas from the individual participants. For scenario construction the steps include (a) individually typing in trends, (b) electronic collection of these trends by the facilitator, (c) projecting the generated trends on a screen, and (d) discussing these one by one for clarification and cleaning of the list (e.g., removing identical trends). As shown in the section on the scenario-building process, these trends can be clustered according to the September formula. For example, in a study conducted for a health care organization, examples of trends are: economic development, individualization in society, ageing of population, etc.

In the next step of the process two trends have to be identified as the two driving forces with which the four scenarios will be constructed. This step is supported by a vote tool. This means that each participant has to vote on each of the relevant trends with regard to the criteria "impact" and "uncertainty" (of the trend for the organization). Both are scored on a scale of 1 to 10. A score of 10 either means high impact, or a high uncertainty. A high uncertainty indicates that it is not well known in which direction a trend will develop in the future. A trend might for example be ageing of the population. In this case most participants will probably assign a low score on uncertainty, because it is quite certain that ageing of the population will take place in the future. However, if one takes economic development as a trend, it will be much less certain if economic growth or decline will be experienced.

Figure 3. Example of a Two-Dimensional Plot of Trends

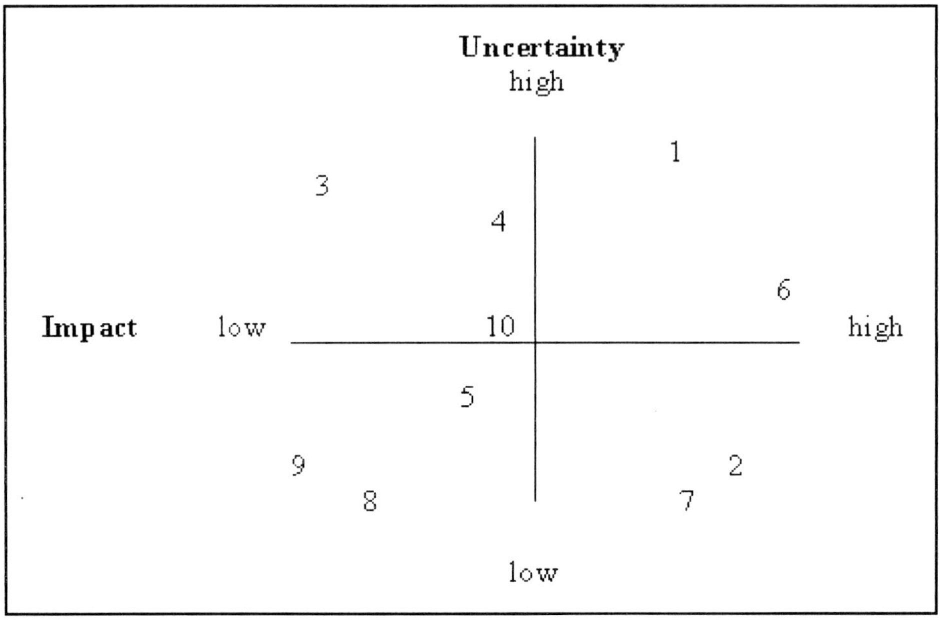

The software system allows plotting of the average scores (and standard deviations) of each trend on the two criteria in a two-dimensional plot. An example of such a plot is given in Figure 3.

In most projects the number of trends is large and the result is a plot with numbers, each referring to one of the generated trends (e.g., 1 = economic development; 2 = ageing of population; 4 = individualization, etc.).

In order to guide the selection of the two driving forces, the discussion focuses on the quadrant with high impact and high uncertainty. It will be clear that one is interested in the effects of trends with a high impact on the organization. Trends which are expected not to have a strong impact can safely be ignored. There is a slightly different argument for selecting trends with a high degree of uncertainty. These trends can develop in two quite different directions (e.g., economic growth versus decline). Focusing on trends with a high degree of uncertainty allows developing of driving forces for which two opposing developments can be explored in order to find out what the implications of these two developments may be.

In a next step the group is faced with the task to generate a number of indicators, which will typically tell how the organization or its transactional environment performs. For example in a study done for a health care organization the system is the health care system. Typical indicators with which to judge the performance of this system include: the length of the waiting lists, efficacy of care, state of health of population, number of complaints, accessibility, etc. Again, generation of these indicators is done by means of electronic brainstorming. In general this produces quite a long list and a selection of this list will have to be made if the process of writing scenarios is to be kept manageable. Voting is again used to bring down this list to about eight to ten indicators which will be used in the construction of the causal loop diagram. In order to support this process of causal loop diagram construction a separate software package is used from the realm of system dynamics, i.e., Vensim®. This package allows easy construction and analysis of causal loop diagrams. (Basically, there are three graphical software packages with which to construct system dynamics models: Ithink, Powersim, Vensim. These have a graphical interface with which causal loop and stock and flow diagrams can be constructed. More information on each of these packages can be found on the following websites: www.hps-inc.com; www.powersim.com; and www.vensim.com.)

CONCLUSION

In this chapter we examined the role of ICT to support scenario-building for competitive intelligence purposes. In particular, we defined the process of scenario-building and how it may be used to arrive at a set of early warning variables. These early warning variables may direct intelligence activities and the scenarios may be used to analyze the specific values of these early warning variables. Next, we discussed how groupware (in particular GroupSystems and software for visualizing and analyzing causal loop diagrams) might enhance the process of building scenarios. In our view, using groupware to support building scenarios and deriving early warning variables may speed up the process as well as it may ensure the quality of the scenarios and early warning variables. Groupware efficiently enables the generation of ideas (driving forces, scenarios, indicators, early warning variables, etc.) in a group and supports online feedback on these ideas. Groupware also helps to start up and maintain an interactive process of strategy formulation. In this way, groupware seems to be an adequate means to build scenarios and derive early warning variables from them.

REFERENCES

Ansoff, H.I. (1975). Managing strategic surprise by response to weak signals. *California Management Review, 28*(2), 21-33.

Cook, M. & Cook, C. (2000). *Competitive Intelligence.* London: Kogan Page.

Ellis, R.J. (1993). Proactive competitive intelligence: Using competitor scenarios to exploit new opportunities. *Competitive Intelligence Review, 4,* 13-24.

Fahey, L. & Randall, R.M. (Eds.). (1998). *Learning from the future. Competitive Foresight Scenarios.* New York: John Wiley & Sons.

Fleisher, C.S. & Blenkhorn, D.L. (2001). *Managing Frontiers in Competitive Intelligence.* Westport: Quorum Books.

Forrester, J.W. (1969). *Urban Dynamics.* Cambridge, MA: MIT Press.

Forrester, J.W. (1973). *World Dynamics.* (2nd edition). Cambridge, MA: Wright-Allen Press.

Forrester, J.W. (1980). *Industrial Dynamics.* (10th printing). Cambridge, MA: MIT Press.

Fuld, L.M. (1995). *The New Competitor Intelligence.* Chichester [etc.]: John Wiley & Sons.

Geus, A.P. de (1988). Planning as learning. *Harvard Business Review, 66*(2), 70-74.

Gilad, B. & Gilad, T. (1988). *The Business Intelligence System.* New York: Amacon.

Hannon, J.M. (1997). Leveraging HRM to enrich competitive intelligence. *Human Resource Management, 36*(4), 409-422.

Heijden, K., van der (1996). *Scenarios. The Art of Strategic Conversation.* Chichester, [etc.]: John Wiley & Sons.

Jessup, L. & Valacich, J. (eds.). (1993). *Group Support Systems. New Perspectives.* New York: Macmillan.

Kahaner, L. (1997). *Competitive Intelligence.* New York: Touchstone.

Kahn, H. & Wiener, A.J. (1967). *The Year 2000. A Framework for Speculation on the Next Thirty-Three Years.* New York/London: MacMillan/Collier-MacMillan.

McGrath, J.E. (1984). *Groups. Interaction and Performance.* Englewood Cliffs, NJ: Prentice-Hall.

McGrath, J.E. & Hollingshead, A.B. (1994). *Groups Interacting with Technology.* Thousand Oaks, CA: Sage Publications.

Nunamaker, J.F., Dennis, A.R., Valacich, J.S., Vogel, D.R., & George, J.F. (1991). Electronic meetings to support group work. *Communications of the ACM, 34*(7), 40-61.

Powell, T. & Allgaier, C. (1998). Enhancing sales and marketing effectiveness through competitive intelligence. *Competitive Intelligence Review, 9*(4), 29-41.

Prescott, J.E. & Fleisher, C.S. (1991). SCIP: Who we are, what we do. *Competitive Intelligence Review, 2*(11), 22-26.

Reibnitz, U. von (1988). *Scenario Techniques.* Hamburg: McGraw-Hill.

Richardson, G.P. (1991). *Feedback Thought in Social Science and Systems Theory.* Philadelphia, PA: University of Pennsylvania Press.

Ringland, G.A. (1998). *Scenario Planning. Managing for the Future.* Chichester, [etc.]: John Wiley & Sons.

Sammon, W.L. (1986). Assessing the competition: Business intelligence for strategic management. In J.R. Gardner, R. Rachlin, & H.W. Sweeney (Eds.), *Handbook of Strategic Planning.* New York: John Wiley & Sons.

Schwartz, P. (1991). *The Art of the Long View. Planning for the Future in an Uncertain World.* New York: Doubleday.

Simon, H.A. (1993). Strategy and organizational evaluation. *Strategic Management Journal, 14,* 131-142.

Sterman, J.D. (2000). *Business Dynamics. Systems Thinking and Modeling for a Complex World.* Boston, MA: Irwin/McGraw-Hill.

Tessun, F. (1997). Scenario analysis and early warning systems at Daimler-Benz aerospace. *Competitive Intelligence Review, 8*(4), 30-40.

Vennix, J.A.M. (1996). *Group Model Building. Facilitating Team Learning Using System Dynamics.* Chichester, [etc.]: John Wiley & Sons.

Vriens, D. & Philips, E.A. (1999). Business intelligence als informatievoorziening voor de strategievorming. In E.A. Philips & D. Vriens (Eds.), *Business Intelligence.* Deventer: Kluwer.

Wack, P. (1985). Scenarios. Uncharted waters ahead. *Harvard Business Review, 63*(5), 72-89.

Glossary

Alerting services
Electronic (Web-based) services that keep a user informed about changes in the content of a specified part of the Internet.

Analysis
The stage of the intelligence cycle in which the strategic significance of environmental data is determined. In this stage, the intelligence is produced. During analysis, intelligence professionals may use different models and techniques to interpret and value environmental data (e.g., SWOT analysis, growth-share matrix or scenario analysis).

Benchmarking
A systematic process to evaluate products, services and processes of "outstanding" organizations with the aim to improve the own products, services and processes.

Blind spots
Problems or shortcomings in the organizational ability to observe the environment, due to which relevant data or developments are missed. Gilad (1996) discusses three blind spot categories: "unchallenged assumptions", "corporate myths" and "corporate taboos".

Bots

Bots (or agents or Web-robots) are "software programs that automatically traverse the hyperlink structure of the World Wide Web to locate and retrieve (user specified) information" (Tan & Kumar, 2002, p. 9).

Business intelligence

The term business intelligence is used in two ways. It is often used as a synonym for competitive intelligence. It is also used to indicate a specific set of ICT tools to support managerial decision-making. This set of tools often consists of a data warehouse and the tools to store, retrieve and present the information it contains (e.g., data mining software).

Business performance management

A process by means of which organizations can identify performance indicators and define and maintain an ICT, human resource and organizational infrastructure to manage their performance.

Causal loop diagram

A causal loop diagram visualizes the causal relations between several variables. A causal relation may either be positive or negative. A positive causal relation between two variables means that both change in the same direction (both increase or decrease). A negative relation means that the variables change in opposite directions. A causal loop diagram may be used in analysis and direction activities, because it can make causal relations between environmental and organizational variables explicit. An insight into these causal relations can support the task of determining relevant intelligence topics and it can support the analysis of the impact of specific (constellations of) values of environmental variables on organizational performance. Chapters VI and XII discuss the use of causal loop diagrams in intelligence activities.

CI

See competitive intelligence

CI cycle

See intelligence cycle

Collection

Stage of the intelligence cycle. In this stage sources regarding the required environmental data are located, accessed and the data are retrieved from them.

Competitive intelligence

In the literature, two definitions are used: a product definition and a process definition. In the product definition competitive intelligence is defined as information about the environment relevant for strategic purposes. The process definition highlights "producing and processing" this environmental information. Process definitions often refer to the intelligence cycle.

Competitive intelligence system (CIS)

A competitive intelligence system may refer to a set of ICT tools to support the intelligence activities, or to a set of infrastructural elements to manage, support and perform the intelligence activities. ICT tools may be a part of this infrastructure.

Competitor intelligence

Intelligence (both product and process) regarding competitors. This term is sometimes (incorrectly) used as a synonym for competitive intelligence

Corporate espionage

The unethical and illegal counterpart of competitive intelligence. Corporate espionage produces intelligence by illegal means (e.g., by hacking, eavesdropping, stealing information, deception, etc.). Competitive intelligence, by contrast, uses open, publicly available sources.

Counterintelligence

Process or activities aimed at protection of information against the intelligence activities of other organizations.

Critical success factors

Robson (1994) defines critical success factors as "those factors that must go well for an organization to flourish." Critical success factors are often determined in order to derive the strategic information requirements.

Data

In the literature, many definitions are available. In Chapter I we defined data as signals external to an observer. These data need to be collected and interpreted before they may become information or intelligence.

Data mining

Set of techniques to discover trends and patterns in (a large set of) data. These techniques are often realized by means of advanced ICT tools (e.g., artificial intelligence applications).

Data warehouse

Inmon (1993) defines a data warehouse as "a subject oriented nonvolatile and time variant collection of data in support of management's decisions." A data warehouse is a large database in which data from various internal (and sometimes external) databases are integrated and reorganized into a format that enables easy and ready access. Most of the time, however, a data warehouse mainly contains internal data and its use for competitive intelligence purposes may therefore be limited (cf., Fuld et al., 2002).

Direction

Stage of the intelligence cycle. In the direction stage one determines the strategic (external) information requirements—i.e., one determines what environmental data should be collected. In this stage one has to identify about which environmental topics data should be gathered. A distinction can be made between a 'rough' data profile (indicating certain data*classes*, e.g., "we need to know something about the logistic capacity of competitor X and Y") and an exact data profile (indicating the exact data within a certain dataclass, e.g., "we need to know the amount of trucks and their capacity"). These topics (both in their exact and rough version) are also known as Competitive Intelligence Needs (Fleisher, 2001), Key Intelligence Topics (Kahaner, 1996) or Essential Information Elements (Sammon, 1984).

Dissemination

Stage of the intelligence cycle. In this stage the intelligence produced in the analysis stage is presented and forwarded to strategic decision-makers.

Early warning system

A system to monitor the early warning variables. This system may refer to a set of ICT tools, or to a set of infrastructural elements to manage, support and perform these monitoring activities. ICT tools may be a part of this infrastructure.

Early warning variables
Variables that indicate the emergence of a trend or development in an early stage. Often these variables are derived from or determined in association with scenarios (see also Chapter XII).

Environment
Prior (1998, p. 67) defines the environment of an organization as that which "encompasses all those factors that affect a company's operations and includes customers, competitors, stakeholders, suppliers, industry trends, regulations, other government activities, social and economic factors, and technological developments." In the literature, several ways to decompose the organization's environment can be discerned. One important decomposition is into a transactional environment (all those factors that directly affect the organization's operations) and the contextual environment (forming the context for the transactional environment—consisting, for instance, of macro-economical factors or demographic developments).

Extranet
An Internet-like network (often an extension of the organization's intranet) to which members of the organization and relevant parties from outside the organization (e.g., suppliers or selected customers) have access.

Game
See simulation game

Game building
Stage in gaming/simulation. During the building stage, game constructors make a model of the problem they want to incorporate in the game. Next, they transform the model into a specific game, and, finally, they define different scenarios that can be played during the game (see also Chapter XI for the use of games for intelligence purposes).

Game using
Stage in gaming/simulation. During the using stage, game facilitators make preparations for playing the game and participants actually play the game (given a certain scenario). (See also Chapter XI for the use of games for intelligence purposes.)

Gaming/simulation

The process of building and using simulation games as a means to deal with complex problems (see also simulation game).

Geographical Information Systems (GIS)

Information systems dedicated to processing, storing and visualizing spatial data. Geographical information systems can be used to support producing and processing intelligence with a spatial component (e.g., to analyze the demographic composition of a region, or to analyze the geographical dispersion of certain relevant variables). In Chapter IX, the use of GIS for competitive intelligence is discussed.

Groupware

Computer systems aimed at supporting communication and decision-making in groups. Most groupware applications include features that allow groups to perform particular "cognitive group tasks", such as generating information (e.g., brainstorming), prioritizing, making a choice through voting and evaluating information (cf., McGrath, 1984).

Human resources infrastructure

The part of the intelligence infrastructure that refers to the human resources needed to manage, support and perform intelligence activities.

Humint

Contraction of *hum*an and *int*elligence. According to Kahaner (1996), humint is "what somebody tells you." Humint is intelligence with a person as its source.

Hyperlinked communities

A group of Web users "organized" around a specific topic. These communities may be implicit or explicit. An implicit hyperlinked community is self-organized, not obvious (hidden), lacks definite membership, has spontaneously evolved, and has an implied social structure. The opposite of implicit communities are explicit hyperlinked communities such as users participating in listservs and newsgroups. Chapter III examines the possibility of mining implicit communities for competitive intelligence purposes.

ICT

Information and communication technology. ICT can be used to indicate the organization's technological infrastructure (comprising of all hardware, software and telecommunications technology) and to indicate one or more specific collections of hardware, software and telecommunications technology (i.e., one or more ICT applications).

ICT-driven approach

Approach to design and implement ICT tools for competitive intelligence in which the functionalities of the ICT tools are the starting point for building an intelligence infrastructure for supporting the intelligence activities. According to Philips (Chapter X) this approach may lead to several difficulties.

ICT selection criteria

Criteria to select ICT for competitive intelligence may refer (1) to the contribution of the ICT to the stages of the intelligence cycle, (2) to the contribution and/or impact of ICT on the intelligence infrastructure, and (3) to costs. See also Chapter I for a treatment of these criteria.

Information

Information can be defined as decoded, interpreted data that are new to an observer (see also Chapter I).

Information overload

The problem that occurs when an information processing system (e.g., a manager, a group, an organization) does not have enough capacity to process the amount of information presented to the system. This problem often occurs during competitive intelligence activities if the information requirements are poorly defined.

Infrastructural approach

Approach to designing and implementing ICT tools for competitive intelligence in which the goal of the CI process and its supportive infrastructure are the starting point for the design and implementation of ICT tools for CI. (See also Chapter X.)

Infrastructure

See intelligence infrastructure

Intelligence

Information relevant for strategic purposes. See Chapter I for a treatment of the concepts of intelligence, information and knowledge.

Intelligence cycle
Cycle of four stages (collections of intelligence activities). The stages are: direction (also referred to as planning), collection, analysis and dissemination.

Intelligence infrastructure
The intelligence infrastructure (or CI infrastructure) refers to the required technology, organizational structure in human resources for managing, supporting and performing the intelligence activities. It consists of three sub-infrastructures: the technological, the human resources infrastructure and the organizational infrastructure. The intelligence infrastructure is treated in Chapters I and X.

Intelligence requirements
See strategic information requirements

Internet
A world-wide network (of networks), linking millions of computers.

Intranet
An Internet-like network linking computers within a specific organization.

Knowledge
Many definitions are given in the literature. In Chapter I, knowledge is defined as "that which serves as a background for observation and action."

Knowledge management
Knowledge management refers to (1) the identification of relevant knowledge for an organization and (2) building and maintaining an infrastructure to facilitate knowledge processes by means of which the relevant knowledge should be produced and processed. Competitive intelligence can be defined as a specific branch of knowledge management, i.e., as strategic knowledge management.

Knowledge processes
In the literature, one often finds four knowledge processes: (1) generation of knowledge, (2) sharing knowledge, (3) storing knowledge, and (4) applying knowledge. In Chapter IV, the knowledge processes for strategy formulation are examined.

Market intelligence
Relevant strategic information about the current or possible market(s) in which an organization operates.

Model of the organization in its environment
A model of the organization in its environment consists of the interrelated essential variables related to the viability of the organization and their organizational and environmental parameters. Without such a model, direction and analysis would be impossible. CI professionals use such models implicitly or try to make it explicit using techniques like SWOT analysis, scenario planning, or the BCG growth-share matrix. In Chapters VI, XI and XII we discuss some techniques to make this model explicit (and the ICT to support this process of explication).

Online databases
Databases that can be accessed from another computer (e.g., via the Internet) to retrieve specific information. A number of commercial online databases exist (e.g., Lexis-Nexis or Dowjones). Search items may be submitted to these databases and search results are returned.

Organizational infrastructure
Part of the competitive intelligence infrastructure, referring to the division of CI tasks and responsibilities.

Outsourcing intelligence activities
Having third parties carrying out a part of the intelligence activities. This can also be done electronically (e.g., by means of online databases, alerting services or Web robots).

PMT
Product market technology combination.

Scenario
A scenario is a description of a possible future.

Scenario analysis
In scenario analysis the effects of different possible futures (scenarios) on the performance of an organization (or on its immediate environment) are assessed. Chapter XII discusses the role of scenarios for competitive intelligence.

SCIP
Society of competitive intelligence professionals.

Search engine
Tool for locating data on the Internet. Common distinctions regarding search engines include general versus specific search engines (the latter focus on a specific topic or region) and search engines (performing a search based on their own "index") and meta-search engines (using other search engines to conduct their search). URLs of well-known search engines are: www.lycos.com and www.altavista.com.

Simulation game
An organized procedure involving particular building blocks allowing participants to improve communication about complex problems by providing a safe and controlled environment to experiment with different interventions under varying circumstances by means of models representing these complex problems. Simulation games may be useful tools to support all the stages of the intelligence cycle. Chapter XI discusses the contribution of simulation games to competitive intelligence activities.

Source
Something or someone containing data and from which the data can be retrieved. Many distinctions regarding sources are given in the CI literature. For instance: open versus closed sources, primary versus secondary sources, internal versus external sources, and a distinction referring to the carrier of the data (human, electronic or paper).

Source identification
Identifying suitable sources (i.e., efficient and containing the relevant data) given a certain data need. See also sourcemap.

Sourcemap
A sourcemap is a matrix linking data classes to sources. In the cells of the matrix the sources are valued according to different criteria (e.g., accessibility, costs, timeliness of the data, etc.). A sourcemap can be used to determine which sources are available to retrieve certain data efficiently. It can also be used to evaluate the collection of sources an organization employs.

Strategic information requirements
The information needs for the process of strategy formulation. For competitive intelligence, the external strategic information requirements are important.

Strategy
In the literature, many definitions are given. A possible definition is the desired portfolio of product-market-technology combinations of an organization.

Strategy formulation
The process by means of which the desired portfolio of product-market-technology combinations is defined and updated.

System dynamics
System dynamics is a simulation methodology that deals with the dynamics of complex systems from a feedback perspective. System dynamics is specifically suited for understanding the dynamic behavior of systems as caused by their internal structure (cf., Vennix, 1996). System dynamics can be used to model the "internal structure" that is responsible for generating the behavior of an 'organization in its environment'-system. Such a model can support both direction and analysis activities. Chapter VI explains how system dynamics may support these activities.

System dynamics software
Software tailored to analyzing the behavior of complex systems modeled according to the system dynamics approach.

Technological infrastructure
Part of the intelligence infrastructure consisting of the hardware, software and telecommunications technology and the associated ICT applications.

Technological intelligence
Intelligence regarding technological trends and developments.

Viability
Viability is the ability of a system "to maintain a separate existence." (Most) organizations are continuously trying to maintain their viability. From the notion of viability the process of strategy formulation can be derived (see Chapter IV).

Viable system model

This model is developed by Beer (1979, 1981) and specifies the necessary and sufficient functions an organization should possess to maintain its viability. This model is used in Chapter IV to identify the process of strategy formulation and to derive the required knowledge for this process.

WWW

World Wide Web. A system by means of which information is organized on the Internet (using hypertext links).

About the Authors

Dirk Vriens (PhD in Policy Science, 1998, University of Nijmegen, The Netherlands) is an assistant professor of Knowledge and Information Management at the Nijmegen School of Management. His research interests include competitive intelligence, knowledge management, cybernetics, and information management. He has published a number of articles and books on these subjects. He also participated in several intelligence and knowledge management consultancy projects.

*   *   *   *

Jan Achterbergh (PhD in Policy Science, 1999, University of Nijmegen, The Netherlands) is an assistant professor at the Nijmegen School of Management. His research interests include systems theory, cybernetics, and knowledge management. He has written a number of articles and books on these subjects.

Paul Hendriks (PhD in the Social Sciences, 1986, University of Nijmegen, The Netherlands) is an associate professor of Knowledge and Information in Organizations. He has worked at the Free University of Amsterdam and the University of Nijmegen where he is currently a member of the Nijmegen School of Management. His current research interests include the role of motivation in knowledge work and organizational structures for knowledge work. He has published several books on research methodology, geographical information Systems and computers. He has also been published in several academic journals, including the *International Journal of Geographical Information Science, Information and Management, Knowledge-Based Systems, Decision Support Systems, Expert Systems with Applications, Geographical and Environmental Modelling* and *Knowledge and Process Management*.

Wendy Jacobs has studied Business Administration at the University of Nijmegen, The Netherlands, where she was granted the master's certificate in 2000. She did her final project at the consumer and marketing intelligence department of the multinational electronics firm that was staged in the article. Her final thesis addresses the connections between groupware and business intelligence. Currently she works at PricewaterhouseCoopers where she joined the Global Incentives Services department. She gives advice to companies and non-profit organizations that want to apply for the incentive programs of The Netherlands and the European Union. She also writes progress reports to inform the Dutch government and the European Commission about their subsidy projects.

Marco van der Kooij is currently working as a manager at Hyperion Solutions (NASDAQ: HYSL) in The Netherlands. He has extensive experience with multinational companies in selecting and implementing a business intelligence platform and a business performance management framework. He is educated in business economics, auditing, marketing and business administration. He started his career in an auditing firm and worked as a controller. Since 1988 he has been working in the information technology industry in sales, marketing, product development and consulting.

Theo van Mullekom is a junior researcher at the Methodology Section, Faculty of Management Sciences at Nijmegen University, The Netherlands. His research centers on using scenario-building as an intervention tool for solving complex problems in organizations.

Özge Pala has a bachelor's degree in Industrial Engineering from Boaziçi University, İstanbul, Turkey, and an MSc in Management Science from CentER, Tilburg University, The Netherlands (cum laude). For the last four years, she has been a junior teacher at the Methodology Section of Nijmegen

Business School, The Netherlands. She is responsible for teaching students how to work with the methodology of system dynamics to make diagnoses of organizational problems with the aim of policy formulation. She is currently a PhD student at the same department. Her research interests are modeling of socio-economic systems using system dynamics, organizational change, and assessment of the effectiveness of system dynamics in decreasing cognitive biases and improving environmental scanning and information processing activities in organizations.

Egbert Philips is assistant professor at the Nijmegen School of Management at the Nijmegen University, The Netherlands. He is a teacher in Business Intelligence and Information Management. He also works as a senior consultant and trainer in Competitive Intelligence, Business Strategy and Innovation Management. His main working areas are the agriculture, pharmaceutical and food businesses, where he has a lot of experience working with multinational companies.

Edna O. F. Reid is an associate professor with Nanyang Business School (NBS), Nanyang Technological University (NTU), Singapore, and president of the Society of Competitive Intelligence Professionals, Singapore (SCIPSgp). She is one of the founding members of SCIPSgp (www.scipsgp.org). Formerly, she was an entrepreneur with an Internet start-up in Malaysia. Her areas of specialization and research are competitive intelligence, web mining and information brokerage. Her Southeast Asia instructional programme includes teaching business intelligence and information technology courses. Prior to her 10 years in Southeast Asia, Edna was at the School of Communication, Information and Library Studies, Rutgers University, USA. Before her Rutgers experience, Edna was a postdoctoral researcher at the University of California, Berkeley, and worked in the Silicon Valley. Before entering the academic field, she was a senior systems analyst and data analyst team leader with a software development company in West Germany and the USA. She has extensive experience in intelligence gathering and analysis while working in the intelligence community. Edna's scholarly activities focus on applying e-learning techniques to information intelligence skills (www.nbs.ntu.edu.sg/Corporate/pdf/wired_age.pdf) and conducting research on Web intelligence (www.e-business.fhbb.ch/eb/publications.nsf/id/214). She has publications in several professional journals. Edna's professional degrees include a Doctorate from the University of Southern California (USC), a postgraduate certificate in MIS from American University, and a master's from the University of Maryland. She is a member of SCIP in USA, Association for Information Systems (AIS), Special Library Association (SLA), and the American Association for Information Science & Technology (ASIST).

Etiënne Rouwette is an assistant professor at the Methodology Section, Faculty of Management Sciences at Nijmegen University, The Netherlands. His research centers on changes in attitudes and behavior as a result of participating in system dynamics group modeling approaches, gaming simulations and electronic meetings.

Jac A. M. Vennix received his PhD from Nijmegen University and is currently full professor of Research Methodology at the Faculty of Management Sciences of Nijmegen University, The Netherlands. He has conducted a large number of projects in a variety of organizations in the areas of system dynamics group model-building and (interactive) scenario construction. He has published a number of articles and books on system dynamics, group model-building, knowledge elicitation, group facilitation and scenario construction. He is editor of the *System Dynamics Review* and received the Forrester Award of the System Dynamics Society. His research interests focus on problem structuring methodology and empirical assessment of problem structuring interventions in organizations; more in particular on how these methodologies (primarily group model-building and scenario construction) can assist in increasing the learning potential of organizations.

Index

L

language barrier 184
leadership 62
linked communities 58
listserv 58
local government 115

M

maintaining the model 250
marketing intelligence 14
MicroStrategy, Inc. 59
model building process 138
model-building stage 254
modeling 165
monitoring 165, 250
multi-criteria analysis 280

O

online communities 58
online discussion groups 64
online marketspace 65
open source 10
organization in its environment 249
organization strategy 274
organizational assets 62
organization's competitive landscape
      209
outlinks 60
outsourcing collection activities 19

P

patents 59
people in models 253
perceived ease-of-use (PEU) 39
perceived usefulness (PU) 39
personal barrier 185
plotting graphs 280
policy experiments 138
press releases 66
primary source 10
pro-active intelligence 271
product-market-technology combination
      88
professional GIS 205

Q

qualitative data 228
qualitative system dynamics 146

R

relational analysis 60
repairing weaknesses in sources 183
reverse link look-up 64
roles 45

S

safety 122
safety plans 122
safety plans development 115
safety problems 123
scenario analysis 269
scenario building 256
scenario-consequences 277
scenarios writing 276
scholarly communications 62
Science Citation Index 60
search engines 19
secondary source 10
self-citation 68
self-organizing 58
simulation-games 248
social interactions 58
Social Sciences Citation Index 60
social structure 58
soft information 64
source adequacy 190
source map 181
source map cells 187
source map implementation 191
sources 189
spatial analysis 195, 203
spatial analysis models 207
spatial data handling 196
spatial decision-making 196
spatial variables 210
stability barrier 185
stakeholder participation 118
stakeholders 58
steering variables 275
strategic implication recognition 216

New Releases from IRM Press

2005 12 22 *ase!*

0 1341 0817803 6

ss Strategies for Information Technology Management

Kalle Kangas
Turku School of Economics and Business Administration, Finland

Business Strategies for Information Technology Management presents the theoretical and empirical research on the business value of information technology, as well as the use of management of information technology for increasing organizational performance and gaining strategic advantages. The betterment of information technology payoff and information systems practice as well as how to link business opportunities to information technology and implementation management are also presented.

ISBN   1-931777-45-4 *(s/c)*; e*ISBN* 1-931777-66-7 • *US$59.95 • 300 pages • © 2003*

"It must be recognized that information needs of various stakeholders vary in different kinds of firms, depending upon industries, resources, and structures. It is, therefore, vital that firms develop business strategies that support IT management."
–Kalle Kangas, Turku School of Econ. and Business Admin., Finland

**It's Easy to Order! Order online at www.idea-group.com
or call 717/533-8845 x10!**
Mon-Fri 8:30 am-5:00 pm (est) or fax 24 hours a day 717/533-8661

IRM Press

Hershey • London • Melbourne • Singapore

An excellent addition to your library